First Steps
to Ministry

A Primer on a Life in Christian Ministry

General Editor, David Markle

Warner Press

Anderson, Indiana

Coordinator of Publishing & Creative Services
Church of God Ministries, Inc.
PO Box 2420
Anderson, IN 46018-2420
800-848-2464
www.chog.org

To purchase additional copies of this book, to inquire about distribution, and for all other sales-related matters, please contact:

W Warner Press, Inc.
PO Box 2499
Anderson, IN 46018-2499
800-741-7721
www.warnerpress.org

David Markle, General Editor
Arthur M. Kelly, Editor and Publication Coordinator
Cover and Layout by Curtis Corzine and Aurora Delgado

ISBN-13: 978-0-87162-899-2

Printed in the United States of America.

11 12 13 14 15 16 / TPS / 10 9 8 7 6 5 4 3

Table of Contents

Foreword

The form, focus, and substance of this book are rightly described as a "primer." The dictionary defines a primer as a book about elementary principles that underlie a subject, area of enquiry, a skill, or service-role. The word *underlie* is crucial because the principles which govern a meaningful ministry to people in matters that pertain to God must be known and honored if needed services are to be effective and sustained. Ministry is indeed based upon, or rooted in, a heart that honors God, a mind nurtured by Christ, an ear opened to God's voice, a disciplined self, a gift-based role, a sense of accountability, and a spirit to serve. This book, addressed to persons taking the first steps to ministry, deals with such matters, and more.

This primer introduces the reader to accented areas of concern for effective, fruitful, and sustained ministry in the church and in the world, and it does so with so much more involved in the writing of each chapter than an apparent simplicity of presentation and understood brevity. Each writer has brought to her or his task a life that reflects the very principles being studied; each one has dipped a pen into the ink-well of his or her own experiences to set forth what has been explicated in their assignment. Having known most of the writers since their student years in college, seminary, and graduate school, and having observed their course of life and labors since those years of preparation, even looked upon as mentor by many of them, I feel both privileged and proud as writer of the foreword to this manual to which they have made timely and noteworthy contributions.

This book abounds in wisdom, offering information balanced with inspired guidance. For those readers taking first steps to ministry, this primer sets forth with plainness the principles which underlie servant ministry in the spirit of Christ. This book also offers a refreshing read for those whose service years have been many, whose first steps to ministry lie well in the past but whose heart and feet are still marching in glad service to the beat of the heavenly Drum.

JAMES EARL MASSEY
Dean Emeritus, and Distinguished Professor-at-Large,
Anderson University School of Theology
May 2001

Preface

In the Hebrew Bible, the word for wisdom carries many connotations. One of those is that wisdom is found in living life in wonder ("fear") of God; another is about living life well, even with skill. Ministry in any age *requires* both; ministry in the murky and indistinct future of the 21st century *demands* both. Persons responding thoughtfully to a sense of God's call to ministry must think wisely about its demands and its promises. The need for thoughtful, committed, passionate Christian ministers has never been more urgent; the need for insight in responding to the call has never been greater.

In 1999 a group of pastors, church leaders, and educators—the Leadership Development Task Force of the Church of God—sat around a table talking about the very real problem of the low supply of new pastors in light of the growing need. They were talking about leadership resources and their lack. They were also talking about the disturbing reality of moral failure in the pulpit. Dr. David Markle, the general editor of *First Steps* and a contributing author, was particularly concerned about the lack of college level ministry texts to help students consider the full spectrum of their calling.

What is needed, they concluded, is a positive and realistic introduction to ministry. What is needed is a text that would help men and women think seriously about the powerful realities of pastoral ministry in the 21st century. What are the forces, realities, and demands of ministry? What are the temptations and the pitfalls—and, more importantly, how can I avoid them? Where are the resources? What are the questions I need to ask? Who are the persons I need to talk with?

This text, *First Steps in Ministry, a primer on a life in Christian ministry,* emerged from that discussion and is a real response to a real need. This book is written by men and women with experience in ministry. It is written by men and women whose lives have been shaped by the church and who have taken the time to reflect on ministry. Each one is worthy of the designation "called." (To check out their "credentials" read the brief biographies at the end of the book.) These are wise essays written by wise men and women who fear God and minister skillfully.

No ivory tower book, *First Steps* is a practical guide for persons who believe God has called them to the high calling of Christian ministry. But it is not about hands on work only; its focus is clearly on the central truth of ministry. It is not about skill, experience, or tricks; certainly it is not about gimmicks: it is about who and *Whose* you are.

The book is organized around four centers, thereby keeping the focus and the flow of ministry in the right place and in the right direction: *Being*—foundations of who we *are*; *Becoming*—disciplining ourselves for fruitful living; *Doing*—discovering what we will do; *Overcoming*—skills for winning the war.

Each author helps us to understand the strategic importance of balancing the tasks for ministry with the relationships of ministry—all in the light of the primary relationship between God and God's called servant. Each author focuses on a particular aspect of ministry, but recurring central themes emerge in the text as motifs in a symphony: the centrality of prayer to significant ministry; the vital importance of the practice of basic spiritual disciplines; the foundational role of continuing study and reflection; the discipline of commitment, that is, doing what one must do; and congruence—strong and visible connection between walk and talk, leading to a life of integrity.

Ministry has never been an easy task, but it is central to the life of the local congregation and key to achieving God's plan. It is at the heart of the church's mission to expand God's rule now and in this place. This book is a check point for all of us: is this, the high, glorious, and demanding call of God, what God calls me to—and, for those who are already in ministry, what God continues to call me to?

I am grateful to be part of this project, to work with David Markle as general editor, and to read and edit each of the writers. I have learned much from the individual and collective wisdom in this book; I am confident that it adds a vital new resource for the kingdom and for life-forming decisions to follow Jesus into full time Christian ministry.

Arthur M. Kelly, Coordinator
Communications and Publishing
Church of God Ministries
June 2001

I.
Being–

foundations of who we are

"'You shall love the Lord your God with all your heart, and with all your soul, and with all your mind.' This is the greatest and first commandment. And a second is like it: 'You shall love your neighbor as yourself'" (Matthew 22:37–39, NRSV).

How is it with your soul?—the early adherents of the Wesleyan movement asked one another this question. And so, dear friend, how is it with yours? A life in Christian ministry flows out of a "life…hidden with Christ in God" (Colossians 3:3 NRSV).

Learning to love God with all that you are is the critical foundation for a life in Christian ministry.

We, who have written, give witness to who we are in Christ Jesus through

    Expression of a heart for God,
    Encouragement of ears that discern our Lord's voice,
    Coming to think of ourselves as "ones who serve,"
    Discovering a passion for life with God in Christian ministry.

Now, we invite you to join us in fuller discovery of who you are in Christ Jesus. Be blessed in that glad journey!

Chapter One:

Diana Swoope, *Growing a Heart for God*

In order for ministry to be truly authentic and applicable, it must flow from the heart of a person filled by the presence of God. There is no enemy to the faith as formidable as the inauthentic witness. Ministry that flows from an obvious relationship with God is powerful and effective. Having a heart that yearns for more and more of God is the essential foundation upon which ministry must be constructed.

Salvation

As contradictory as it may sound, there are those who occupy places and positions in Christian ministry who are not professed Christians. For whatever reason, they are not saved. This next statement may sound very simple to some and unnecessary to others. Yet, the risk of redundancy must be taken: Those who seek to minister in the name of Christ must be saved themselves.

An unconverted minister is definitely an odd concept, but it is more common than one would think. A man, who returned to seminary to pursue a Doctor of Ministry after ten years as pastor of a church, admitted in class one day that he had never believed in Jesus Christ for himself. There were too many unbelievable and unconfirmed notions in the Bible. Personal belief in and acceptance of the gospel was untenable. He entered the pastorate to please his parents and remained for so long because it "felt good and paid well!" Obtaining another degree was simply a means to one more raise in pay. This is a sad but true story.

Ministers of Christ must be able to persuade others that Christ is, for all situations, "the way, the truth and the life" (John 14:6). How can one propose to bring the help of God to someone if they have not already believed themselves in the ability of God to help? The prerequisite for all ministers is that they believe on the Lord Jesus Christ. Understanding the gospel will come, but only as one has a heart that can first affirm that "I know whom I have believed...(2 Timothy 1:12).

Passionate Desire for God

People yearn for authenticity in a world filled with holographic modes of living. They know the difference between a person who has just reached entry level in their relationship with God, and those who are allowing Christ to fill them through and through. They know the discrepancies that are apparent in a woman or man who is lackluster in their pursuit of God.

Please heed this word of caution: Diligently be on guard against the spirit of complacency that masks itself in personal confidence. The tasks of ministry are often repetitive and rushed. Whether preaching, praying, singing, writing, visiting, or comforting—whatever the area of ministry—there will be times in which it seems as though one task is hardly ended before it is time to begin another. In these situations, it is very easy to begin to rely upon experience, gifts, personality, or a combination of all the above. One's gifts and skills, no matter how proficient or inspiring, however, are not enough to bring together the hurting hearts of people and the healing hands of God.

The power to make the difference in people's lives is in the presence of God. God's presence is what distinguishes the effective minister from just being another person with a call to ministry. Develop a desire for God that is passionate and partisan. Don't be satisfied with just the "presents" that God gives through "successes" in ministry.

Settle for nothing less than God's presence. Seek it. Pursue it with all your heart. You will find it. For it is true that one receives what one diligently pursues (see Matthew 7:7–8).

Get a hunger and thirst in you that can be satiated by none other than the God who is aptly named "presence" in Exodus 33. Read Psalm 43, 63, and 143 over and over until the insatiable quest for God articulated by the authors becomes personal. The Apostle Paul, a worthy example for any aspiring minister, passionately exclaimed, "I want to know Christ" (Philippians 3:10). Nothing else mattered in the grand scheme of things. Ministers cannot possibly have any greater descriptive attached to them than that which was said of the New Testament apostles: "They have been with Jesus" (Acts 4:13).

Disciplines of the Heart

While the pursuit of God's presence must be the passionate occupation for the minister, growing a heart that can adequately host the presence of God must be a concomitant drive. It is true that one receives what one diligently pursues. It is also true that one becomes what one purposefully practices.

Anything that experiences growth has been subject to some form of discipline and dedication. The person who is serious about the call to ministry will need to learn to practice some disciplines of the heart. These are stretching exercises, so to speak, that condition the heart and mind for the vision and direction of God. While there are no magic formulas that will enact the purpose of God, there are some habits that, when diligently practiced and consistently applied, will be useful to understanding how to live and move in the presence of God.

DISCIPLINE #1: CONSECRATION

Fair or not, there is a higher expectation and perhaps a greater responsibility for the minister in the area of consecration. While the call is not to be humanly perfect, there should be a high level of concern for ones spiritual condition. The pure heart is the "wineskin" into which God will pour the Holy Spirit.

In the wake of the recent rash of moral and ethical failures of several prominent church leaders, many Christian groups are talking more and more about holiness and the need for righteous living. The impact and influence that Christian leaders can wield in the body of Christ cannot be treated lightly. Whether right or wrong, people watch carefully and take their cues for living from their leaders.

For this reason, ministers must lead by example. They can ill afford to take their cues from the people around them or from society. The lifestyle of the minister must be principled. The Spirit and Word of God dictate those principles. The Bible is very forthright and firm about lifestyles and habits that are unbecoming to those in ministerial leadership. Open immorality should not be named once among any Christian, but especially among ministers.

Morality, however, is just one aspect of living about which the minister must be concerned. The overall character of the minister must be carefully cultivated and guarded. Character issues concern more than choosing right from wrong. The issues of character encompass the overall attitude and approach to the public and private life of the minister. To be sure, one's character will be "heard" before the mouth ever moves. The character of the minister is the primary source of personal influence. In ministry influence is everything.

It is of utmost importance that the conduct, conversation, and customs of the minister be consistent with the word of God so that one's influence will not be compromised. The Fruit of the Spirit evidences true Christian character. "Love, joy, peace, patience, kindness, goodness, faithfulness, gentleness, and self control" (Galatians 5:23) should be applied in every area of life.

Far too many have placed convenience of lifestyle ahead of issues of character. There is a level of implicit trust associated with the office of a minister. Unfortunately, some ministers have hidden questionable habits behind this implicit trust, thereby abusing the office. While some life habits may be convenient, they are not expedient for the growth and overall witness of the minister. A consecrated life that is fully under the control of the Holy Spirit and consistently aligned with the word of God must be the daily occupation of the minister. Pursue holiness with all diligence in every facet of life, from relationships with the opposite sex to matters of finance. Holiness is the sentinel of the heart, the dwelling place for the presence.

DISCIPLINE #2: CONFESSION

One of the most dangerous attitudes to have is overconfidence in one's spirituality. Many have fallen into the trap of thinking more highly of themselves than they ought. Rather than being true to what is known about personal strengths and weaknesses, some often tempt the Holy

Spirit by carelessly flirting in areas of life that are personally over-whelming.

Let's face it. Everyone has a dark side. Each has leanings in the heart that if not held in check may cause one to wander. Without the help of God, these tendencies will often give birth to sin and ultimately spiritual death (see James 1:13–15). The discipline of daily confession is vital to maintaining a healthy spiritual life.

The word confession basically means "to speak the same thing" or to "agree with." True confession begins with personal honesty. One must have an attitude that acknowledges personal insufficiencies: "I am not all that I ought to be." It is good to know, however, that God still choos-es to employ us in divine service despite this fact.

The person whose heart yearns with passion for God must be ruthlessly honest in recognizing areas in her or his life that need cleansing and strengthening. No one knows you better than you know yourself. You know if you have problems with the quick, unsupervised access to the illicit sites on the World Wide Web. You know if you are harboring secret jealousies of peers and friends even though you have somehow managed to hide these from them. You know if your desire for power and control has lead to unhealthy interactions with others. You are more aware of your "tendencies" than anyone else—other than God.

You don't need to wait until a senior minister or peer confronts you. Honestly and reasonably evaluate yourself. Confess your insufficien-cies and sins to God. Pray that you may be healed (see James 5:16). Recognize that you cannot overcome the leanings of your heart without daily reliance upon the strength of God. Tell God all. Be confident in God's unfailing love for you and the unwavering promise of imminent, effectual help for your needs.

There are times in which, for your own spiritual conscience, cleansing, and restoration, you may need to confess shortcomings and failures to another spiritually mature individual (see Galatians 6:1). It may even be wise to surround yourself with several mature Christians, whether they are "ministers" or not, who can serve as an accountability group that helps you to keep your weaknesses in check and your strengths in focus. Seek God's counsel to determine what accountability structure is best for you. But, once knowing the counsel of God, submit to the process. The "Lone Ranger" approach to ministry is suicidal. Make yourself accountable to someone who will indeed hold you accountable.

Others often see what we do not see in ourselves. Praying, perceptive accountability partners can apply pressure in areas in which we tend to be careless and casual, steering toward growth. They can also relieve pressure in areas in which we are too hard on ourselves. In the diligence to be spiritually sound, we can sometimes make everything sinful, including natural tendencies in our personalities that are distinctive but not corrupt.

Confession should certainly be offered directly to persons whom you have knowingly injured or offended. Effectiveness in ministry can be hindered where there is conflict that has not been confessed and resolved. Stop whatever you are doing and fix it (Matthew 5:24). This keeps your heart transparent and your service to others truthful.

DISCIPLINE #3: CELEBRATION

The call of God to ministry can be exciting and invigorating, but the actual outliving of that call can be exasperating and often disappointing. Growth may not come as quickly as anticipated. Rejection may come in ways unimagined. Receptivity to one's service may be less than encouraging. Betrayal may come from the people into whom you poured vast amounts of time, energy, and resources. Add to this the fact that the tasks of ministry can be boring and tedious, setting the stage for ministry burn out.

It is in these times that you may feel as though God deceived you by calling you into ministry (see Jeremiah 20:7-9). Hard times will come in ministry. Working with people is tough and sometimes thankless work. It is very easy to lose sight of the goodness of God when you are regularly confronted with the decadence of people—especially those whom you thought were thoroughly filled with God's spirit. The discipline that keeps the heart fertile and the spirit encouraged in these times is celebration.

Celebration acknowledges the goodness of God despite the gravity of the situation. It brings perspective to an imbalanced picture. The problems, pressures and pains associated with life in general and ministry specifically take on realistic dimensions. Celebration reminds you of who has called you into ministry and whose responsibility it is to provide for the calling (1 Thessalonians 5:24). It sets you free to simply obey God and not try to be God.

Celebration is praise. Praise is a guaranteed way to engage the presence of God (see Psalm 22:3). Celebration puts God back in the rightful place of preeminence. People and problems take on less prominence when God truly has the preeminence. It takes discipline and practice to learn to celebrate when complaining is easier and seemingly more effective. Yet, a celebrating heart is a confident heart. A celebrating heart is a comforted heart. A celebrating heart is a conquering heart.

DISCIPLINE #4: CONVERSATION

Daily, personal, focused conversation with God should be the primary occupation of every minister. An old saying is that "prayer changes things." While this is definitely true, the greater accomplishment that God seeks through the daily conversation is to change you. Prayer is the avenue by which we learn more about God's presence. Corporate prayers are simply not enough to maintain the vital connection between the minister and the powerful presence of God.

In conversations, one not only talks, but one listens. Great conversationalists usually listen more than they talk. The same should be applied to prayer. Listen to God keenly. God will speak to your heart. It is through the conversations of the heart that God grants us information that is critical for good success.

It is really amazing how little time the people who have been called to speak for God actually spend speaking *to* God. Prayer must be learned and practiced. It takes discipline, particularly when praying seems ineffective and ineffectual. The sense that conversations with God are senseless has caused many to cease to pray. Yet, the admonition to "pray without ceasing" (1 Thessalonians 5:23) continues to be valuable. Conversing with God is an action and an attitude. Jesus actively engaged in prayer. On many occasions he removed himself from the crowd and even his disciples to engage in focused conversation with God. There is a need for the minister to withdraw, on a daily basis, to a place of solitude and quiet to actively engage in prayer. Jesus' prayers were most often centered on his knowledge of the word of God. A rich knowledge of God's word provides a powerful springboard for conversation with God. To be sure, conversations that begin with God's word will always catch God's attention. Allow the Bible to be a source of personal enrichment, not just a resource for preparation of the next sermon. "Let the word dwell in you richly" (Colossians 3:17), it will enhance your prayer life, feed your soul and empower you for living.

To keep the devotional time lively and fruitful, it is advisable to have a plan of action. First, establish a place to which you can go regularly and remain undisturbed. It may be your office, a room or corner in your home, even a literal closet. Take your Bible, pen and paper, a devotional book, and a hymnal. Carry a printed directory of names of those associated with your ministry. Write down names of people and situations that come to your mind. This is often God directing you to pray for these persons. You may even carry the newspaper or other chronicle of current events.

Vary the order of your prayer time. Read your prayers sometimes. Sing your prayers. Meditate for a portion of the time. Write your prayers. Pray from passages in the Bible, from names listed in your directory or from the headlines in the newspaper. Kneel. Stand. Bow. Lie prostrate. Whatever your mode of operation, it is imperative that you spend time just "hanging out with God" in prayer. Regular conversations with God is your source of power and your time of refreshing. Actively, fervently pray.

Prayer is not only an action, but it is also an attitude. Conversation with God does not take place in the closet only. God speaks through our daily interactions with people, through our daily routines, and even in the interruptions. Listen to what God is saying and respond in obedience.

DISCIPLINE # 5: CONSIDERATION

The minister, who truly seeks to grow a heart for God, should give careful consideration to what is in the heart of God. The biblical record supports the assertion that at the very core of God's heart is considerable love and compassion for all people (John 3:16). Yet, there also seems to be considerable support for the assertion that God's heart leans toward those who are downtrodden, marginalized, and locked in unjust situations. Jesus announced, in Luke 4:18, that liberty for these people would be the focus of his ministry.

It is impossible to love God and not be concerned with the plight and condition of people suffering from the effects of the evil actions of people and the evil results of unjust systems. Indeed, one's claim to love God loses its authenticity in the absence of a willingness to help one's neighbor (see Luke 10:25ff).

Consideration for people that leads to acts of justice and mercy is evidence that one understands and follows the heart of God (Micah 6:8). This may necessitate widening one's boundaries to include persons of different cultures, religions, or socio-economic backgrounds. The verses recorded in Matthew 25:25-31 suggest that we can feel the pulse of God and see into the heart of God when we perform deeds of compassion for "the least of these."

Developing a servant's heart, then, follows the pattern set by Jesus who affirmed that he came to serve, not to be served (see Luke 22:28; also John 13:3–17). True religion is not solely to be found in ritual expression or cognitive assent, but also in the positive pursuit of righteousness expressed in the area of social compassion. It takes discipline to discern the difference between works born out of true consideration and love for people and works done for consideration by the people. Humility is required, yet a person who truly yearns for the presence of God will also yearn for that which is in the heart of God—love and mercy. This is the essence of an authentic walk with God and the basis for authentic ministry.

Summary

Growing a heart for God does not happen out of desire alone. It requires discipline and consistent practice. It requires *consecration*—a resolute determination to do the will of God, to be holy as God is holy. It requires *confession*—the recognition that perfection has not been realized and without the cleansing of God, sinful tendencies yet threaten to be actualized. It requires *celebration*—to keep life and ministry in proper perspective. When God has the preeminence, troubles have less prominence. It requires *conversation*—daily, focused prayer and devotional times that are supported by the Word of God. This empowers and enriches the heart. It requires *consideration*—doing justice, loving mercy, and walking humbly with God, so that the healing hands of God may be effectively applied to the hurting hearts of people.

Chapter Two:
David Markle, *Nurturing the Mind of Christ*

Did our Lord Jesus think of himself first and primarily as servant? Or, did our Lord think of himself first and primarily as leader? These questions became relevant for me in a painful, yet instructive pastoral experience.

"No vision, no relationship, no leadership." The words from a key leader in our congregation struck me dumb. They seared my consciousness for weeks. Many times I have reflected upon that particular congregational leadership retreat setting and what had led up to it. I had served as pastor there for nearly four years.

The ministry had exceeded my expectations. The number and reach of small and large groups had increased in a healthy manner. Growing attendance in worship reflected a respectable portion of new followers of Christ. The church provided continuing education funds that enabled studies at a leading seminary. I endeavored to "bring home" the benefits of those enriching educational opportunities, particularly in the area of leadership. What went wrong?

Let us look at my friend's statement one segment at a time: *Vision*? It was just as alive in my heart as at any time in that pastorate. But looking back, I could have communicated it more creatively and more often. *Relationship?* Certainly my brother desired something more in our relationship than had developed. I was losing influence with a portion of the influencers in our congregation and his statement served as a "wake-up" call to me. *Leadership?* Relationship and shared vision are key factors in gaining and keeping permission to lead. There is no question that these factors impacted the necessary trust to continue leading in that situation.

Yet there remains one more layer. As our ministry grew in fruitfulness, my confidence in my ability to lead in Christ's kingdom grew. That was good. As I received fresh insights from pastoral mentors and graduate studies into functioning as an "initiating leader" in the congregational setting, I attempted to implement them in my life in ministry. That was good, too. In this season, however, nearly imperceptibly, my sense of identity as a leader shifted. I was moving from seeing myself as a servant leader (where the role of servant is primary) to a self-perception as a servant *leader* (where leadership is primary). That is worthy of deeper examination.

As I unpack a bit of my personal heritage, I invite you to examine your own inclination toward ministry today. Specifically, do you come at the opportunity of investing your life in Christian ministry from a *serve first* or a *lead first* mindset?

Two of the "giants" in my life are my parents. They focus on servant-hood to the exclusion of leadership. They have simply sought to live the life and serve as they are gifted. My father worked in automotive components plants for 35 years. On a number of occasions he was invited to move into a supervisory role. Each time he declined. He did, however, pursue training for a greater level of technical sophistication in a service role to others. In the local church, he served as treasurer for an even longer period. My mother has been a "behind-the-scenes" servant in the church. She typed and mimeographed the worship bulletin for many years; she ordered, delivered, and distributed the church's Sunday school booklets; she served in the nursery well beyond her grandchildren's age of eligibility for that service. One of the few times she has been on the platform was when the congregation honored her lifetime of quiet service in their midst. In sum, both of my parents served faithfully, neither is obviously a visible leader. I value this heritage and recognize that my family of origin "leadership DNA" shaped me to become a servant leader.

Others come to the opportunity to serve in ministry with greater motivation on the *leadership* side of the equation. Perhaps this is your experience. You tend to become the leader of each group that you join. You enjoy exercising responsibility when crucial decisions must be made. The desire to lead may burn brightly in your soul. Others may look naturally to you to "take the lead."

It is my glad affirmation that God works with and through persons of both primary motivations to accomplish his kingdom work. How have the "giants" in your life shaped you for service and leadership in God's kingdom?

Another avenue of approach may come to light as we place ourselves in the story of the morning of Jesus' resurrection. In John's account, Mary Magdalene rushes to tell Peter and "the one who Jesus loved" (John 20:2) the news of her discovery of the empty tomb. The following verses depict a footrace to the tomb. The Apostle John outruns Peter, but waits, peering in: "He bent over and looked in at the strips of linen lying there but did not go in" (John 20:5). Peter betrays none of John's hesitation: "Then Simon Peter, who was behind him, arrived and went into the tomb. He saw the strips of linen lying there, as well as the burial cloth that had been around Jesus' head. The cloth was folded up by itself, separate from the linen" (John 20:6–7). John describes his own participation: "Finally the other disciple, who had reached the tomb first, also went inside. He saw and believed" (John 20:8).

Do you identify yourself with Peter, bursting into the tomb, assessing the situation, drawing a conclusion, at the ready for quick response? Or do you see yourself as John, thinking carefully about the meaning of the empty tomb, waiting for another to arrive, hesitant to take the initiative?

The good news is that God worked with and through both Peter and John in significant ways! The good news is that persons moving toward Christian ministry may learn and grow from some "giants" who modeled servanthood most dramatically and from others who more readily modeled leadership. In the seminal work, *Servant Leadership*, Greenleaf describes the reality of the range of human motivations toward a leadership role:

> The servant-leader is servant first.... It begins with the
> natural feeling that one wants to serve, to serve *first*.
> Then conscious choice brings one to aspire to lead.
> That person is sharply different from one who is *leader*
> first, perhaps because of the need to assuage an unusual
> power drive or to acquire material possessions.
> For such it will be a later choice to serve—after leader-
> ship is established. The leader-first and the servant-first

are two extreme types. Between them there are shadings and blends that are part of the infinite variety of human nature (Greenleaf 1977, 13).

Greenleaf describes well the range of human motivation concerning service and leadership. Yet, as disciples of Jesus Christ, we must find our primary identity in relationship to God in Christ. Thus, our Lord's self-perception in this matter is formative for us.

Our purpose in this chapter is to examine who we are in light of the resources of the biblical witness that both inform and reflect the self-perception of Jesus as a servant who leads; and by extension, to ask how do those same passages shape our self-perception as persons engaged in Christian ministry in the 21st century? We will look at the shaping of our identity as we examine the servant songs of Isaiah, explore our motivation and ambition for a life in Christian ministry as we hear Jesus' statement of purpose in the gospel of Mark, and view our attitude toward others in light of Jesus' humility described in the first century hymn in Philippians 2:5–11. Finally, we will ready ourselves for a life of intentional servanthood as did Jesus in John 13. I believe that we will find clear answers to the questions that opened this chapter and clear guidance for the formation of our identities as servant leaders.

Living with Paradox

There are a number of paradoxes present in the Christian experience. Though they stretch our capacity for integration, we are stronger in our faith as we learn to hold their seemingly opposing ends in dynamic tension. Among them are the tensions between the sovereignty of God and the free will of human persons, the goodness of God and the presence of evil, the possibility of living free from willful sin and God's readiness to forgive us when we sin. The skill with which we hold both ends of these tensions together indicates something about the depth and balance of our faith.

The members of the religion and Christian ministries department in our college engaged in lively discussion regarding the tension between the emphases of the local congregation and that expression of the church wherein we serve, the Christian college. As emotions rose to a fever pitch, our academic dean wisely called "time out." He declared to us, "Feel the tension, get used to it, it's not going away."

One of the inescapable paradoxes experienced in a life in Christian ministry is felt in that tension between servanthood and leadership. The question is at the heart of our identity as ministers of the gospel. Am I primarily a *servant* who leads? Or, am I primarily a *leader* who serves? Let us draw out this distinction further. The servant who leads holds a primary focus on servanthood. This person's prime mode of being in the world is to serve, whether that service is consciously focused upon God or upon another person. For this minister, the prime motivation for leadership is to serve. Leadership is only one option among others as a means of service. In contrast, the leader who serves exercises primary focus upon leadership. This person's primary mode of being in the world is to lead another person or group of persons in the name of Christ. For this minister, the prime motivation for service is the opportunity to lead. Serving others is viewed as one means of leading them.

In *Leading the Congregation*, Norman Shawchuck and Roger Heuser assert, "The desire to serve others must be stronger than the desire to lead—so that leadership becomes a means of serving" (Shawchuck and Heuser 1993, 35). It appears that the weightier side of the servanthood-leadership paradox is on the side of servanthood. I would hold that however we have entered this preparation for a life in Christian ministry, we must move with our Lord toward a self-perception as a servant who leads. Will this position pass muster with Scripture, in particular with passages that focus upon our Lord Jesus? Do they reveal a person who primarily thinks of himself as a servant who leads or as a leader who serves? We turn our attention now to see.

The Identity of a Servant Leader

The servant songs of Isaiah (Isaiah 42:1–9, 49:1–7, 50:4-9, 52:13—53:12) contain important material determinative of Jesus' sense of identity. Scholars, viewing them through the lens of the Hebrew conception of "corporate personality," aid us in discovering a formative message both for the people of God (Israel) and for an individual who would emerge in their midst (a suffering servant).

Pastors often embody the presence of the entire church in their acts of ministry. In a symbolic way, when a minister calls on church members or prospective members in the hospital, she acts in behalf of the whole body of Christ. When the pastor stands with a gospel word amid a unique and temporary community of mourners comprised of both believers in Christ, believers in other faiths, or persons with no faith at all, he embodies and speaks for the community of faith in Jesus. As the pastoral prayer is voiced in Lord's day gatherings of worship, the sensitive pastor prays not merely her own prayer, but rather the prayer made in behalf of the whole people of God in that place. At the close of that prayer (and perhaps throughout it), it seems natural for the people of God to identify her prayer as their own by saying, "Amen, so be it, Lord!"

In a similar way, a specific servant would emerge historically who would embody the identity and purpose of a servant people. The servant songs are formative to the identity of both the people of God and this emerging person. Let us examine each song, especially sensitive to discover whether it emphasizes a "servant who leads" or a "leader who serves."

In Isaiah 42:1–4, God describes this people or individual as "my servant." This servant will "bring justice to the nations" (Isaiah 42:1b) with sensitivity to human frailty and with unswerving purpose. This will be accomplished not by the servant's own wits or resources, but rather by the agency of the Spirit of God. Indeed, the promise of God extends the blessing of the servant's ministry to all peoples: "I will keep you and will make you to be a covenant for the people and a light for the Gentiles..." (Isaiah 42:6b).

The identity, established by God, is as a servant. The activity spawned by his Spirit is leading others into the reign of God's justice. The person (or people) depicted in Isaiah 42 seems clearly to be a servant who leads.

As we move to Isaiah 49, the predominance of the purpose of God becomes even more striking. Here, the servant affirms God's purpose that predates the servant's birth: "You are my servant, Israel, in whom I will display my splendor" (Isaiah 49:3). Verse 4 describes the frustration of unfulfilled aspirations each of us encounters in Christian ministry, yet also affirms the assurance in which we serve. In verse 5, the servant "owns" the identity of servanthood assigned by the Father in preparation for rehearsing that word for us in verse 6. The Lord promises that the impact of the servant will extend to all peoples: "It is too small a thing for you to be my servant to restore the tribes of Jacob and bring back those of Israel I have kept. I will also make you a light for the Gentiles, that you may bring my salvation to the ends of the earth" (Isaiah 49:6).

Again, the purpose of God is for a people who will serve him in displaying his splendor to all the peoples of earth. This primary purpose of servanthood is owned both by God and by the recipient of this identity.

In Isaiah 50:4–9, the servant is identified by what the servant does. The servant listens to God and thus may speak with an "instructed tongue" (Isaiah 50:4) to the weary. Hearing that the servant must suffer, the servant submits himself to the abuses of humanity confident of God's ultimate vindication. The spirit of humility and submission to God and God's way reveal the identity of the person in focus here. It is not by name but by internal sense of being and purpose that we view the servant who leads in this song.

The final and most familiar song overtly names "the servant" (Isaiah 52:13) and most closely resembles our Lord in his passion. It is a picture of deep irony—this one whose very form would be marred and whose appearance is no drawing card—will still the voices of kings (Isaiah 52:15) as they recognize one who is greater than they. Indeed, it deepens, "he was despised, and we esteemed him not" (Isaiah 53:3b).

Beautiful, poetic words describe the horror of his suffering and the wonder of his sacrifice for us:

> Surely he took up our infirmities and carried our sorrows, yet we considered him stricken by God, smitten by him, and afflicted. But he was pierced for our transgressions, he was crushed for our iniquities; the punishment that brought us peace was upon him, and by his wounds we are healed. We all, like sheep, have gone astray, each of us has turned to his own way; and the Lord has laid on him the iniquity of us all (Isaiah 53:4–6).

He went to his suffering in silence. He died without earthly descendant.

Neither wicked nor rich, his death and burial identify him with each in turn (Isaiah 53:7–10).

Our God called the tune and the servant fulfilled the difficult dance. Now, he will be exalted forever:

> After the suffering of his soul, he will see the light of
> life and be satisfied; by his knowledge my righteous
> servant will justify many, and he will bear their iniq-
> uities. Therefore I will give him a portion among the
> great, and he will divide the spoils with the strong,
> because he poured out his life unto death, and was
> numbered with the transgressors. For he bore the sin
> of many, and made intercession for the transgressors
> (Isaiah 53:11–12).

Here again, the name is significant: "servant." That service is poured out with greatest humility and suffering. The servant leads us by his suffering. He humbly makes the way for each of us. No greater leadership—no greater service—has ever been rendered.

Irrespective of the practice of our family of origin, our origin and identity in Christ point us to one whose primary sense of self was focused upon serving the will of the Father. For Jesus that will included suffering in behalf of all the peoples of earth that they might enter his grace and his reign of righteousness. His identity is one of servanthood. Thus, we receive a "double portion" of servant identity—both as a member of the people of God and as individual followers of Jesus Christ. With our Lord, we must begin by viewing ourselves primarily as servants who lead.

The Purpose of a Servant Leader

Is the focus of our ministry upon our own fulfillment in exercising leadership or upon meeting the needs of those whom we serve and lead? Greenleaf proposes that the distinction between the person oriented primarily to service and the one oriented primarily to lead is found at the point of whose needs are primarily in view: "The best test, and difficult to administer, is: Do those served grow as persons? Do they, _while being served,_ become healthier, wiser, freer, more autonomous, more likely themselves to become servants? And, what is the effect on the least privileged in society; will they benefit, or, at least, not be further deprived?" (Greenleaf 1977, 13–14).

The quest of human ambition is as old as humanity. For us, ambition simply is. The issue is this: what will we do with it? Among Jesus' inner circle, James and John came to Jesus with a request for the best seats in heaven (Mark 10:35–37). They desired to be named "the greatest" by God. Jesus informed them that though each of them would suffer mightily for him, it was not his call as to who would receive those chief seats in heaven. Meanwhile, the rest of the apostolic company became outraged, either by the hubris of their companions or perhaps that James and John thought to ask first. Nonetheless, Jesus nipped the incipient conflict in the bud with a lesson on the nature of great leadership and a pronouncement of his purpose in ministry.

First, he told them how it was *not* to be in his kingdom: "You know that those who are regarded as rulers of the Gentiles lord it over them, and their high officials exercise authority over them" (Mark 10:42). *Leadership* among peoples of the world is often a matter of *rulership.* The attitude of leader to follower may often be: "I am over you. I am in charge of you. I will tell you what to do and you will do it." Jesus denies this mode of leadership to his followers and redirects their ambition: "Instead, whoever wants to become great among you must be your servant, and whoever wants to be first must be slave of all" (Mark 10:43–44). It is as if Jesus said to the disciples, "You aspire to be a great leader? Fine. Let me show you the way: become a great servant!"

Earlier we looked at the anticipation of a servant messiah arising amid a servant people. Now, we hear Jesus' own perception of his purpose in coming to earth. The correction of James's and John's misguided ambition serves as the context for Jesus' declaration of his chosen mode of being in the world: "For even the Son of Man did not come to be served, but to serve, and to give his life as a ransom for many" (Mark 10:45).

Jesus' purpose is to serve his Father and serve other persons made in his image. This is not only his destiny, this is his choice. He comes to serve and, especially, to lay down his life on the cross as his ultimate act of service. Lamar Williamson, Jr., cinches the application for us: "The argument is of the 'how much more…' type. If the Lord Jesus was a servant, how much more ought his disciples to be servants" (Williamson

1983, 193). Servanthood is his primary purpose in life, and by relationship with him, becomes ours as well.

The Attitude of a Servant Leader

A third primary view of Jesus' perception of himself comes from the early Church. At the end of his earthly life, how did others view his self-perception as he had fleshed it out in his living? This goes beyond what he had said to an assessment of how he had lived.

In his letter to the church at Philippi, Paul cites what is often regarded as a first-century hymn (Philippians 2:5–11) as he exhorts the members of the body of Christ to work together with a common mind and heart (Philippians 2:1–4). There is no greater, more far-reaching example of how we should view ourselves in relationship to other persons than that of our Lord.

Though his personhood and his work are unique in that he alone is Son of God, we who are sons and daughters of God find our identity and purpose most securely in relationship to him. Indeed, this sense of identity is primary, coming prior to what we shall *do* in life and shaping *how* we shall do it. The passage depicts both our Lord's voluntary humiliation (Philippians 2:5–8) and the Father's resulting exaltation (Philippians 2:9-11) of him. Our focus centers upon his humility.

The mindset to which we are exhorted is not alien to us in Christ. It is alien to those whose existence is merely in the realm of the current world order apart from Christ. It is, however, a mindset that becomes ours when we belong to Jesus Christ. Thus, living in him, this attitude about ourselves is not something external like a piece of clothing that we don for a particular day, but rather wells up within us out of our fundamental relationship to God in Christ. Thus, an exegetical translation of Philippians 2:5 might read: "Have this same mind among you which [is] yours in Christ Jesus...."

Jesus' attitude of humility must not be defined by any attribute of deity that he gave up in becoming human, but rather defined, oddly enough to our sensibilities, by the fact that he, being God, chose to become human. This is his primary act of humility—becoming one of us. Yet, he remains markedly different from us, in that he remained fully God.

This "incarnation" means that Jesus placed himself within the dilemma of sinful humanity. He is liable to suffer all that being human entails. He is tempted just as we are. He, too, will die. In the midst of becoming fully human, Jesus is always distinguished from us in that he chose to be in this dilemma, while we were born into it. We bear the sin of corporate humanity by birth; he bears it to the cross, not by birth, but by his own choice. Thus is the grace of our Lord Jesus Christ revealed to us as he chose not to sit idly by while we remained immersed in sin; rather he "emptied himself" by taking on the very essence of who we are.

The first and primary step in his humility was becoming human. But he added richness and depth to humility when he laid down his life for us. "Greater love has no one than this, that he lay down his life for his friends" (John 15:13).

This is what a life in Christian ministry demands of us: that we lay down our lives for others—one day at a time, one sermon or lesson at a time, one formative relationship at a time, one act of mercy at a time— in all of our days. Is this an attitude toward life that you are willing to take? Are you willing to be a person whose life is primarily lived as an act of service to others in the name and Spirit of Jesus? If your answer is "yes" then by all means let us journey on! If not, you may need to reconsider the course that you are pursuing.

Jesus lifted the path of humility to its ultimate level by dying on a Roman cross. There existed in his time no more horrible or humiliating way in which to die. From a heart of servant love and a mind of servant sacrifice, he made the ultimate sacrifice for you and me. The Christ willfully journeyed from the highest height to the greatest depth in order to redeem humankind.

A third element in Jesus' self-perception comes into place—seeing himself as a servant in relationship to others. In vital relationship with him, we find ourselves moving toward a like attitude about our own relationships to other persons. We have arrived at a matched set, our identity, our purpose, and our attitude each primarily shaped by our Lord's own choice for a posture of servanthood.

Choosing a life of servanthood

As always, our Lord has gone first. He has charted the way forward before us. The intentionality with which Jesus acts as servant on the last night of his earthly life is striking. John 13:2-5 records:

> The evening meal was being served, and the devil
> had already prompted Judas Iscariot, son of Simon,
> to betray Jesus. Jesus knew that the Father had put all
> things under his power, and that he had come from God
> and was returning to God; so he got up from the meal,
> took off his outer clothing, and wrapped a towel around
> his waist. After that, he poured water into a basin and
> began to wash his disciples' feet, drying them with the
> towel that was wrapped around him.

Jesus knew who he was. Jesus knew where he was going. Jesus knew what the Father had entrusted to him. He could be trusted to lead for he was wholly committed to serve. Each deliberate step expresses his decision to serve. This grew from the essence of his being. Having made this decision within, Jesus enacted the washing of the disciples' feet as the penultimate act of his life.

A number of implications are suggested by our journey into these key biblical passages. First, "servant who leads" ministry depends upon an ongoing vital relationship with God in Christ. While informed by "state of the art" research related to the local church as she most effectively serves today, primacy must be given to and remain upon the identity, purpose, and attitude that we find fleshed out by Jesus. It is not that we become Jesus, but rather in intimate relationship with him, we grow more and more like him. As he gave primacy to servanthood in his earthly ministry, his Spirit propels us toward a like identity, purpose, and attitude in our life in Christian ministry. Indeed, to choose the opposite course, to take the tack of a "leader who serves," runs the risk of living out a denial of our primary identity in Christ.

Second, an expression of this primacy of servanthood is that the opportunity to serve remains its primary motivation. A "feetwashing mindset" permeates each act of ministry. Whatever gifting we have received becomes primarily a means of serving others (the original purpose of spiritual gifts) rather than primarily a means of self-discovery, self-actualization, or worse, self-aggrandizement. There is great satisfaction experienced by the doer in doing what we have been designed by God to do. Indeed, it is a wonderful experience to discover what we are to be and do in God's kingdom, yet that motivation recedes in importance as we are captured by "the more excellent way" of love as we grow to serve others for their sake and for the sake of Christ.

Third, we will never outgrow the need for the primacy of servanthood. A "servant spirit" becomes determinative of the way in which leadership is carried out. Oden (1983, 54) views it as fundamental:

> No well-conceived view of the pastoral office can ever
> set aside or leave behind this basic diaconal pattern:
> serving God through service to the neighbor. *Diakonia*
> is an essential layer of every theory, grade, or proper
> definition of ministry.

No matter how "high" one might go in ministry, servanthood remains irreplaceable in the foundation of that ministry. Let us grow beyond giving mere lip service to servanthood while with a "wink and a nod" we move on to the real business of leadership. Let "servant of God" be primary in our sense of identity, purpose, and attitude so that whether we preach, teach, lead worship, shepherd children, relate with teens, or care for adults, our particular function remains an expression of servanthood unto God and persons.

Fourth, having made a case for the primacy of servanthood in the servant leader paradox, let me emphasize that the paradox must stay in place. We are in danger of surrendering the "grown up" servant of Christ that we are to become if we abandon or neglect the leadership role that God entrusts to us. Servanthood does not imply weakness, but rather, as in the case of Jesus, true meekness or "strength under control" (Messer 1989, 103–115; Oden 1983, 54–57).

Finally, we find here a decision that must be re-affirmed on a consistent basis. The wear and tear of life in Christian ministry tends to convince us that our primary identity comes from our perceived degree of success. That perception may be by our own measure or based upon what we think others think of us. Jack Hayford puts the reminder in terms that apply to every day ministry: "Fruitful leadership is not getting others to fulfill my goals (or even my God-given vision for our collective enterprise and good), but helping others realize God's creative intent for their lives—personally, domestically, vocationally and eternally" (Barna 1997, 67–68). Without denying the appropriateness of the desire to bear fruit (John 15), let us affirm that our primary identity, purpose and attitude will remain in Jesus Christ. It is a perennial temptation for the minister to find her/his primary identity in what is done and how that effort is received by others. We seek here to give first place to relationship with Christ in these crucial internal matters.

Our Lord and Us

And so we return to where we had begun: Did Jesus think of himself first and primarily as servant? Or did our Lord regard himself first and primarily as leader? Through the lens of Scripture we have examined his sense of identity, purpose, and attitude. The former seems clearly to be the case. All the giftings, all the power, all the graces entrusted to Christ by God the Father were made effectual because it was so. May it be so in you and in me! Amen.

Reference List

Greenleaf, Robert K. 1977. *Servant Leadership*. New York: Paulist.

Hayford, Jack. 1997. "The Character of a Leader," in *Leaders on Leadership*. Edited by George Barna. Ventura: Regal.

Messer, Donald E. 1989. Contemporary Images of Christian Ministry. Nashville: Abingdon.

Motyer, J. Alec. 1993. *The Prophecy of Isaiah*. Downers Grove: InterVarsity.

New International Version Bible. 1984. Grand Rapids: Zondervan.

Oden, Thomas C. 1983. Pastoral Theology. New York: Harper and Row.

Shawchuck, Norman, and Roger Heuser. 1993. *Leading the Congregation*. Nashville: Abingdon.

Williamson, Jr., Lamar. 1983. *Interpretation: A Bible Commentary for Teaching and Preaching: Mark*. Atlanta: John Knox.

Chapter Three:
G. Samuel Dunbar, *Developing an Ear for God's Voice*

One of a growing Christian's great challenges is to determine what God is saying to him or her about his divine will for the future – especially when that word from God has implications for vocational choice and career direction.

There is, of course, a sense in which each and every follower of Christ is a "minister" of the gospel. Jesus' directive recorded in Matthew 28:19 to "go and make disciples of all nations" is not given exclusively to career ministers, but to all who would live in obedience to his commands. Whatever one's occupation may be, as believers we can minister to others God's love and message of salvation.

For some, however, God's leading will be to enter into a life of vocational Christian ministry. It is essential to understand that such vocational Christian ministry is not a "chosen profession," but rather a "sacred calling." That is what the word "vocation" implies: a calling.

The Call to Follow Christ

In a number of places in the New Testament there is a general use of the concept of God's "calling" to all believers to follow Christ.

In Acts 2:38 Peter responds to inquirers at Pentecost that they should "Repent and be baptized, every one of you, in the name of Jesus Christ so that your sins may be forgiven." Then verse 39 records the inspired apostle's conclusion affirming that "The promise is for you and your children and for all who are far off—for all whom the Lord our God will call." There Peter teaches that the life of salvation involves persons discovering that the life mission of the Lord Jesus was about God calling or inviting persons to leave behind *self*-dominated living and join in the exciting discovery of what it means to live in Christ. We may also reasonably assume that such "calling" involves the leading, nudging, and persuasive work of the Holy Spirit.

Again in the Apostle Paul's experience there was a "heavenward" call referred to in Philippians 3:14. Here Paul testifies to the fact that he personally has heard God's invitation to complete successfully the Christian pilgrimage which was begun some years prior. Thus God's voice reaches out to those beginning the Christian pilgrimage as well as those completing it, and no doubt at many points in between encouraging, pleading, drawing believers to a life of pursuing the obedient footsteps of Christ.

This is what we refer to as the general call for all to believe, obey, and follow the Christian way. But there are also references to God's specifically calling certain individuals to enter into what would become a new, lifelong Christian vocation for them.

The Call to Vocational Christian Ministry

Among those whom God called to vocational Christian ministry is Peter. The Gospel of John, chapter 21, records that very special exchange between the resurrected Christ and Peter wherein Christ glances around at the fishing boats and nets by Galilee and asks, "Simon son of John, do you truly love me more than these?" "Yes, Lord," Peter responds, "you know that I love you." Jesus' rejoinder to Peter's response is, "Then feed my lambs." A second time the risen Lord asks, "Do you truly love me?" and when Peter again answers in the affirmative, Jesus says, "Take care of my sheep." A third time Jesus asks the question and the third time Peter says "yes" and Jesus responds again with, "Feed my sheep." With that command Peter is launched on a new career. No longer just a fisherman, he becomes the premier preacher of the Gospel in Jerusalem and a leader among the apostles.

Then in Acts 13 we find the Holy Spirit-empowered church in Antioch "worshiping the Lord and fasting" when "the Holy Spirit said, 'Set apart for me Barnabas and Saul for the work to which I have called them.'" The church responded by placing their hands on Barnabas and Saul, later re-named Paul, and sending them off to a new ministry. Later in both Romans 1:1 and 1 Corinthians 1:1 Paul verified that he was "a servant of Jesus Christ, called to be an apostle and set apart for the gospel of God."

Peter, Barnabas, Paul, and others experienced a divine "call" that sent them down new paths of service and adventure in God's will. How did they "hear" their "call from God?" Did an audible voice speak in each case? We know that was what happened in Peter's case, but what about at Antioch when the Holy Spirit spoke? We cannot know with absolute certainty through which medium each person's call comes. It is certainly within the realm of God's possibilities to speak audibly wherever and whenever he chooses. But even in these biblical accounts it is safe and reasonable to determine that the call didn't come in an audible voice.

An Inward Impression

The Greek language, in which the New Testament was originally written, uses at least nine different words that are translated as "call" in the English. Each implies different kinds or ways of God's calling. Only one of these Greek words, *phoneo*, means to make a literal sound out loud. Several of the Greek words, especially the frequently used klesis, suggest something closer to an impression, sense, or inward inclination. Another one of the words may mean a written invitation as well as spoken word.

How can we know for a certainty then whether or not God may be calling us to vocational ministry? What "impressions" should I look for and where should I seek? One clue may be found in the young Isaiah's experience recorded in Isaiah 6. Here Isaiah has gone to the temple to worship and pray during a time of national anxiety and grief. King Uzziah, who had been a righteous leader, guiding Judah in paths of obedience to the Lord, had died. A concerned Isaiah was moved to seek God and there in the temple the young prophet "saw the Lord." Isaiah was overcome by the utter holiness of God and, as is so often true, when one gets a clear vision of the holy God the worshiper is led to confess, "I am ruined! For I am a man of unclean lips, and I live among a people of unclean lips, and my eyes have seen the King, the LORD Almighty" (verse 5).

This confession opened the door for a cleansing from God and a renewed Isaiah "heard the voice of the Lord saying, "Whom shall I send? And who will go for us?" And in response Isaiah said, "Here am I. Send me!"

Honesty before God

Whether in a formal house of worship or elsewhere getting honest before God in prayer and earnestly seeking him with one's whole heart and deepest sense of longing is a good way to open the door for God to speak. Such seeking cannot be an isolated or "one time" occurrence. It must become a way of life for those who would be certain that it is God's voice speaking. By developing an attitude of openness and receptivity to God's Word, by striving for disciplined devotional practices, by fasting and prayer, we are better able to hear God and be assured it is the Divine Voice which speaks.

Confirming the Call to Vocational Christian Ministry

As each of us sincerely seeks God, God will send other confirmation of the call to Christian ministry. Spiritually sensitive people around us will verify to us that they also sense God is calling us to his service.

A Personal Encounter

After plenty of ups and downs in attempting to live a Christian life, I got quite serious about serving the Lord and seeking his will for my life when I was sixteen years old. I was in worship services regularly, read my Bible, began to be more disciplined in prayer, and was more and more active in my local church's youth program.

In the spring I attended our state youth convention along with about fifteen other youth from our local church. It was always a lot of fun and I enjoyed being around the other kids. We attended the worship services, conferences and group activities and on the first night settled in late, as usual, but just couldn't get to sleep. I tossed and turned and lay awake for several hours while my roommate quietly slept.

Finally, I threw back the covers, got on my knees beside the bed and quietly prayed. "Okay, Lord, I'll do whatever you want me to do with my life."

I got back in bed, but still couldn't sleep. So I got up, knelt, and prayed again: "All right, Lord, I'll go into the ministry." To this day I do not know why I said that because I really hadn't given any specific thought to being a minister and I never recalled anyone talking to me about it. I had become active in speech and debate at school and had already received some special recognition for public speaking. Since public speaking was what I then thought a minister's primary task was that may have had some effect on my thinking. Anyway, I was finally able to go to sleep.

Confirmation from Others

The next evening I had been asked to serve as "Chairman" for the evening service. I led in prayer, gave the announcements, introduced the speaker and at the conclusion offered the benediction. I remember glancing over my right shoulder after the "Amen" to notice that a number of people had clustered around the speaker on the other side of the wide platform. This was a regular occurrence and while I had thought about walking over to greet and thank him for his message, I decided not to since he was engulfed, and turned to my left to walk offstage.

Just as I got to the edge of the platform I felt a hand come down on my shoulder. I turned, and there was the speaker, Dr. Robert Coleman. He had broken away from the crowd, strode across the platform and began speaking directly to me. His words were, "Son, have you ever considered that God might have his hand on your life for Christian ministry?"

Even now as I write these words tears come to my eyes when I think how God was at work in my life. I was startled at Dr. Coleman's question, but I responded: "Yes. Yes, I have." With that he turned and walked back to his seekers and I walked off the platform. No one else had heard our exchange, but I was deeply impressed by it.

That night I was able to sleep easily, but before I did I offered another prayer. One of my most influential Sunday school teachers, Jean Fish, had said to us one time: "When you make an important decisions share it publicly at your earliest convenience. A public declaration will help prompt you to keep your word." So, since my prayer the night before had been private and since my exchange with Dr. Coleman had been private, I now prayed: "Lord, at my earliest convenience I will publicly declare my call to Christian ministry." I slept peacefully.

A Public Declaration

The next day was Sunday, the closing day of the convention. I said nothing about my "call" at breakfast to my fellow youth or to any of our counselors. There was no opportunity to share during the morning worship hour or at the conference time. The conference leader was an old family friend and former missionary, Merlene Huber. When she began the conference she said her assigned topic was about Christian disciplines, but she felt impressed to spend most of her time talking about how important it is to obey God when he reveals himself to us.

We ate lunch. Afternoon service time came and was being concluded with wrap up remarks by our state youth president, when Dr. Robert Coleman came back to the pulpit and asked if he could say "one more thing." He was obliged and then he spoke: "As we conclude this convention, I would like to have our closing prayer be a prayer of dedication. If there are any persons here who have dedicated their lives to Christian ministry or missions during this convention, I would like them to stand so we can have a special prayer of commitment offered for them." I stood along with a number of others. Several members of my youth group gasped a bit when I stood that day. My father and mother had driven in just for that service to help transport our group back home. They shed some tears. Now, more than thirty years later, I have never looked back. At the time of this writing, I will soon complete twenty-seven years in active vocational ministry.

Initial Efforts in Ministry

Another important development that helped to confirm my call to ministry came as I returned home following that youth convention. The Sunday evening after the convention concluded it was customary for the youth to share about their convention experiences with our entire congregation. I shared about my perceived call to Christian ministry and my acceptance of that call. I don't know whether or not every person there took seriously my sharing, but my pastor certainly did. That very night, following the evening service, our pastor approached me and said, "Start preparing a message. In a few weeks I'll schedule you to preach on Sunday night." I was scared, flattered, and excited all at once. Years later, as I reflect back, those first few sermons were pretty shallow and trite, but the members of my home church, including our pastor, were nothing but encouraging. I was shocked when following one of my fledgling messages our pastor extended an invitation and a friend of mine came forward to receive Christ. All of these experiences helped to confirm my call.

Another affirming development came when about a month after my convention call experience my pastor invited me to join him one day in making hospital visits. He coached me on how to dress and outlined what we would do with each visit.

As we approached the first room he handed me his New Testament and Psalms and instructed me to read the marked passages on his cue. As we entered the patient's room he introduced me, began a brief conversation with the patient and then said, "Now, Sam is going to read us a few verses of Scripture." He nodded. I read. Then he offered prayer and we left. He complimented me on my reading as he reached to take his Bible back. "At the next stop, you pray," he said. So I offered prayer at his directive and by the time we had made five or six visits I was fully entering into the process of visiting, encouraging, reading Scripture, and praying. It felt good, even natural, and further confirmed my sense of call. It also began to teach me that ministry is a lot more about building relationships and nurturing spiritual development in other persons than it is about public speaking and preaching.

God works in different ways in different person's lives, and there are other steps that can be taken to help discern God's will. Completing a spiritual gifts inventory can be a helpful step toward affirming whether or not God has equipped or is equipping you with those gifts that would tend to affirm any inclinations toward ministry. Psychological tests can also help by indicating factors that would enhance ministry or need to be addressed in avoiding pitfalls. There are a variety of inventories and tests that are available through counseling centers and your schools to help confirm your readiness and your preparation for ministry. As I completed college and, later, seminary I benefited from these types of indicators.

Attending conferences and workshops that deal with Christian vocations is another way of helping to assess whether or not impressions of "call" are accurate or misplaced. Certainly "apprenticeships" are helpful in determining what God is saying.

Once I had shared my sense of call to ministry, my local church pastor began to "test" both my resolve and willingness to be trained. He invited me to attend ministers' events with him. He took me with him to do other pastoral calls and gave me several good books to read. He frequently asked me to prepare messages and he and my home church graciously allowed me to practice on them. All of these experiences at the hands of loving and caring Christian people helped affirm my call.

Some may experience a "call" to ministry like that of the Old Testament's Esther, who found herself in circumstances where her opportunities, gifts, and abilities made it obvious that God was calling her to a special ministry. In Esther's case, God's people were held in captivity and were in jeopardy of perishing. Esther was aware of the need for intervention and as Queen she was in a position to effectively act. Nevertheless, she was fearful and needed the urging of her foster father Mordecai who said to her, "And who knows but that you have come to royal position for such a time as this?" (Esther 4:14).

For some of us a call may come because we carefully observe the circumstances—or have someone like Mordecai point them out to us—and perceive that we are appropriately gifted to make a difference. If we know that God has so gifted us and also positioned us to be useful in his kingdom work, by the processes already noted of worshipful reflection, prayer, fasting and consultation with trusted spiritual advisors, we too may find that God has called us for such a time as we discover we are in. Once again, persistent earnest seeking and confirmation by our fellow church members will be valuable in affirming our call.

It is worth noting that along the way many other worthy and dedicated Christians have sensed that God might be calling them into vocational Christian ministry, but after a period of exploration through worship, prayer, fasting and consultation have moved in other directions. As long as they are serving Christ, they too are in the "ministry." God's voice does not send every earnest pilgrim down the same path. Time and careful testing will prove whether or not his voice is calling to the profession of Saint Paul or to some other worthy walk.

Reference List

Gushee, David P. and Walter P. Jackson, eds. 1996. *Preparing for Christian Ministry: An Evangelical Approach.* Wheaton: BridgePoint, 1996. See especially "Toward a Biblical View of Call," 65-79.

Huber, Randy and John E. Stanley. 1999. *Reclaiming the Wesleyan/ Holiness Heritage of Women Clergy: Sermons, A Case Study and Resources.* Messiah College, Grantham, PA: Wesleyan Holiness Women Clergy.

Messer, Donald E. 1989. *Contemporary Images of Christian Ministry.* Nashville: Abingdon. See especially "A Theology of Ministry," 62-80.

Oden, Thomas C. 1983. *Pastoral Theology: Essentials of Ministry.* San Francisco: Harper and Row. See especially "The Call to Ministry," 18-25 and "Women in the Pastoral Office," 35-46.

Vision-2-Grow Monograph Series on "Call to Ministry."

Chapter Four:
Jeannette Flynn, *A Passion for Ministry*

Consider your own call, brothers and sisters; not many
of you were wise by human standards, not many were
powerful, not many were of noble birth....so that no
one might boast in the presence of God. He is the
source of your life in Christ Jesus (Hebrews 1:26,
29–30 NRSV).

The call and preparation to ministry engages a person at every level
and in every way. Attention is given to doctrinal issues; skills must be
developed and honed; education is pursued that will help the minister
be mentally equipped; and practical applications are rehearsed so that
baptism, communion, weddings and funerals are handled appropriately.
Courses and conferences regarding people-skills, group dynamics, and
church growth methods are all offered for those aspiring to respond to
the call of God and excel in ministry.

One area, however, that is seldom given thorough attention or thoughtful life planning is that of maintaining "passion" for ministry. Far too
often we feel the initial passion that stirs us to respond to the call of
God on our life, but we fail to realize that this is the very element we
need in order to persevere and finish well.

Derric Johnson, in his book *Easy Doesn't Do It,* tells a revealing true
story.

> *In the Spring of 1967 a passenger express ran right up the back
> of a plodding freight train in Central California. Both trains were
> derailed and 36 lives were lost in the wreckage and flames.*

During the investigation that followed, it was discovered that the automatic signaling system had been malfunctioning since early that day. One of the railroad employees was told to take a warning flag and station himself at the inoperative light to warn all engineers of impending traffic hazards.

Seeing the slow freight pass first...followed just a few minutes later by the speeding passenger express, the signalman sensed the imminent disaster and frantically waved his flag.

During the investigation that followed, the Judge asked the engineer, "Did you see the flag?"

"Yes, sir, I did," was the answer.

The Judge went further, "Why didn't you stop?"

The flag was the wrong color, your Honor," the engineer replied.

The signal-man jumped up. "I waved the red flag. Anybody knows that means STOP!"

"It was a yellow flag meaning PROCEED SLOWLY WITH CAUTION." The engineer replied.

"The flag was red!"

"The one we saw was yellow!"

The Judge's solution was simple. "Get the flag. We'll see for ourselves."

Guess what! Years ago the flag had been a bright red. But in the passage of time, the cloth had faded into a dull yellow. It had been so long since the flag had been used, no one even noticed (Printed by Y.E.S.S. Press, 1991, pp. 99-100).

More often than anyone wants to count, we have known, read, or heard about the wreckage of a ministry where the passion for Christ had gradually faded over the years and "no one had noticed." The symptoms may vary, but the results are similar. When the passion faded, so did the sense of call to ministry. When the passion ebbed away so did clarity of moral boundaries and ethical standards. When the passion became dull so did leadership zeal and inspired preaching. It is possible to possess all the skill, know all the methods, be informed regarding all the programming, and still lack the power of effective leadership and sense of fulfillment that God always intended his ministers to experience.

The writer of Hebrews states, "…let us lay aside every weight and the sin that clings so closely, and let us run with perseverance the race that is set before us, looking to Jesus the pioneer and perfecter of our faith,…" (Heb12:1–2 NRSV).

The Greek word for race is aganon from which we get our English word agony. It refers most closely not to a sprint or dash but to running a marathon. We are challenged to prepare ourselves so that we might finish the distance.

It is to that end that we turn our attention toward the vital area of maintaining a passion in ministry.

…all the members of the body, though many, are one body….
(1 Corinthians 12:12 NRSV)

The journey of ministry begins when persons:

- Acknowledge the great love God has for them personally,
- Receive Jesus Christ as their personal Savior,
- Submit to his rightful authority in their lives,
- Seek the leadership of the Holy Spirit in directing and gifting their life, and
- Begin to find ways to respond to all that God has brought to their life.

As a result, habits are changed, relationships are made different, service in the kingdom and to others begins, and the witness of what God has done in their life is shared.

When salvation comes to the hearts and minds of individuals, they often find themselves filled with a powerfully strong sense of passion for loving God. The realization of all he has done for them causes great appreciation and a sense of indebtedness. It is important to affirm that journey for every person and recognize that each one who accepts Christ has a vital place in the body of Christ.

However, this response to God's work in a life does not and should not necessarily cause her or him to seek credentialing or full time professional ministry. The deep passion that fills us in the act of salvation can cause some individuals to believe their response to salvation must be to enter full time professional ministry–maybe, but maybe not. This grows out of a lack of understanding that while we are all called to minister as part of the body of Christ we are not all called to vocational ministry. The acceptable response to God is faithful obedience to all that his word sets before us through our lifestyle, our attitudes, our actions, our thoughts, and our service.

There will be some who will have a distinct, unmistakable call to ministry that becomes their vocation in life. That call and the passion that accompanies that call exceeds the response to simply use your gifts as opportunity and opening allows. It becomes the compelling urgency upon one's life. It transcends the local place where we live or the local body of believers we know and call family. This chapter is meant to speak to those who have sensed this larger call upon their life about the passion that must accompany that calling.

For the love of Christ compels us....
(2 Corinthians 5:14 NKJV)

Passion must not be defined simply as the intensity of our feelings, or even as zealous action. Nor should passion be identified as having strong emotions. While a measure of those elements are involved, the passion of which the word of God speaks and the Spirit brings to our life is quite different. In fact, the Greek term for passion, *pathos*, is often interpreted as "suffering."

Editor Colin Brown in the *New International Dictionary of New Testament Theology* states that, "...the Synoptic Gospels are, in a sense, passion accounts extended both backwards and forwards in time, the passion is their central theme.... In John the whole life of the incarnate Logos is presented as his passion, though as a passion in which he was glorified" (Zondervan Publishers, 1978, Vol 3 pp 722–723).

Passion is the deep motivation that gives us the encouragement and courage to fulfill—for a lifetime—that vocation to which God has called us. It is the sturdy frame that keeps the tent of our life upright and open. Godly passion is the energy that fuels us when our human spirit wearies. It does not take the place of the Holy Spirit, but is the tool of the Holy Spirit in our life. Passion does not take the place of our relationship with Christ, but it is the fire that burns within us as a result of the relationship. Passion is the constraining determination to remain true to the calling and life that Christ has set before us. Passion for the ministry to which God called us makes strong the fortress of our life against the temptation of compromise for success, fame, finances, church politics, or the lure of the world. Passion for the ministry to which God called us serves as a strong anchor when the adverse winds of suffering, criticism, misunderstanding, and unfair judgment blow upon our life. Passion is a balm that promotes godly healing when woundedness has taken place in relationships. Passion rises from the depths to motivate us to try again when our dreams have come to an end and our human energy has run out!

This kind of passion has no source of existence outside of our relationship with God. Passion for ministry grows out of an understanding of who God is in our lives; the unconditional love with which he loves us; and the sacrifice of his own Son to bring salvation to us. Passion for ministry grows out of a deep awareness of what God has done through the ages of time because "He so loved the world." True passion for ministry must grow out of a divine, unmistakable call of God upon our life to a purpose, task, and mission that God has set before us.

There are people who have a great desire or deep-seated need to be in ministry. Do not confuse this with passion for ministry that grows out of a calling. There are people who use ministry as a "fix." They will tell you they teach or preach because it helps them grow. Everything they read, study, or hear is quickly developed into three points and an illustration to be delivered next Sunday. There are people who use ministry as a means of meeting their own emotional needs. They like being needed and desire to be the person everyone comes to for the answer. They relate what they do in ministry as their self worth or value. It gives them a sense of significance. They may have the correct rhetoric, but their motives are amiss. Instead of exhibiting genuine passion for ministry, they are often grasping for recognition and accolade. True passion for ministry does not seek significance for self. Rather genuine passion lifts Christ as the focus of significance and places self as the servant to others—sometimes at great personal cost. Still others approach ministry as a power base out of which to operate. They are frustrated when decisions don't go their way; they are disillusioned when programs don't produce results. They are "driven" by their desire to control or succeed. There is a great chasm between being "driven" and being filled with a godly passion.

There are people who begin ministry because of the expectations placed upon them by themselves or by others. "My parents and my grand-parents and five uncles and two aunts are in ministry." "Everyone has always told me I would make a great worship leader." "My best friend is called to ministry and we do everything together." Expectations of others or even expectations of self will direct you in a path that God had no part in choosing. There are people who go into ministry as a means of "paying God back for all he has done for me." They feel as though they owe him something and ministry is the payment. They are con-fused and disappointed when ministry leaves them hurting or doesn't develop like they dreamed.

A genuine passion for ministry that grows out of a calling upon our life holds us steady when programs succeed and when they fail. It keeps our focus clear when growth is phenomenal and when decline seems inevitable. Passion organizes our priorities when everyone calls on us and when no one wants to hear our name, much less our sermons. Genuine passion compels us to train others, empower those around us, and equip and disciple for kingdom expansion. Passion stirs us not to be concerned with self acknowledgment but rather to pray for and lift oth-ers into greatness because that benefits the kingdom of God. Passion in ministry guards us from being jealous for "the credit," but rather focus-es on the success of others for the sake of the kingdom.

Richard Kriechbaum writes a prayer for ministers that reminds us of who we really are under the call of God.

Unless your Spirit informs and encourages me, I will
not know how to play my part. I will stand foolishly
silent on the stage, not knowing what I can do or even
what I truly like to do. Worst of all, I will not know
what I cannot do. Unless you intervene, I will blow my
lines and miss my cues and confuse all the others. Help
me sense my spiritual gifts so I will attempt only what
you especially enable me to do and lead only where you
are at work (*Leadership Prayers*, pp 2–3).

May our passion rise out of our communion with God and not just
grand ideas or fanciful dreams. May our passion harness the emotions
of our life and bring focus on the goals of the Kingdom. May our passion give us courage to risk doing that to which we are called and wisdom to not do what we are not called to but simply tempted by.

… I have this against you, that you have left your first love.
(Revelation 2:4)

One of the great challenges before the individual who is called to ministry is to be wise about the elements that will cause us to "leave our first
love" and quench our passion. First and foremost we must be careful
that our passion is for God and our relationship to him. While we can
truly enjoy the ministry and be fulfilled by our efforts in ministry– ministry must never become our first love. That place belongs to God and
God alone. One of the easiest places to lose your passion for ministry
is in ministry. If our call to ministry and our passion for ministry were
birthed and grew out of our intimate relationship with God, then we
must recognize that is the wellspring where passion is refreshed.

In a marriage, it would be easy for a zealous, diligent wife to spend
a majority of her time cooking, cleaning, fixing, washing, and caring
for the physical needs of the family. Though she labors for her family
from sun up till sun down, it would not take long for her children to
grow distant from her emotionally and her husband to feel neglected
and detached. A husband feels the strong need to earn a living that will
feed, cloth, and house his family. Yet if all his waking hours are given
to a job or jobs that meet the physical demands of his family, the family
will soon resent both the person and the job. It is not only what we do
for those we love and who love us, but rather the intimate relationship

and communication we have with them that keeps the passion of human bonds strong. So also in ministry. While God has called us to vocational ministry, let us never forget that he first called us to himself and then out of that relationship he entrusted us with a call to minister.

We must be ready to deal effectively with the hurts and disappointments of ministry. Jesus was very forthright in telling us that if the world hated him, it would hate us as well. There are times of pain in every person's life. It is part of being alive. How we deal with the wounds and disappointments makes all the difference. We cannot simply cover them up, ignore them, or pretend they don't really hurt. As previously mentioned, the word passion actually comes from pathos—suffering. We are not called to be self appointed martyrs who simply go about receiving every unfair action and word without response. Neither are we called to be so ethereal that nothing can dent our armor. Some would like to pretend that pain can never pierce their heart. Some have distorted the infilling of the Spirit to mean that we never feel the full array of human emotions. Godly passion is the deep resource that helps us to resist bitterness. Passion demands that we be "real." While we are in deed vulnerable and can be wounded, there is a resolve that pain will not dissuade us from the path God has chosen for us.

A balance between the needs of the soul and the body must be measured and honored. Our soul needs times of refreshing, regular nourishing from mentors, friends and leaders. We are built for fellowship with others in ministry and in the body. Passion grows most effectively in the quiet times we spend with God. Time that is not fraught with seeking God's blessing for a new program, profound wisdom for our next sermon, the course of ministry, or his help to get to the next level. Instead what is needed is quiet time designed for simple communion with the lover of our soul and for our own soul's sake!

Our physical needs impact our spiritual passion. We are designed and woven so that the physical and spiritual threads interweave to form one fabric. Exercise, appropriate rest, times of vacation, proper nutrition, laughter with family and friends, and interests that broaden us and build us are as vital as our devotion and prayer life. We live in a society addicted to adrenaline. We applaud the symptoms of that addiction. We admire the one who works twelve or fourteen hours a day and never takes a vacation. We were not designed for that kind of activity. It is

why so many of God's passionate leaders in the Bible spent significant
time in deserts, wildernesses, and quiet sea sides. Rest, reflection, evaluation, and mediation are fuel for a healthy passion that will last a lifetime.

On the other end of the spectrum, however, passion also grows out of
good and faithful labor. The old phrase, "You can be so heavenly minded
that you are of no earthly good," still holds true. A real life analogy was
quite visible to the early church leaders. The Dead Sea is a significant
body of water that ought to bear a great variety of sea life. Water flows
into it regularly, but there is no outlet. As a result, the concentration and
contaminents kill any life that would grow there. In our country, the
Great Salt Lake is similar in its diseased state. It is not only valueless,
it steadily continues to absorb healthy farming land, homes, and even
streets. Passion is nourished by the healthy balance of work and rest.

There are perceived and real expectations in ministry. The expectations
of others and ourselves are powerful. We can even distort the expectations God has of us. One of the sure passion killers is when we try to
live up to any expectation other than God's true vision for us. The disciples in the sixth chapter of Acts understood this trap well. The church
was growing. They were the talk of the town. Miracles were happening
around them. New people were coming every day. So much to do and
so much to maintain. Then conflict broke out. Given the tremendous
coming together of so many diverse cultures and backgrounds, it is little
wonder. So, of course, the congregation sought the Apostles. I would
imagine many thoughts went through their heads. There were some type
A's in that group—Peter, James, John, Simon the Zealot. Surely the
thought crossed their minds, "We've got to fix this. We can't let this get
out of hand." But look at the response of the Apostles. They would not
yield to the expectations of the congregation. Their passion made them
stay the course. "We will give ourselves to study of the scripture and
prayer." The needs were real. The disciples were the leaders. However,
a wise leader with a healthy godly passion for the ministry is called to
will help others find their place in the body and service so that God is
honored through each one.

Jealousy and pride are double first cousins. The temptation to resent the
opportunities or positions of others can rob us of our own passion for
what we do. In fact, when we begin to focus on what we don't have or

can't do, we being to resent the very place God has sent us to and our passion for ministry is quenched. Comparing ourselves to others can create an undue sense of unworthiness and unholy pride. Both damage the true passion of ministry for the place and calling God gave to us. Passion helps us to love those to whom we were sent to be filled with God's vision for that place and these people regardless of size or prestige.

A challenge of our economy today is to live within our means. Perhaps a greater challenge is to live content within our means. Our passion can be wooed to another love if we do not guard our hearts. There are many ministers who find it necessary to be bivocational in order to provide for the needs of our families and lives. Paul himself proudly proclaimed that he was bivocational; however, he never forgot his first love! He never forgot that his vocation was the proclamation of Christ and that he made tents so he could pursue his vocation freely. We must not be trapped by the appeal to make money and proclaim Christ on the side. I doubt seriously that Paul used his relationships with those to whom he preached Christ so that he could sell them tents. Rather, I believe he probably used his relationship with those to whom he was selling tents to proclaim Christ. Christ said you cannot serve two masters for you will love the one and hate the other (Luke 16:13).

So many families today find themselves in debt. While this is not a treatise on financial planning, it is a study on passion in ministry. One of the most deadly traps to passion occurs when we become encumbered by the things of this world. Indebtedness will choke the joy and passion from our walk with Christ as well as ministry. Larry Burkett often makes the statement, "Show me your checkbook and I'll tell you the condition of your heart." Indebtedness will cause us to become consumed with the frustration of being in bondage. Over stretched financial obligations will pull us between two great forces. On the one hand we must earn enough money to repay our loans and a large portion of our disposable income must be set aside. On the other hand the call of God on our life tugs at us to "travel light" (Luke 10:4) so that our availability will not be limited.

Finally, we must nourish our passion with regular worship, confession, and praise. Ministers can be guilty of being sure that these elements are provided for everyone else but failing to ensure that their own souls are nourished. The responsibilities that surround every minister during times of corporate worship make it difficult at best to allow the minister to truly experience genuine worship. The truth is that a minister must find regular times to practice worship, confession, and praise without being the one responsible for leadership. Even personal devotions can become little more than times of sermon preparation if we do not understand the significance of nurturing the passion for ministry through genuine reflective worship.

Therefore, I remind you to fan into flame the gift of God....
(2 Timothy 1:6)

We must realize that true godly passion is a great flame that burns within us. I hear ministers talk about winning "this generation" or the importance of having a certain style of worship. The passion of God is not just for a specific generation of people or for a certain mode of worship. The passion of God is for the loveable and the unlovely, for all ages and all races. Paul exemplifies the true passion in ministry when he stated, "I have become all things to all people that I might by all means save some [to Christ]" (1 Corinthians 9:22).

The passion of God reveals itself in a heart that is humble. God is the spokesperson; we are simply the vessel. Stirring up the passion of God is not simply getting psyched up like a runner in the Olympics. We misunderstand this passion. God is the message; we are the messengers. Stirring up the passion of God means that we participate in stirring our love for him within ourselves and not just preparing for a good message or planning for great programs. Stirring the passion of ministry means reconnecting with "the great cloud of witnesses" that have gone before us. Ministry does not rest in our hands alone or in the success of this moment.

I am confident of two truths about the great reformers John Huss and Martin Luther. First, it was passion that compelled them to withstand the flames of persecution and to raise the hammer to nail the message to the door. Second, their passion was magnified by their awareness of those who had gone before them and the truths for which they stood. Neither of these men nor most of the reformers who followed them could have fathomed the far-reaching effects of their actions. We must keep our eyes on Christ, recognize the heritage that surrounds us, and trust an almighty God that while we cannot see the results we hope for, he has a plan.

Wesley L. Duewel writes of the necessity of this passion in his book *Ablaze For God.*

> A passionless Christianity will not put out the fires of hell. A passionless leader will never set the people ablaze. A passionless youth leader will never set the youth ablaze for Christ....
>
> Can the *Shekinah* fire that set the desert bush ablaze set our hearts aflame until we are burning bushes for God? The *Shekinah* fire on Mt. Sinai suffused the whole being of Moses till his face radiated the glory of God. Can we draw near enough to God until that Shekinah fire begins to transfigure our vessels of clay and our people see glimpses of the glory of God upon us and in us?
>
> It is not to be earned, worked up, or simulated. Only God can baptize with fire. Only God can send Shekinah. Only God can meet your need and mine. We have labored too long without it. We have come far short of God's glory without it. We have left our people too largely unmoved without it.
>
> We cannot light this fire. In ourselves we cannot produce it. But we can humble ourselves before God... We can seek God's face... God's holy fire descends upon prepared, obedient, hungry hearts" (Francis Asbury Press, 1989, pp. 28-31).

"Our eyes fixed on Jesus the source and goal of our faith. For he himself endured a cross and thought nothing of its shame because of the joy he knew would follow his suffering; and he is now seated at the right hand of God's throne. Think constantly of him enduring all that sinful men could say against him, and you will not lose your purpose or your courage" (Hebrew 12:2-3 JBP).

Reference List

Blackaby, Henry T. & Henry Brandt. *The Power of the Call.* Broadman
   & Holman Publishers, 1997.
Duewel, Wesley L. *Ablaze For God.* Francis Asbury Press, 1989.
Johnson, Derric. *Easy Doesn't Do It.* Y.E.S.S. Press, 1991.
Leadership Prayers. Tyndale House Publishers, Inc. 1998.
London Jr., H.B. & Neil B. Wiseman. *The Heart of a Great Pastor.*
   Regal Books, 1994
Neuhaus, Richard John. *Freedom For Ministry.* William B. Eerdmans
   Publishing Company, revised 1992.

II.

$\mathfrak{B}$ecoming–

disciplining ourselves for fruitful living

The word of our Lord and the writing of the Apostle John give us a starting place as well as a "never-ending" context for the process of our becoming in Christ Jesus. Jesus proclaimed that faith provides a death-to-life passage that begins here and now: "Very truly, I tell you, anyone who hears my word and believes him who sent me has eternal life, and does not come under judgment, but has passed from death to life" (John 5:24 NRSV).

The unfolding of that person that you are to become took on new life the minute you said yes to Jesus Christ as Savior and Lord. It shall continue through endless eternity: "Beloved, we are God's children now; what we will be has not yet been revealed. What we do know is this: when he is revealed, we will be like him, for we will see him as he is" (1 John 3:2 NRSV).

A growing sense of who we are in Christ Jesus gives birth to the vision that "what I become is my gift to God." We invite you, however, to discover and enact specific disciplines in prayer to God, in accountability with others, and service as a bridge between Word and world. We believe these disciplines will set the stage for living with God-given purpose. We believe that these disciplines will enrich your personal contribution to the kingdom of God and set a climate that encourages your emergence as a fruitful servant of God.

Chapter Five:

Louis Foltz, *Becoming the Gift*

We are fearfully and wonderfully made....[1]

I could see the bus coming from almost a mile away. When I was of pre-school age, twice a week my mother would take me with her into town to do our shopping. Dad was gone to work long before daybreak, taking the tin-and-wheels we used for a car with him. So we rode the bus. It was a half-mile walk to the highway where the Greyhound made its morning run down the Napa Valley into town. As regulars, the driver knew where to look for us; waiting beside the mailbox at the edge of our dirt road. My heart would leap as the bus motored down upon us, gleaming in silver and glass. Seeing our wave, slowing down, easing forward slowly to keep from blowing dust, the Greyhound driver stopped his magnificent traveling machine right at our very feet. Grabbing the large, chrome handle, Bob Brown would open the door wide and I would gaze up into his smile as he sat high above the boarding staircase. There could never be anyone else so much in command of things, so confident and powerful, so enviously dashing as Mr. Brown. He sported a gray uniform with a matching billed cap. A chrome hound at full stride raced above its bill. His black shoes glistened as they rested against the large foot pedals. His "good morning" boomed off the great windshield as we ascended into his protective custody. I knew then that God needed me to become a Greyhound bus driver. The power, the control, and the respect that came with the uniform were my dream for many years.

Little could I understand at age four that driving a Greyhound bus was more complicated than growing up to be big enough to fit into a shiny uniform. Nor could I understand that the responsibilities of the driver were far more complex and difficult than pushing pedals and turning the wheel. Yet my ambition was quite understandable. It wasn't the occupation of bus driver that I envied as much as what that position represented. It wasn't the uniform I wanted; it was to be respected as a competent individual. It wasn't the bus I wanted to drive as much as it was a sense of power that I wanted to control. It wasn't as much about the "what" that I wanted to do as it was about the "who" that I wanted to become—someone needed, admired, and responsible.

From the viewpoint of many children, careers are clothing to be put on, like a bus driver's uniform. If one acquires the right uniform one can become a bus driver, a lawyer, a physician, or a pastor. To a child, professions seem to be made up of roles to be donned, rehearsed, and practiced with the skill of a good actor. The adult behind the wheel of the Greyhound also "plays bus driver," and is able to do so with a real bus. The lawyer appears to have gone through years of schooling to acquire a set of legal attire, robes made of the finest juris prudence. When a sufficient amount of legal knowledge has been acquired, the person will become a lawyer. In the same way, the pastor is often seen as having acquired and donned a persona of the clergy, carefully woven together with skills of Bible study, counseling, and preaching.

Careers can appear to be a matter of making the right uniform: weave the threads, wear the role.

Many students come to college with the intent of "becoming" a new identity. Quite a few believe that if they diligently pursue a course of study they will be rewarded with the ability to profess a role, that is, to enter a "profession." The value of who we are, and whose we are, can be confused with the performances we are able to carry out. If one engages in a great deal of effort-filled "doing", they will "become" somebody of value. Students who expend four years of labor in the study of the biological sciences, followed by four years of medical school, a year of internship, and a few years of residency may believe that they will "become" a physician like the great missionary, Albert Schweitzer, or like the physicians portrayed on television—Dr. Mark Greene of "ER" or Hawkeye Pierce of "M.A.S.H." Students who invest many hours in the study of the Bible, biblical history, Greek, Hebrew, hermeneutics, homiletics, exegesis, pastoral counseling, and Christian education, may believe that they will star in the role of a Billy Graham or of their beloved local pastor. Their motive for service is noble; their desire to gain recognition as a person of value is understandable, but there is an intrinsic flaw in the plan.

We are not called to become a profession. *We are called to become ourselves. What our God calls us to "become" is a more authentic version of our own unique self.* One cannot "do" a set of difficult tasks and "become" a professional title, a doctor, a teacher, or a pastor. There is no such person as "a doctor": There is a wonderful variety of unique individuals who practice medicine. There is no such person as a pastor: There are uniquely gifted believers who have been specifically called by God to gain skills to minister distinctively through their uniqueness. Every one's calling from God is unique and so is each and every ministry. Each of us becomes a gift from God to others. As that gift of his love we find direction toward what he would have us do.

In examining God's call on each of our lives, Christian scholar and author Henri Nouwen makes a significant distinction between personal vocation and a career (Nouwen 1982). Nouwen reminds us that the word "vocation" comes from the Latin *vocare*, to call. He urges us to remember that our calling, our vocation, is much larger than our career. Our particular career should include our vocation, but not exclusively imprison it. We are called by our Lord to become everything unique and beautiful he intends for us. And to that unique calling, that vocation, he will enable us to acquire skills for ministry which can be practiced with a uniqueness which is also our own.

In the title phrase of our chapter—becoming the gift—the term *becoming* always remains a present tense verb of strong action. We never become. We never *arrive.* We are continually in the process of increasing development and maturation. We never reach a place of completed spiritual growth. To study for a vocation in ministry is not only to study vigorously the nature of God, but also to study aggressively the nature of one's self. To study for the ministry is, first, to engage in continuing conversation with the Holy Spirit to labor toward personal identity. The process of *becoming* requires a life-long dialogue. The disciple of Christ is one who is known, by the very word itself, to be disciplined. The serious ministerial student disciplines his or her life with rigorous prayer, meditation, study, and personal honesty. This on-going assignment can be, and should be, rigorous. The challenge in becoming what the Lord intends is a lifetime effort, and the gift we become is expensive. It is paid for with personal inconvenience and frequent significant sacrifice. It is truly "bought with a price"; first by our Lord and Savior's sacrifice at Calvary and then through the perseverance of our own discipleship.

Train up a child in the way he should go....[2]

Solomon's wisdom to "train up a child in the way that he should go" is extremely important as we look at the variety of natural talents and spiritual gifts which our Lord has distributed among his people. The word train (Hebrew *chanak*) is the same expression used when referring to the cultivation and training of plants. It is very difficult to force a plant to grow in a manner other than what has been given to its nature. Try to retrain a climbing vine to grow counter-clockwise instead of clockwise. It will fall off the string. In a similar way, the natural learning styles built into us demonstrate the ways in which we may be trained up in the way we were designed to grow. We have a natural bent, too. If we allow the Lord to train us to become who he would have us be, then doing what he would have us do comes naturally. Then we shall receive a sense of fulfillment that will steady our professional, vocational course.

What do you enjoy doing in your free time? The tasks, games, and hobbies that you enjoy in your spare time give clues to the natural style of learning God has given you. Over the past fifteen years, Harvard University psychologist Howard Gardner and his research staff have examined the many psychological styles which people apply to go about living in the world. (Gardner 1985) These researchers have examined attributes valued by different cultures as well as the habits of people who have recognized gifted abilities for particular tasks and specific situations. They also identified abilities which can be linked to specific processes in the brain and nervous system. From these continuing investigations, eight separate styles of thinking have been identified so far. This current notion of diverse and innate "intelligences" is replacing the notion of a single form of human "intelligence." The uniqueness of the gift we continue to become is even implanted in our genetics.

It would seem that there are people who are born with a natural propensity to understand and appreciate music. Others have a gift for introspection, while others are more gifted at conversation and thinking in the presence of others. Some people have a natural spatial ability to enjoy and engage in the visual arts. Some people are born with an inner ability to appreciate nature and enjoy finding, identifying, and categorizing animals and plants. Some people are truly born to move and need movement to think and play. Others deeply enjoy solving problems using reasoning and mathematics. And there are some individuals who are naturally fluent with words. This list is not exhaustive. As research continues into how we use our neurological wiring, researchers are certain that more "intelligences" will be added to the list.

Sometimes we observe people who are obviously gifted in a single one of these styles of processing the world. We frequently label them "talented" or "gifted" as their unique ability is easily recognized, but the rest of us are gifted, too. Most of us are gifted in a combination of two or more areas; our uniqueness being recognized in the combination of natural "intelligences" and valued in the situations in which we can apply them. For instance some individuals may demonstrate a combination of talent in introspection and visualization. Watch them creatively doodle, paint, or sculpt. Other people may have a combination of logic and musical ability. Watch them invent tunes or compose musical scores. A combination of natural intelligence in introspection, movement, and appreciating the out of doors may find a person sharing God's nature with others through out-of-doors activities. There are a vast number of combinations of activities which may find their expression through the natural interests which we can recognize as gifts from our Heavenly Father.

Some are called to be apostles, some prophets, some pastors and teachers....[3]

The many tasks needed in the work of Christ's church can use all the various combinations of natural skill. The tasks of preaching, teaching, discipling, organizing, designing, directing, managing, negotiating, consoling, and reconciling are used in a wide variety of settings within every congregation's calling. The congregation needs to look to individuals whose personal uniqueness matches the needs of the ministry. How interesting it is to observe other members of the church body thoroughly enjoying tasks which we find to be tedious, difficult, or almost impossible. For individuals whose natural style of intellectual processing matches the task, doing compatible work helps them in the richness of their own authenticity. For people who are assigned (or assign themselves) to tasks which do not apply their natural abilities, the job will require the donning of a role and the performance of tasks which separate us from our sense of calling.

This difference in compatibility may be seen in tasks within the church congregation. One Sunday school teacher is energized by her active class of primary age children. Another is emotionally drained by the very same experience. One individual finds great joy in managing the church books. Another is overwhelmed by the thought of the task. Not all people called into the pastorate share the same combination of natural abilities. For example, some effective ministers may show a powerful gift for preaching, an adequate ability at the teacher's lectern, but very poor counseling ability. Other effective pastors may be inspired by God's ability to use them in personal and family counseling, but find preaching to an assembly a very unnerving and reluctant responsibility. As Paul reminds us in 1 Corinthians, the body of Christ necessarily needs each of us and is not made to function with only one or two people in Jack-of-all-trade leadership positions. It takes us all, and each of us effectively placed, to become the gift.

In their book, *Discovering Your Natural Talents: How to Love What You Do and Do What You Love*, authors John Bradley, Jay Carty, and Russ Korth provide six "suitcases" or arenas in which to discover the combination of natural abilities and life experiences which identify the uniqueness of their calling (Bradley, Carty, and Korth, 1991). The authors also emphasize that institutions such as the organized church depend upon different combinations of skills to minister to God's people. The church needs people who are energized by working with groups of unfamiliar people rather than drained by the task. The church needs people who enjoy completing tasks as well as people who are comfortable engaging in never-ending processes. The church needs people who enjoy working alone as well as people who need others to get the assignment done. The key to accomplishing the wide variety of ministries found in the church is discovered in becoming the person God intended and answering the call to tasks requiring the unique combination of honed natural talents and skills.

There are giants in the land....[4]

Stories of giants are found in many cultural traditions around the world.

In the *Holy Bible*, giants are mentioned in several places. Besides Goliath of Gath, there were Ammorites who inhabited the Land of Milk and Honey prior to the coming of the children of Israel. The Book of Numbers tells us that when the spies of Israel were sent from Kadesh Barnea, only Joshua and Caleb were not paralyzed by fear of the giants' potential power. The terror of apparent certain destruction kept the children of Israel at bay, wandering in the desert for almost four decades. Becoming a unique gift in the service of our Lord is frequently hampered by the lack of completing one particular phase of childhood development: the conquering of our personal giants. The terror of personal giants may keep children of all ages wandering in a personal desert of uncertainty for much of their lives.

All children face giants: those individuals who are larger, more powerful, and appear more in control of the environment. Adults face giants, too. Each of us encounters people who appear to have more physical or social power, seeming to relegate those about them to a position of helpless dependence.

To a toddler, all adults look much larger, are obviously more powerful, and appear always to be right in what they say and do. A small child cannot judge an adult's thinking to be correct or in error. The sheer size and apparent competence of adults defines their correctness in the eyes of a vulnerable child. Grownups are able to define physical and moral reality and how to model competence in each. A child can not judge the appropriateness of an adult's behavior. Sometimes the necessary responsibilities of loving parents are not going to be seen by the child as pleasant, but the sense of personal care is consistently felt. Medical check-ups aren't fun and the process of discipline isn't either. But these are necessary circumstances for effective parenting. Good parents always endure some amount of misunderstanding. This is one of the costs of training up children and setting them free. Even when it hurts, children sense the expression of love by nurturing parents to be consistent through both pleasant and unpleasant circumstances. Through this training, children learn how to behave independently, working toward the increasing sense of personal identity, competency, and responsibility which are the hallmarks of adulthood. As children rightfully struggle toward competency and their unique calling, the parents relinquish increasing degrees of behavioral freedom, attached to increasing responsibility for personal consequences. Developing through mutual love,

First Steps to Ministry

children become more responsibly independent and the giants become increasingly multi-dimensional human beings.

Tackling the giants is one of the significant steps in the psycho-social development of children. A major task of growing up is this transformation of the giants of childhood into significant and unique individuals. Erik Erikson has termed this process of giant-killing "individuation." With the ability to employ the new found tool of speech, the two year old begins to carve out a personal identity unique from that of his or her parents and other significant adults. Every parent is aware of the most frequently used word in the vocabulary of the child which has reached the age Arnold Gessell has termed the "terrible twos." The great roar of "no!" from the mouth of the defiant toddler has less to do with the immediate situation as it does with an on-going declaration of autonomy. The child is deeply aware of vital dependence upon significant adults for nurturance, affection, and interpretation of the world. At the same time the growing need to be treated as a unique human being forces interpersonal defiance in the effort to be recognized as an independent soul. This process of individuation is, for some, a lifetime struggle to be recognized by significant others as an autonomous spiritual being. "Individuating," a first step in "becoming," is a strong drive in all of us.

By becoming more than a giant's appendage, the child is learning how to think, act, and love independently. As the parent permits the toddler to have ideas and emotions which are unique, the child gains a sense of what Erikson terms "autonomy." The parents and other caregivers then become unique people to be reckoned with. With this sense of autonomy comes the ability to generate ideas and feel emotions which are not dictated by the immediate thinking or present emotional state of the caregivers.

In many cases, however, this process of "becoming" or "individuating" is incomplete. Parents, for a variety of intentional or inadvertent reasons, expect the child to see situations from their giant-sized point of view or to mimic their feelings about the immediate surroundings. Even if the child is unable to take the parent's perspective, the toddler may feel coerced to respond as if he or she did. An unaware parent may not have the skill to deal with a cranky child. The parent facing emotional difficulties may not know how to respond to an otherwise playful toddler. Responding to the obvious power of the giants, these children develop a consistent sense of physical and emotional dependency. The striving for individuation erodes into a state of emotional subordination to those who appear to be more competent. These giants in the child's Promised Land can create a sense of incomplete autonomy, a sense of what Erikson termed "shame." Shame is a sense of personal identity which is counter to the concept of individuation—of becoming. Shame is a sense of stagnation which can last a lifetime. Shame-based people do not have a healthy sense of making mistakes; they consider themselves to be a mistake. Shame-based people feel they are fruitlessly wandering in their own desert for decade after decade. This sense of incompleteness can be contagious within a family, passed down from parents to children, generation to generation.

Often, to compensate for this feeling of shame, individuals will strive to mask their sense of incompleteness through donning the attire of a competent social role. Adults who still feel their sense of self identity to be in the grip of their personal giants often attempt to demonstrate their worth to those who appear more competent through the playing of respected roles. This would include the mistaken scenario that one can become a bus driver, a doctor, or a pastor by mastering the behaviors required of that particular social position. There are individuals who strive to enter professions, including those in full-time ministry, more out of a responsive struggle to conquer psychological shame than out of a genuine vocational call. Some individuals are not truly studying to become the gift but to gain the autonomous respect and social influence that all persons strive for as unique children of God. Out of that hunger many will try to enter a profession which does not match their God-given intelligences but will elicit dignity and command social respect. There are persons studying for the ministry who find the tasks of ministerial work quite foreign to their natural talents, but the desire for personal respect and social approval will drive them to endure a course of training which is extremely taxing due to its personal incompatibility.

Persons and Personages

In his book, *The Meaning of Persons*, Christian psychologist Paul Tournier describes how all children develop a manner of effectively presenting themselves to others through the construction of what he calls the "personage" (Tournier 1957). Our personage is our best foot forward, the intentional image of ourselves we present to other people. Our personage is the set of behaviors others see as we represent to them the person that we are. Ideally, our personage is a transparent reflection of who we are becoming, presenting ourselves to others with visible areas of strength and need. Our personage is an intentional construction of ourselves. We construct our personage deliberately, deciding what to display, emphasize, and disclose as a public image of who and whose we are.

While the person we are becoming should easily be seen through the personage we present, the transparency often may be clouded by the dust of doing battle with the giants of our lives. The feelings of dependency, incompetence, and shame which result from inconsistent or over-demanding relationships may cause individuals to construct a misleading personage for defensive protection. Rather than remaining transparent, the personage of someone who has an incomplete sense of appreciated individuality may become a piece of hard, opaque, self-protective armor. In an attempt to conceal a sense of inadequacy, to present an image of competence, and to fill a need to be needed, shame-based individuals may strive to present to others a personage which more represents a set of respected, stereotypical roles than a unique set of talents and styles of intelligence. In some cases, the hurting person may take on ministerial studies to protect themselves from an internal sense of inferiority or social impotence. For some, the challenge of a ministerial profession is more a process of constructing a somewhat compatible occupation than a vocational response to the call of God. The typical result of such a misfit of identity and effort is emotional discouragement and burn-out. God's call to each of us is to personally become the gift, not to futilely attempt to manufacture it.

Human Doings

In his best selling book which examines shame-based family dynamics, psychologist John Bradshaw refers to individuals growing up in toxically shaming environments as becoming "human doings" rather than "human beings" (Bradshaw 1986). Human doings are those who use the attributes they have cultivated in their personage in a futile attempt to seek wholeness. Not understanding the gift of grace, human doings work not only for their salvation, but also for their personally defined identity. These shame-based people view their worth in the world in terms of the contributions their roles can make. Many are persons still looking for giants in their lives to approve of what they accomplish.

As role players, human doings are very motivated to do things in the right way. Rather than enjoin their unique personality to that of another in holy matrimony, human doings attempt to play the role of *ideal* husband or wife. Rather than apply their unique set of intelligences to the rearing of children, they attempt to play the role of *ideal* father or mother. Rather than apply their spiritual gifts to Christ's work, they play the role of *ideal* pastor, teacher, counselor, or elder in the congregation. Rather than letting the Lord develop their personage as a gift from himself to his people, human doings fill their personage with social scripts and struggle to act them out. There appears to be a lot of maturity left to be unfolded. They are much like the child who admires the bus driver, thinking that if they could only wear the correct uniform they would be capable of driving the bus.

Some individuals go into ministry out of an urgency to be needed and respected. They find the role of clergy to hold an image of respect, power, and influence for the most worthy of causes, the kingdom of God. Many of the tasks of congregational work, however, may not fit the spiritual gifts and natural talents God has given them. The inevitable fatigue and feelings of frustration are wrongly justified as suffering sacrificially for the work of Christ. Total burn out may be only a short while away. They fight back at the sense of failure with yet a stronger personage of righteous work, not realizing that the Lord has a gift of a unique calling for them in the activities which they do well.

When you were younger, you girded yourself and went where you pleased....[5]

In the very last chapter of John's Gospel we find an account of the very first men's fellowship breakfast. Seated around an early morning campfire are the disciples and the risen Christ. Simon Peter is drying himself as he had stepped out of their fishing boat, splashing into the Sea of Galilee a little while before. (Was he trying to please the Lord by again walking on the water; this time without being commanded to do so?) For three years Peter had tried to follow our Lord through his own grit. He had witnessed the miracles and beheld the transfiguration. He had walked on water; at least until he realized what he was doing. It was revealed to him by the Holy Spirit that Jesus of Nazareth was, indeed, the awaited Messiah. He swore to follow him to the bitter end, only to be reprimanded with a promise of being sifted like wheat. And sifted he was. On that darkest of human nights Peter the Rock found that all the best intentions, the finest manufactured personage, is not enough. Left on his own, pressed in the midst of a hostile crowd, Simon the son of Jonah repeatedly denied ever even knowing Jesus Christ.

Around that daybreak campfire, soaking wet more with his own humiliation than with sea water, Peter heard Jesus repeatedly ask him the simplest of impossible questions: "Simon, do you love me?" And that is the same question asked of each of us: do we really love him? Do we love him enough to become the wonderful gift that he would have us become? Or do we merely seek his approval in the same way that we seek to please the other honored giants in our lives? Do we want to please the Lord through our own attempts to walk on water, build tabernacles out of sticks, and swear our allegiance to the heavens? Will we go to school, study with great determination, and work at ill-fitting tasks until we, too, find in our exhaustion that we cannot follow Jesus on our own?

"Do you love me?" was the question. And it still is. Peter confesses that he does, indeed, love the Lord with his whole person. It is the beginning question for Peter's ministry and also for the ministry of each one of us. As the Holy Spirit reveals to us our love for our Lord, he also reveals to us the gift we can continually become. Intensive study and work within the church are completely transformed with this confession of whose we are. We do not work to wear the role of clergy but strive to unfold the uniqueness of God's creation within us. We do not select occupations and try to fit into them. We listen for our vocation and follow Christ's leading into it.

"Truly, truly, I say to you, when you were younger, you used to gird yourself, and walk wherever you wished; but when you grow old, you will stretch out your hands, and someone else will gird you, and bring you to where you do not wish to go" (John 21:18). Just like Simon Peter, we stretch out our hand and begin the process of becoming the gift. In becoming the gift, in becoming ourselves, we find that Christ has a unique calling for the combination of talents and intelligences he

Wow...

has put into us. Often that calling includes ministry in places which we would never choose on our own, but to become a gift is to take it to places it was meant to be given.

Taken, Blessed, Broken, Given Away

When we participate in holy communion we are recognizing the greatest gift God has given to us: the life of his only Son. In the taking of the bread and the cup we are remembering that gift of eternal life. In one of his final writings, *Life of the Beloved,* Henri Nouwen speaks of Christ's people in the terms of holy communion (Nouwen 1992). Since we are the body of Christ at work on God's earth, in a sense we, too, should be remembered in the communion bread which honors the body of our Savior. Nouwen reminds us that at the Last Supper, Jesus took the bread and blessed it. He then broke it and gave it away. That is how we, too, become the gift of Christ to others. In becoming the gift, Jesus takes our lives in his hands and richly blesses them for the Father's sake. Then, like the bread, he breaks us. Cracking through the crust of our social roles and the self-protective armor we have placed around our fragile inner person, he exposes the inner tenderness of each of us. He then does with the gift of our lives what the bread shows us was intended all along: he gives us away. We become the gift to be given away. A gift is of no use unless it is given. We are not to be a gift to ourselves, but to others. In the kingdom of God the passion of ministerial study is not for gain but for giving. The more we become the gift, the more we are given. The more we can confess our love for our Savior and join our talents with others into a single body, the more we are surprised as we become the intended recipients of the gifts of those who join us in mutual ministry.

Beautiful.

End Notes

[1] Psalm 139:14.
[2] Proverbs 22:6.
[3] Ephesians 4:11.
[4] Numbers 13:28.
[5] John 21:18.

Reference List

Bradley, John, Jay Carty, and Russ Korth. 1991. *Discovering Your Natural Talents: How to Love What You Do and Do What You Love*, 4th ed. Colorado Springs, Colorado: NavPress.

Bradshaw, J. 1986. *Bradshaw On: The Family*. Deerfield Beach, Florida: Health Communications, Inc.

Gardner, H. 1985. *The Mind's New Science: A History of the Cognitive Revolution*. New York: Basic Books.

New American Standard Bible. 1977. Nashville: Thomas Nelson Publishers.

Nouwen, H., McNeill, D., and Morrison, D. 1982. Compassion: *A Reflection on the Christian Life*. Garden City, New York: Doubleday.

Nouwen, H. *Life of the Beloved: Spiritual Living in a Secular World*. 1992. Crossroads Publishing Co.

Tournier, P. *The Meaning of Persons*. 1957. New York: Harper and Row.

Background Readings

Erikson, E. *Childhood and Society*. 1993. New York: W.W. Norton.

Fossum, M. and Mason, M. Facing Shame. 1989. New York: W.W. Norton.

Kegan, R. *The Evolving Self*. 1983. Cambridge, MA: Harvard University Press.

Satir, V. *The New Peoplemaking*. 1988. Mountain View, CA: Science and Behavior Books.

Yancey, P. *What's So Amazing About Grace?* 1998. Grand Rapids, MI: Zondervan.

Chapter Six:
Stephen Carver, *A Life in Word and World*

One of the greatest challenges I have had in attempting to share the Bible with others was when I became involved in prison ministry, first as a Bible study leader and then later as a chaplain intern at a state penitentiary. The situation of this ministry group was so harsh and the needs of the inmates were so great that at times I felt overwhelmed with the responsibility of bringing a relevant message from the Bible into that setting. In order to go into that setting, I had to know for certain God was calling me to do so, and I believe this certainty is necessary for all those who feel led to share the Bible with others.

In order to be effective in any ministry setting, the minister must begin with a personal foundation of an inner awareness of the presence of God, having a deep and abiding sense of the call of God on her life.[1] Also, in order to be constantly in tune with God's will, the minister needs to develop a devotional life in which prayer is central. The daily time of prayer reminds the minister of the calling of God, encourages the minister's ongoing dependence upon the Spirit of God, provides the minister an opportunity to lift the needs of the people before God, and aids the minister in deepening the quality of her character.[2]

The next step in preparing to become a minister who is able to share the Scripture with others is to realize the need for a disciplined approach to preparing a message.[3] Preparing to share a message from the Bible involves an awareness of the context of the biblical passage as well as an awareness of the context of the ministry group with whom the message is going to be shared. Whether the ministry group is a church congregation, a small group meeting in a home, or Bible fellowship on a college campus, the minister who is attempting to be biblically accurate in his ministry must go to a great deal of effort in order to interpret the biblical text and then apply the interpretation in a ministry setting in such a way that the people receiving the message will be able to interact with it productively. If properly prepared, the minister can serve as an interpretive bridge between a specific biblical passage and the ministry group as is demonstrated in the following diagram.

Diagram 1

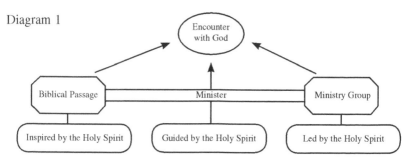

In Diagram 1 the point of the minister's interpretive activity is to facilitate the ministry group's encounter with God. Therefore, both the minister and the ministry group need to be aware of the presence of God moving among them and directing their paths. It is the objectivity provided by the Spirit that enables the minister to go beyond her own personal agenda to share a message that is as much for her as it is for others. It is the convicting power of the Spirit that places the biblical message deep into the hearts of people, producing fruit unto eternal life.

Yet, as important as the role of the Spirit of God is in this process of sacred communication, the minister still needs to do her best to dig into the meaning of the text and to apply it to the ministry situation, because this effort will help the minister to avoid misinterpreting a passage.[4] Fortunately, there are interpretive approaches available that will greatly aid the minister's work in this area, including the interpretive approaches known as Historical Criticism, Grammatical Criticism, and Literary Criticism.[5]

To demonstrate how each of these interpretive approaches can facilitate the interpretation of a biblical passage, an interpretive issue in Psalm 51 will be addressed in this portion of the chapter (if the reader is unfamiliar with this psalm, it would be best to read through it before continuing). After doing a preliminary reading of this psalm, the minister encounters a range of issues, but perhaps none more central than the

issue of forgiveness of sin and its basis for being granted. Having identified a key issue, now the interpreter's task is to use the interpretative
approaches to dig deeper into the meaning of the text.

Historical Criticism

Often the best starting point is using Historical Criticism which helps
the interpreter to understand why a passage was written and what is
the cultural background behind the passage. For example, consider
the possible background of Psalm 51. One of the first steps in doing
Historical Criticism is to determine who wrote this psalm and why. For
some psalms, this is a very difficult task because the text does not tell
us who wrote it (e.g., Psalm 1). When encountering a passage like this,
the interpreter needs to read the text carefully for clues as to what the
author's purpose is and what that purpose indicates about the author's
situation. Also, consulting biblical commentaries can be helpful in
gaining some ideas why a particular psalm might have been written.
However, in the case of Psalm 51, there is a title or what is known
as a superscription, giving the interpreter some details about not only
who wrote the Psalm but why it was written.[6] According to the title of
Psalm 51, this psalm is "for the choir director. A Psalm of David, when
Nathan the prophet came to him, after he had gone in to Bathsheba" (all
quotations are from the *New American Standard Bible* [1977] unless
otherwise indicated).[7] As can be seen, David wrote the psalm after
being confronted by the prophet concerning David's relationship with a
woman named Bathsheba. But a question arises: what was the problem
with this relationship that would require the intervention of a prophet?

For those who know the Bible well, this is an easy question; however,
for those who do not, there will need to be more work done to determine the fuller historical context. The history of David's life is given
in the books of 1 and 2 Samuel, and the account of David's relationship with Bathsheba is given in 2 Samuel 11—12. According to these
two chapters, David stayed home from battle one time, and he noticed
Bathsheba bathing from his vantage point on top of the king's palace.
Desiring her, he had her brought to him, and he had relations with her
even though she was a married woman. Soon after this event, Bathsheba
sent him a message indicating she was pregnant. This was a serious
problem for David because Bathsheba's husband Uriah was out fight-
ing in the battle, so there was no way the child would be considered

his. So David moved quickly to have Uriah brought back from the front
in hopes Uriah would have relations with his wife so when the child
was born it would seem to be Uriah's. But once again a problem arose
for David. Uriah refused to enjoy the comforts of his home while his
comrades were "camping in the open field" (2 Sam 11:11). So David
decided to have Uriah killed and then take Bathsheba to be his wife. It
is at this point in the narrative Nathan the prophet comes on to the scene
and confronts David with his sin. As a result of David's sin, the child
born to David and Bathsheba dies, and David's family is cursed by God
(i.e., "the sword shall never depart from your house" [2 Sam 12:10]).

The historical background of the writing of Psalm 51 informs us David
is in a great deal of pain when he writes this psalm. He has offended
God, lost a child, received a curse on his family, and endangered the
stability of the kingdom of Israel. Out of his pain, David writes this
psalm in an attempt to regain God's favor on him, so God's favor will
not leave David nor Israel. There is much at stake.

While the use of Historical Criticism up to this point has provided the
interpreter with information about the issues behind the writing of the
psalm, there is more to be done with this interpretive approach. There
still remains the task of addressing the issue of reception of forgiveness
as it would have been understood at the time of David. One of the striking elements of Psalm 51 is David's lack of appeal to animal sacrifice
as the immediate avenue for his forgiveness. In fact, in verse 16 David
even indicates God does "not delight in sacrifice," although David does
foresee a time when sacrifices will be favored by God once again (v
19). Given that David lived at a time when animal sacrifice was being
performed regularly, often by David himself (e.g., 2 Sam 6:17), why
didn't David make his appeal for forgiveness based on the sacrificial
system? An examination of the system of sacrifice helps to answer this
question. Even though David lived during the time when sacrifices
were being offered according to Levitical law (see Lev 1–8), he could
not appeal to them, because his sins were not covered by the system of
sacrifice. Often the view is promoted that animal sacrifice was a way
to atone for all sins, but the stipulations of the Mosaic covenant clearly
indicate some sins could not be atoned for, such as the sin of adultery
(Lev 20:10) and the sin of murder (Exod 21:12–14) (Knight 1982, 239;
Tate 1990, 28). Moreover, in Numbers 15:24–31, there is a distinction
made between unintentional sins and sins done defiantly, with the for-

mer able to be atoned for but the latter unable. Since David has intentionally committed two sins requiring punishment by death, on what basis could he appeal to God for forgiveness?

Grammatical Criticism

To address this question, it is best to move into the interpretive approach known as Grammatical Criticism.

This interpretive approach helps the interpreter to determine the meaning of a passage by providing the means by which key words in the original language of the text can be identified and understood in light of the grammatical relationships with the rest of the words in the passage.[8] One of the first things an interpreter can do in determining if any words or phrases are problematic concerning the issue of forgiveness in Psalm 51 is to compare some of the major translations. Consider the following comparison of the first four verses of Psalm 51 in the New American Standard Bible (NAS) and in the New International Version (NIV) (italics were added):[9]

NAS	NIV
Be gracious to me, O God, according to Thy *lovingkindness*; According to the greatness of Thy compassion blot out my transgressions.	*Have mercy on* me, O God, according to your *unfailing love*; according to your great compassion according to your great compassion blot out my transgressions.
Wash me *thoroughly* from my iniquity, And cleanse me from my sin. For I know my transgressions, And my sin is ever before me. Against Thee, Thee only, I have sinned,	Wash *away all* my iniquity and cleanse me from my sin. For I know my transgressions, and my sin is always before me. Against you, you only, have I sinned
And done what is evil in Thy sight, So that Thou *art justified* when Thou dost speak,	and done what is evil in your sight, so that you are *proved right* when you speak
And *blameless* when Thou dost judge.	and *justified* when you judge.

As can be seen by reading through these two translations, there are a few significant differences in some of the verses, especially in verse 1 where the basis for David's request for forgiveness is anchored. In the NAS version, David asks for God's mercy based on the "lovingkindness" of God, but in the NIV David asks for God's mercy based on the "unfailing love" of God. While both expressions have the word "love" involved, there is enough of a difference to make the interpreter pause and ask what David has in mind here, but there is no way to determine this with just the English versions. The interpreter has to go back to the Hebrew text.

There are several avenues back to the Hebrew word behind these expressions, but the use of an exhaustive Bible concordance is the most accessible to everyone, so it will be used here to determine the meaning of the Hebrew word in question.[10] It was indicated above that in the NAS version the Hebrew word of interest is translated "lovingkindness." The next step then is to use the *New American Standard Exhaustive Concordance of the Bible* to locate this word's Hebrew root (if the interpreter is using another version, a concordance matching that version will need to be used). With the concordance in hand, the interpreter begins by turning to the word "lovingkindness" (it is found on page 764). Then the interpreter should run her finger down the list of passages containing this word until she comes to the following citation for Psalm 51:1.

> to me, O God, according to Thy l;   Ps 51:1   2617a

As can be seen, to the right of the Scripture reference is a number— 2617a. This is the number corresponding to the Hebrew word behind "lovingkindness," which can be found in the lexicon in the back of the concordance. Looking in the lexicon, the interpreter will find the number 2617a on page 1521 and see the Hebrew word behind "lovingkindness" is dsj which is pronounced *chesed* (pronounced with a hard "ch" such as in "Bach").[11] Immediately below this word, the interpreter sees numerous possible meanings for *chesed* used by the NAS translators, including "devotion," "faithfulness," "favor," "kindness," "lovingkindness," "loyalty," "mercy," and "unchanging love." These definitions of the word *chesed* provide the interpreter with a possible range of meanings for *chesed*, although more options for this word are possible.[12]

Now the interpreter must decide which meaning is best for the context of Psalm 51. How is this done? Since this word is being used in a Davidic psalm, the most relevant data will be verses in the other Davidic psalms using *chesed* . An examination of the relevant sections in the concordance reveals that the word *chesed* occurs in numerous Davidic psalms, including Psalms 5, 6, 13, 17, 18, 21, 23, 25, 26, 31, 32, 36, 40, 52, 57, 59, 61, 62, and 63. The question then is what should the interpreter do with all of these occurrences of *chesed*? What passages are most relevant for an understanding of how *chesed* is used in Psalm 51? In the context of Psalm 51, David asks God to be gracious to him in spite of his sin, and David believes this grace is anchored in the chesed of God. So the passages most helpful for an understanding of chesed in Psalm 51 would be passages where David's relationship with God is being strained and he appeals to the *chesed* of God. One such passage is Psalm 6. In this psalm, David believes God is angry with him, and so he asks for God's grace and healing, and then he states: "Save me because of Thy *chesed*" (v 4b). The connection between being in right relationship with God and the chesed of God is also found in Psalm 25:7 where David states: "Do not remember the sins of my youth or my transgressions; According to Thy *chesed* remember Thou me, For Thy goodness' sake, O LORD." In Psalms 6 and 25, then, there is a recurring theme of David knowing estrangement from God is possible, and yet, based on the chesed of God, David still believes he can have a relationship with God. In the contexts of these Psalms, one could contend David is appealing to something other than God's love which he could have referred to but does not (love in Hebrew is *'ahabah* [hbha]). Support for this contention is found in 2 Samuel 7:15, where God makes an eternal covenant with David and God indicates that His *chesed* "shall not depart" from the house of David. Hence, following this line of evidence chesed would more closely be connected to the faithfulness of God as it is anchored in his covenant relationship with David, and this view has found support among certain scholars (e.g., Glueck 1967).

However, clearly the NAS and NIV translators have chosen a different avenue for interpreting *chesed*, and they have support in prominent lexicons (e.g., Brown, Driver, and Briggs 1979, 339) and theological dictionaries (e.g., Harris 1980, 307). So given the discrepancy between the data gathered via Grammatical Criticism and the choice of the translators, is there any way to resolve this issue? Exactly what is the basis for David's request for forgiveness?

Literary Criticism

It is at this point where the interpreter will find some help from the use of Literary Criticism,[13] an interpretive approach which promotes a close reading of the text, including an examination of the genre (i.e., form) of a passage and its accompanying characteristics. Psalm 51 is of the genre of psalm poetry, and as such it has its own peculiar way of expressing its ideas.[14] As was noted above, one characteristic of psalm poetry is the title which gives information on musical performance, authorship, and historical background. Another characteristic of psalm poetry is that psalms are generally divided up into categories according to their type of content and form.[15] Some biblical scholars place the Psalms into numerous categories (Gunkel 1998; Mowinckel 1967),[16] while others use a simpler scheme (Brueggemann 1984).[17] The one followed here is a four-category schema with praise, royal, wisdom, and lament psalms (Bellinger 1990, 23),[18] and Psalm 51 is clearly of the fourth type.[19]

Lament psalms are known for their intensity of expressing sorrow and for their five part development: a cry out to God (e.g., "how long, O Lord?"), an indication of the nature of the complaint (e.g., enemies, personal sin, or physical pain), a prayer for deliverance, a remembrance of what God has done in the past, and a decision to yet praise God (Ryken 1984, 114). This five-fold division can provide the interpreter with a format for reading closely the details within Psalm 51.

While Psalm 51 does not begin with the frustration of the speaker, there is still the cry to God: "Be gracious to me, O God" (v 1). In the second half of verse 1, David's problem is identified as "my transgressions," [20] defined in verse 4 as an action done directly against God and in verse 14 as "bloodguiltiness" which corresponds with what has already been discovered through the study of the historical background (i.e., he had Uriah, Bathsheba's husband, killed). So in defining the nature of his problem, David repents, giving a dramatic confession of the depth of his depravity before God, anchoring his sinfulness even into his conception (v. 5).[21] Having presented the depth of his problem, David then asks for deliverance through the cleansing from sin, emphasizing this need through the words "blot out" (vv 1, 9), "wash" (vv 2, 7), "cleanse" (v 2), and "purify" (v 7). David's hope is that this cleansing will enable him to remain in God's presence and keep the Spirit of God in his life (v 11). David knows that his sin has jeopardized his relationship with

God, so he is hoping God will "hide" his face from David's sins even as the sins are being cleansed. David appears to have some confidence this request will be responded to because of his understanding of the nature of God as one which accepts a broken spirit (v 17). The fourth part of the lament psalm (the remembrance of God's goodness) is tightly connected to David's prayer of deliverance as David remembers the "greatness" of God's compassion (v 1), the purity of God's judgment (v 4b), God's desire for inner truthfulness (v 6), and the type of motivation that must accompany a request for forgiveness (vv 16–17). Moreover, as David remembers the attributes of God, he is inspired to praise God (the fifth element of lament psalms). For example, in verse 13 David promises to teach sinners about God, so they will be converted to God. He follows this with more praise in verses 14 and 15:

> Deliver me from bloodguiltiness, O God, Thou God of my salvation;
> Then my tongue will joyfully sing of Thy righteousness.
>
> O LORD, open my lips,
> That my mouth may declare Thy praise.[22]

As can be seen from the above analysis, a close reading of the psalm in light of its genre (i.e., a lament) is helpful in understanding the overall flow of Psalm 51 and the extent of David's request for forgiveness within the context of praise for God. However, there is more that can be learned from applying Literary Criticism. Along with enabling the interpreter to understand the overall movement of the psalm, Literary Criticism can also help the interpreter to unpack the smaller movements within a psalm in terms of how each line of poetry builds on the one that precedes it (this is known as parallelism).[23] This element involves being aware that each verse of poetry is composed of two or more lines of poetry, usually divided by a comma or semi-colon. There are several types of parallelism, with some scholars primarily promoting three (e.g., Bellinger 1990, 13) and others four or more (e.g., Ryken 1984, 103f.). The type of parallelism helpful to know for the issue at hand in Psalm 51:1 is synonymous parallelism (italics and underlining are added):

Line 1: *Be gracious to* me, O God, according to **Thy** *chesed*;

Line 2: According to the greatness of **Thy compassion** *blot out my transgressions.*

Synonymous parallelism involves a repetition of an idea in both lines, sometimes with expansion of that thought in line 2. As can be seen from the above quotation, line 1 contains a request for the grace based on God's *chesed*, and line 2 builds on this request by specifically asking for removal (i.e., blotting out) of sin based on God's great "compassion" which can be defined as "the idea of the feelings of a mother toward her baby" (Tate 1990, 14). So *chesed* and "compassion" are parallel terms, and thus they inform and define each other. So David's appeal for forgiveness is not just anchored in a covenantal approach to God, but it also includes an appeal to God's character as being one of a caring parental figure. David has an intense relationship with God that has not ended with his sin.

In this section of the chapter, one interpretive issue in Psalm 51 was pursued in an effort to demonstrate what can be learned from three interpretive approaches: Historical, Grammatical, and Literary Criticisms. Now it is appropriate to draw some conclusions. From the application of Historical Criticism, the interpreter knows David has committed grievous sins which cannot be removed through animal sacrifice. So his life is at stake as well as the stability of the nation of Israel. From the application of Grammatical Criticism, the interpreter knows one of the key words in the text is *chesed*, and this word has covenantal implications. From the application of Literary Criticism, the interpreter knows the overall movement of Psalm 51 and how David bases his request for forgiveness on his repentance, his understanding on the nature of God, and the relationship he has with God. Based on the evidence gathered from these approaches, the interpreter can then summarize his thoughts in a fashion similar to the following paragraph.

According to both the historical and literary context of Psalm 51, David has clearly abused his relationship with God, but his status with God is not based solely on these sinful choices. For a significant portion of his life, David had stayed in good relationship with God, and as a result of that relationship, God had promised always to keep a Davidic king on the throne of Israel. As was noted above, in making this promise, God says in 2 Samuel 7:15 that his *chesed* "shall not depart" from the house of David. Unlike the conditional relationship which God had established with King Saul's house, David's house could rely on God's continual provision and care. This does not mean that David could do whatever he wanted. God did punish him for his sin with Bathsheba. Yet, the punishment did not lead to a complete break in the relationship. David experienced his punishment and went on, as did the Davidic kingship, but not because of David's faithfulness, his ability to gain God's pity, nor his performance of animal sacrifice. But rather, the relationship continued because of the covenant loyalty of God and God's ability to care for and forgive David as a child who has repented of his sin. So perhaps it is best to translate chesed as "loyal parenthood" because this would carry with it the idea of God's care as well as his desire to keep his word to David in spite of David's shortcomings. Thus David is able to ask God for forgiveness based on a long-term covenantal relationship David has with God as well as on David's knowledge of God's character as being one of willing grace to a repentant sinner.

As can be seen from addressing an interpretive issue in Psalm 51, there is much that an interpreter can learn from using Historical Criticism, Grammatical Criticism, and Literary Criticism. If a minister has done her homework well, she can speak about the deeper meaning of a biblical passage, opening the scripture to the ministry group in a manner which will lead them into a deeper encounter with God. So the application of Historical, Grammatical, and Literary Criticisms to Psalm 51 demonstrates that approaching the Scripture from different angles helps the minister to be aware of the world of the text. This can be demonstrated by adding to the previous diagram:

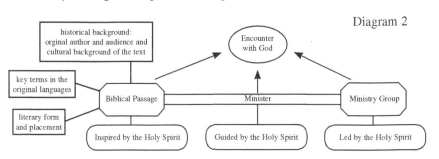

Diagram 2

Up to this point, a great deal of time has been spent working with the biblical passage; however, once the minister has come to the place where she is feeling quite certain that the text has been interpreted appropriately, she is still not ready to deliver a message to the people. The research into the biblical passage has given the minister a strong sense of the different issues that the passage can address, but the next question is which issue is the most relevant for the ministry group on a specific week? What are they dealing with in the world? How should the biblically based message be contextualized? To address these questions, there are two more steps the minister needs to take before sharing from the scripture.

First, the minister needs to spend time in prayer specifically seeking God's guidance in terms of what is most relevant for the audience. As a servant of God, the minister should seek to bring a message to the people reflecting the leading of God. The exegetical work has revealed a great deal of relevant and important information about Psalm 51, but what aspect of the passage needs to be highlighted the most? Should it be the tragic consequences of sin? Should it be the need to have a repentant heart before God? Should it be the loyal parenthood of God? Only God knows what will have the most influence on the people at a particular moment in time. By spending time in prayer, the minister is open to the movement of the Spirit of God, and the emphasis of the message or Bible study is selected not on the basis of the whim of the minister but on the guidance of God.

A particularly effective way to prepare for this time of prayer is for the minister to spend some time reflecting on the spiritual, emotional, and physical needs of the ministry group. Fellowships, Bible study groups, and congregations all go through cycles. Sometimes everything is going well on all fronts, and sometimes several areas are problematic. In a sense, the minister needs to be continually "taking the temperature" of the ministry group, and this cannot be done from a distance. The minister should be visiting homes and places of employment as well as attending events within the community. Seeing the members of the ministry group in settings outside of the church building will help the minister to get a clearer sense of where the ministry group is spiritually. People can come to the church and act as though everything is fine for one or two hours, but how are they doing the rest of the week? The minister might find out through her work in the community that those who seem least comfortable in the church building are doing well the rest of the week and those who exhibit the most social graces in the church building are really struggling. By getting to know the people well and bringing their needs before God as a part of preparing to share a message from the Bible, the minister is consciously attempting to serve the role as a conduit for the grace of God to the people.

Second, once the minister has a strong sense of which elements of the passage to emphasize in light of God's leading and the needs of the people, the message needs to be contextualized for the ministry group in light of the its background. For example, one area the minister needs to consider is the educational level of the people. If the ministry group is largely college educated, then the level of vocabulary used will be different from what one can use with a ministry group having an eighth grade or high school education. If the ministry group makes connections between a wide variety of ideas through the means of traditional liberal arts categories, the minister can use this sort of language in connecting elements in the message with what is happening politically, socially, economically, and religiously. This does not mean that a minister should "dumb down" his message for a ministry group with a lower level of education. But rather, the minister should make connections between ideas the way the ministry group makes those connections. It might not be via the language of college, but the connections are made nonetheless, perhaps through how the workplace is affected or the price of gas is affected. For example, a minister who uses Veblen's concept of "conspicuous consumption" in making a point about the dangers of riches will probably not communicate this idea as effectively to a ministry group that is unfamiliar with the field of sociology as the minister would if he talked more concretely about how some people's desire for huge homes is making it more difficult for the average person to afford the lumber for a moderate size home. In the case of a widely diverse ministry group, it is best to aim for the median of the ministry group, even though some will feel left out and others not challenged enough.

Another area the minister needs to be aware of in preparing her message is the culture of the ministry group. Some stories just don't translate well from one culture to another. If the minister is in a farming or ranching community, an illustration about the problems office workers face or about traffic problems will probably not be as effective as an illustration which has some sort of agricultural symbol or image. It is in the area of culture that the minister must be particularly careful. Some areas are more bound to their own specific culture than others, and in some cases the locals are not too eager to share their traditions. It takes time to know what makes certain communities unique. The minister should not assume one city is just like another or one rural area is just like another. Every community, indeed every ministry group, has its own peculiarities that are part of its culture, including holiday customs, sports, entertainment pursuits, and idiomatic phrases. There is a "way of doing things" that some members of the ministry group will insist upon, including the way that a sermon should end (such as with a prayer) or what the outline of a Bible study should include. It is best to discover what the culture is, try to communicate within that culture, and attempt changes gradually. More often than not, ministers who have thought a ministry group was backwards or behind the times and have attempted to force change have been invited to minister somewhere else. Loving and caring for people must begin with appreciating where the people are. If the minister has a need to remake a ministry group into her own cultural and educational image, the minister and the ministry group are going to be very frustrated.

To demonstrate the movement from interpretation to a message based on an understanding of the context of the ministry group it is best to provide an example in this section of the chapter. In the opening portion of this chapter, I indicated that I have led Bible studies in a prison setting, so how would I take the interpretive work done on Psalm 51 in this chapter and apply it in that setting? As was noted above, I would begin by spending time in prayer, reflecting on the needs of the inmates as they were shared with me at the last Bible study and during times of visitation throughout the week. For example, one of the ongoing needs the inmates expressed was for forgiveness and release from guilt. Being in prison, they are confronted with the consequences of their sin every day, and the atmosphere can be stifling, especially since they are around others who feel exactly the same way. Moreover, visitation from family and friends often heightens their sense of guilt because they see the stress their incarceration has placed on those closest to them, particularly the stress on spouses and children who often experience severe poverty.

Concerning the educational level of the inmates, many of them do not have a high level of education, so it will be important to construct a Bible study using terms which are understandable. Unusual or complicated terminology will need to be eliminated and replaced with simpler terms that communicate the same basic message. Moreover, care will need to be taken not to use what some call "church" language. Those who have been in a community of faith for a period of time develop a certain jargon, including such lengthy terms as justification, sanctification, and propitiation. Many of the inmates have not grown up in a religious context, and so theological terms have to be explained to them.

Concerning the cultural background of the inmates, it is varied in terms of where they were prior to coming to prison, but obviously they have been forced to adapt to a common culture in prison. The prison environment is mostly one of oppression, depression, and forced uniformity. Inmates are required to wear the same kind of clothing, to be on guard against violence at any time, to be responsive to the demands of prison guards, and to become used to bars, cement, and barbed wire. To find some sort of relief from the drudgery, inmates will turn to any educational and vocational opportunities provided by the prison, and they will also look to physical activities such as sports to pass the time of day. Inmates are very cautious about forming relationships with each other and rarely want to talk about why they are in prison, because there is a pecking order in prison. Those who have committed certain crimes are looked down upon by the rest of the inmates and in some cases are beaten and abused. Anyone coming into their world is viewed as an outsider who cannot possibly grasp what they are going through. So to contextualize a message for this ministry group involves being sensitive about the hardships the inmates face on a daily basis and the atmosphere of intimidation and fear that encapsulates their existence.

Taking into consideration all of the observations about the ministry setting made so far, how can a minister construct a message from Psalm 51 that would be relevant to these inmates? In the interpretive work done on Psalm 51, it was observed that the psalm primarily addresses David's request for forgiveness after committing adultery and murder to cover it up. This context of sin and forgiveness lends itself to a Bible study about what to do about feelings of guilt. However, as was observed above, the minister does not want to go too quickly into this subject, because inmates will be reluctant to talk openly about their crimes. So below is an outline of a Bible study that could be used to help connect this ministry group to the message in Psalm 51.

Opening: Connect to Their Understanding

Ask the ministry group the following questions:

> What does the word "embarrassment" mean to you?
> Have you ever been embarrassed? I have. (Share several personal stories but don't expect them to volunteer their own stories.)
> What does the word *guilt* mean to you?

Do you think there is a difference between feeling guilty and being embarrassed? What is the difference?

Share a time when I have felt guilty. Again don't ask them to share their feelings of guilt unless they openly volunteer to do so; it takes time to build a safe environment to share about themselves.

Transition to the Biblical Passage

Ask the following questions:

> Do you think any people in the Bible ever did anything that they felt guilty about?
> Who were they?
> What did they do?
> How did they handle their guilt?

Allow for conversation to take place about a variety of biblical characters such as Adam and Eve, Noah, Abraham, and Peter.

Direct the conversation toward David. Present an overview of his life, highlighting particularly the successes he had as king and the depth of his spirituality.

Then ask the following questions:

> Do you think the great king David ever had any difficulties?
> What challenges might he have faced as a king?
> Do you think he ever did anything he felt guilty about?

Discussion of Psalm 51

Read the psalm aloud.

Comment on the title of the psalm and how it connects to events in 2 Samuel 11–12.

Discuss the details of David's sin and how he could have made such tragic decisions.

Talk about contemporary events and leaders who have made tragic decisions.

Talk about the human condition and the difficult choices we make as humans, some of which lead us into sin.

Ask the following questions:

According to the psalm, on what basis does David ask for forgiveness?
What does David connect to being forgiven? (Be prepared to discuss the concepts of cleansing from sin as well as the renewal given by the Holy Spirit.)

Discuss the following issues:

Removal of sins in the Mosaic covenant.
How David's sins cannot be removed by the system of sacrifices.
The meaning of the word chesed in the passage.
The idea of loyalty.
The idea of parenthood (be careful here; many inmates do not have parents who are good role models.)
The basis on which David can ask for forgiveness given all of the evidence.

Conclusion

Emphasize the willingness of God to listen to us and to forgive us of our sins as we openly confess them to him.

Note that God's forgiveness does not necessarily mean we will not have to suffer at least some consequences for our sin. David had to suffer severe consequences, even though God forgave him.

Hence, their continued incarceration should not be taken as a sign that God is unwilling to forgive them or renew them.

Close in prayer. Leave time for them to pray silently to God about their feelings of guilt and their need for forgiveness.

The above example Bible study demonstrates how knowledge of the context of a biblical passage and the context of a ministry setting can be brought together by the minister in order to promote an encounter with God. The complete diagram of this overall process is given below:

Diagram 3

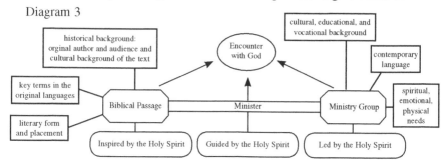

Ministers who have done thier homework in the "Word" and in the "World" are able to help bridge the gap between the two as they are empowered by the Holy Spirit, thereby facilitating an encounter between God and the ministry group.

End Notes

[1] The word "minister" will be used throughout this chapter to refer to anyone called by God to serve a given group of people, whether the group is in a traditional church setting or in any other setting, such as a Bible study group in a prison.

[2] The Apostle Paul indicates the qualifications for someone in leadership have to do primarily with issues of character such as being "temperate, prudent, respectable, hospitable" (1 Tim 3:2) and being "free from the love of money" (1 Tim 3:3).

[3] As Peterson notes: "Few things are more important in the Christian community than reading the Scriptures rightly. The holy Scriptures carry immense authority. Read wrongly, they can ignite war, legitimize abuse, sanction hate, cultivate arrogance. Not only can, but have...do. This is present danger" (1996, 8).

[4] As Fee notes, the Bible is to be read "intelligently, not willy-nilly or with a kind of laziness that gives credit to the Holy Spirit for every imaginable wrong interpretation of the text, simply because we were too lazy to do the hard work of study" (1996, 32).

[5] For a full discussion of each of these interpretive approaches see Hayes and Holladay 1987, chapters 6-8.

[6] Selecting the appropriate approaches to interpreting the text is an essential step for the interpreter to make, especially since not every approach is equally helpful in promoting an encounter with the text of Scripture. As Wolff notes, it is best for the interpreter to "avail himself of the possibilities of philological, historical, and literary interpretive technique" in an effort to "betake himself to the place of the text" (1969, 165).

[7] Superscriptions also contain indications of psalm types and musical information, but unfortunately the meaning of some of the terms used is very difficult to determine. For a discussion of these terms, see Kidner (1973, 36-43), Oesterley (1953, 9-19), Pfeiffer (1948, 642-644), and Robinson (1960, 115f.).

[8] Kidner notes that the authorship of psalms connected to David are challenged on aesthetic, theological, spiritual, historical, linguistic, and textual bases, but Kidner believes "some of these objections are arbitrary and simplistic; none is adequate to the task of proving a general negative, even though some isolated questions remain unanswered" (1973, 34). One of the major issues in assigning authorship to the Davidic psalms has to do with the meaning of the preposition l (lamed) in Hebrew which precedes David's name. As Craigie notes, l in this position can mean "for," "by," "to," "with reference to," or "for the use of" (1983, 33). Craigie concludes that l "need not, and probably does not, imply authorship," even though he acknowledges David could have composed some of the psalms (1983, 35).

[9] As Harrison notes, many of the Davidic psalms have superscriptions that correspond well with the narratives about David's life, but there are some that do not including Psalms 34 and 56 (1969, 977f).

[10] Leupold contends Psalm 51 could not be Davidic, because it does not mention David's specific sin, seems to consider the sin to be only against God, indicates the walls of Jerusalem needed rebuilt when they did not, and is too spiritually advanced for David's day (1969, 399). However, Harrison includes it in the list of psalms which correspond well with biblical narrative about David's life, although he does realize the correspondence may be due to an informed editor (1969, 978).

[11] In the Hebrew text, these four verses are actually verses 3-6 instead of 1-4 because the superscription in the Hebrew text is counted as verses 1-2.

[12] An exhaustive concordance is a text which contains the biblical reference for every occurrence of every word used in the Bible. Moreover, it also has corresponding numbers assigned to those words which can be used to look up the Greek or Hebrew word behind the English word in question.

[13] The hard "ch" sound is represented in transliteration with an h and a dot under the h. Using Hebrew letters, the word chesed is spelled dsj with the hard "ch" sound corresponding to the letter j (it is important to note that Hebrew is read from right to left when trying to connect the sounds to the Hebrew letters).

[14] Other possible options include: "covenant loyalty" (Anderson 1972, 391), "unshakeable covenant love" (Knight 1982, 241), "steadfast love" (Leupold 1969, 401), and "loyal love" (Tate 1990, 3).

[15] The other main types of literary genres in the Bible are historical narratives, wisdom poetry, visionary literature (prophetic and apocalyptic), gospels, and epistles, each with its own distinctive literary elements. For a full discussion of the elements of each of these genres see Ryken, 1984.

[16] Prior to the development of Literary Criticism, the classification of a psalms according to genre or form was based on the use of Form Criticism.

[17] For a helpful overview of Gunkel's and Mowinckel's perspectives see Bellinger 1990, 18ff.

[18] Brueggemann has three categories for psalms: orientation, reflecting on "satisfied seasons of well-being"; disorientation, reflecting on "anguished seasons of hurt"; new orientation, reflecting on "turns of surprise" (1984, 19).

[19] It should be noted that Bellinger also provides subcategories for two of these classifications (praise and lament). Concerning the three types other than lament, Praise psalms offer praise to God for something he has done or for the attributes of his character (e.g., Psalm 8). Royal psalms are prayers for the king of Israel, with some of them being messianic in tone (e.g., Psalm 2). Wisdom psalms give the reader guidance concerning the way of the righteous versus the way of the wicked, and usually there is a reward indicated for the righteous and a warning of judgment for the wicked (e.g., Psalm 1). These first three types of psalms usually express their ideas in a three-fold pattern with a thesis statement in the first few verses, poetic development in the middle of the psalm, and a resolution (i.e., summing up) at the end of the psalm. Ryken uses this three-

fold structure for what he labels "lyric" poems (1984, 111-112), but I believe the structure can be applied more widely.

[20] Anderson categorizes Psalm 51 as a "penitential" psalm, a subset within the wider category of laments in his system (1972, 389).

[21] Some scholars maintain the Hebrew word behind "transgressions"— uvp—should best be translated "rebellious acts" or "revolt," and this fits well with the nature of David's sins as being done defiantly (for a discussion of this term see Tate 1990, 15).

[22] Some theologians see in this verse proof of the doctrine of original sin, but it should be noted that within the context of Hebrew poetry, this statement is probably best understood as hyperbole (i.e., exaggeration for effect), emphasizing David's emotional response to his sin, rather than a statement on human depravity in general.

[23] Metaphors are used throughout the Psalms as a way to give readers concrete images communicating in depth thought. In the case of building the "walls of Jerusalem," the application of the metaphor would be in matching the need for protection from physical enemies with the need for protection from spiritual ones—in David's case his own lust.

[24] Hyssop is used in the sprinkling of blood on the doorposts for the first Passover (Exod 12:22), for the ritual cleansing of a leper (Lev 14:4f), and for cleansing someone defiled by contact with a corpse (Num. 19:6f).

[25] As Robinson notes, parallelism is a "fundamental principle of Hebrew verse form" as "every verse must consist of at least two 'members,' the second of which must, more or less completely, satisfy the expectation raised by the first" (1960, 21).

Select Bibliography

Alter, Robert. 1992. *The World of Biblical Literature.* New York: Basic Books.

Anderson, A. A. 1972. *The Book of the Psalms.* Vol. 1. New Century Bible, edited by Ronald Clements and Matthew Black. Greenwood, S. C.: The Attic Press, Inc.

Beitzel, Barry. 1988. "Jerusalem." In Baker *Encyclopedia of the Bible*, vol. 2, edited by Walter Elwell, 1123-1135. Grand Rapids, Michigan: Baker Book House.

Bellinger, W. H., Jr. 1990. Psalms: *Reading and Studying the Book of Praises.* Peabody, Massachusetts: Hendrickson Publishers.

Brown, Francis, S. R. Driver, and Charles Briggs. 1979. *A Hebrew and English Lexicon of the Old Testament.* Based on the Lexicon of William Gesenius, translated by Edward Robinson. Oxford: Clarendon Press.

Brueggeman, Walter. 1984. *The Message of the Psalms.* Augsburg Old Testament Studies. Minneapolis: Augsburg Publishing House.

Bullock, C. Hassell. 1979. *An Introduction to the Poetic Books of the Old Testament.* Chicago: Moody Press.

Craigie, Peter. 1983. *Psalms 1-50.* Word Biblical Commentary, edited by David Hubbard and Glenn Barker, vol. 19. Waco, Texas: Word Books, Publishers.

_____. 1986. *The Old Testament: Its Background, Growth, and Content.* Nashville: Abingdon Press.

Dahood, Mitchell. 1968. *Psalms II (51-100).* The Anchor Bible, edited by William Albright and David Freedman, vol. 17. Garden City, New York: Doubleday and Company, Inc.

Elliger, K., and W. Rudolph, eds. 1983. *Biblia Hebraica Stuttgartensia.* Stuttgart: Deutsche Bibelgesellschaft.

Fee, Gordon. 1996. "History as Context for Interpretation." In *The Act of Bible Reading: A Multidisciplinary Approach to Biblical Interpretation,* edited by Elmer Dyck, 10-32. Downers Grove, Illinois: Intervarsity Press.

Fee, Gordon, and Douglas Stuart. 1982. *How to Read the Bible for All Its Worth.* Grand Rapids, Michigan: Academie Books.

Gabel, John, Charles Wheeler, and Anthony York. 2000. *The Bible as Literature.* Oxford: Oxford University Press.

Gillingham, S. E. 1994. *The Poems and Psalms of the Hebrew Bible.* Oxford Bible Series, edited by P. R. Ackroyd and G. N. Stanton. Oxford: Oxford University Press.

Glueck, Nelson. 1967. *Hesed in the Bible.* Translated by A. Gottschalk. Hebrew Union College Press.

Goldingay, John. 1981. *Approaches to Old Testament Interpretation. Issues in Contemporary Theology,* edited by I. Howard Marshall. Downers Grove, Illinois: Intervarsity Press.

Gunkel, Hermann. 1998. *Introduction to Psalms: The Genres of the Religious Lyric of Israel.* Completed by Joachim Begrich. Translated by James Nogalski. Macon, Georgia: Mercer University Press.

Harris, R. Laird. 1980. "hsd." In *Theological Wordbook of the Old Testament.* Vol. 1, edited by R. Laird Harris, 305-307. Chicago: Moody Press.

Harrison, R. K. 1969. *Introduction to the Old Testament.* Grand Rapids, Michigan: Eerdmans Publishing Company.

Hayes, John, and Carl Holladay. 1987. *Biblical Exegesis: A Beginner's Handbook.* Revised Edition. Atlanta: John Knox Press.

Hill, Andrew, and John Walton. 1991. *A Survey of the Old Testament.* Grand Rapids, Michigan: Zondervan Publishing House.

Kidner, Derek. 1973. Psalms 1-72: *An Introduction and Commentary on Books I and II of the Psalms.* The Tyndale Old Testament Commentaries, edited by D. J. Wiseman. London: Inter-Varsity Press.

King, Philip. 1992. "Jerusalem." In *The Anchor Bible Dictionary,* vol. 3, edited by David Noel Freedman, 747-766. New York: Doubleday.

Knight, George. 1982. *Psalms.* Vol. 1. The Daily Study Bible (Old Testament), edited by John Gibson. Philadelphia: The Westminster Press.

Leupold, H. C. 1969. *Exposition of the Psalms.* Grand Rapids, Michigan: Baker Book House.

Mowinckel, Sigmund. 1967. *The Psalms in Israel's Worship.* 2 vols. Translated by D. R. Ap-Thomas. Nashville: Abingdon Press.

Murphy, James. 1977. *A Critical and Exegetical Commentary on the Book of Psalms.*

Minneapolis: Klock and Klock Christian Publishers. New American Standard Bible. 1977. Chicago: Moody Press.

Oesterley, W. O. E. 1953. *The Psalms.* London: S. P. C. K.

Peterson, Eugene. 1996. "Forward: Caveat Lector." In *The Act of Bible Reading: A Multidisciplinary Approach to Biblical Interpretation,* edited by Elmer Dyck, 7-9. Downers Grove, Illinois: Intervarsity Press.

Pfeiffer, Robert. 1948. *Introduction to the Old Testament.* New York: Harper and Brothers Publishers.

Robinson, Theodore. 1960. *The Poetry of the Old Testament.* London: Gerald Duckworth and Co. Ltd.

Ryken, Leland. 1984. *How to Read the Bible as Literature.* Grand Rapids, Michigan: Zondervan Publishing House.

Sarna, Nahum. 1993. *On the Book of Psalms: Exploring the Prayers of Ancient Israel.* New York: Schocken Books.

Stuart, Douglas. 1984. *Old Testament Exegesis: A Primer for Students and Pastors.* Revised Edition. Philadelphia: The Westminster Press.

Tate, Marvin. 1990. Psalms 51-100. *Word Biblical Commentary,* edited by David Hubbard and Glenn Barker, vol. 20. Dallas, Texas:Word Books, Publishers.

The Holy Bible: New International Version. 1978. East Brunswick, N. J.: New York International Bible Society.

Thomas, Robert, ed. 1981. *New American Standard Exhaustive Concordance of the Bible*. Nashville: Holman Bible Publishers.

Weiser, Artur. 1962. The Psalms: A Commentary. The Old Testament Library, edited by G. Ernest Wright, et. al. Philadelphia: The Westminster Press.

Wolff, Hans Walter. 1969. "The Hermeneutics of the Old Testament." Translated by Keith Crim. In *Essays on Old Testament Hermeneutics*, edited by Claus Westermann and James Mays, 160-199. Richmond, Virginia: John Knox Press.

Young, Edward. 1958. *An Introduction to the Old Testament*. Grand Rapids, Michigan: Eerdmans Publishing Company.

Chapter Seven:
Dwight Grubbs, *A Life of Prayer*

Let me say it at the beginning: *A vital prayer life is absolutely essential for effective ministry. It is the foundation, the integration center, the structure, and the focus.* Perhaps we've heard that before, but we've often chosen to act as if we haven't. We gladly do the work the Master sent us to do and study to learn more about the Master's plans, but in the process, we neglect our relationship with the Master (see Mark 1:35; 3:13–15; 6:30–32). The result of this neglect is a ministry based on personal charisma, energy, and technology—each strongly influenced by secular ideologies. We fall back on trusting our ideas, our efforts, and our skills to accomplish a ministry.

In reality, we are often tired, frustrated, lonely, and unsure; perhaps we are even ineffective. Could it be that we have used many resources in ministry other than our Source? Have we found our own resources inadequate?

When we are seekers after God, pilgrims on a journey, beggars searching for bread, disciples looking for guidance, wounded children needing healing, sinners in need of grace – then prayer connects us to the Source that satisfies and enables.

What I'm saying is this: Prayer is for those who need God—*and we all need God.* When we turn to God, we find that the Spirit stands beside us, the Word instructs and feeds us, and the church nurtures and corrects us. We have to ask, however, and receive through the continuing conversation we call prayer. Are we ready to say that our life in Christ takes precedence over our labors *for* Christ?

In this chapter I invite you to examine your definition of prayer, understand the contemplative approach, deal with difficulties in prayer, consider ways to integrate your ministry with your life of prayer, and create a practical plan for personal prayer.

Definitions

Our definition of prayer emerges from our understanding of God. If that is true, the task of defining prayer is a formidable one and simplistic conclusions will not suffice. Typically prayer is defined as asking or seeking God's intervention, so our lists become longer as our requests increase. We really are quite adept at informing God about our needs! These are prayers we initiate based upon human circumstance.

Another perspective views prayer as a response to God who offers the free gift of relationship. Thus prayer becomes a continuing conversation with God (at God's initiative) in order to cultivate that relationship which enables us to live more holy and serve more fully. We might say that prayer is *less* about asking God to act on our behalf and *more* about seeking after God.

Obviously a balance is needed between active (*kataphatic*) praying and receptive (apophatic) praying. The former includes intercession, which is seeking God on behalf of self and others. The latter includes listening, waiting, and meditating as one seeks to experience the presence of God. This form is often called contemplative praying.

Contemplative Prayer

A contemplative is a God-seeker who looks *for* God, at God, to God, and *with* God. Contemplatives are journeying toward God, looking to God the Source; interpreting life and the world through the eyes of God; *fundamentally* seeking to behold the face of God.

Contemplative praying, then, is God-focused. The goal is continuous conversation or communion with God. It is precisely this vital connection that will sustain the labor of intercessory praying. Contemplatives have been faulted for being "so heavenly minded that they are of little earthly use." I doubt that this is the case. Besides the fact that we cannot avoid culture's pain and sin, a contemplative with a true vision of God is quickly driven to God's world and people.

In my experience the church teaches, preaches, and practices intercessory prayer quite well. Generally, however, we have been uninformed about or neglected contemplative prayer. My exhortation to ministers and Christian leaders is this: Set about developing your contemplative prayer life.

If my exhortation strikes a responsive chord, consider these suggestions for growing as a contemplative:

Search—Do an examination of heart, life, ministry, and health. Is there a God-shaped vacuum? Is God trying to tell you something or call you to prayer? Find some good resources for this search.
Solitude—For part of this search, you may need to get away in order to be alone with God. Solitude is more a matter of space than place.
Surrender—Learn to let go. Relax. You weren't called to manage the universe. Incorporate Sabbath principles. Reject religious hype and hucksterism as the methods of choice.
Silence—Let your body, mind, and soul experience stillness. Schedule quiet moments and hours, even days. Avoid noise—including the sound of your own words.
Supplication—Pray for yourself, using confession, adoration, care-casting, and thanksgiving.
Servanthood—Having nourished your own mind, body, and spirit, go care for others. But not before!

Eugene H. Peterson has written helpfully to pastors who may be experiencing confusion regarding their call and the loss of a sense of vocation. He says,

> We look at the job descriptions handed to us,
> we look at the career profiles outlined for us,
> we listen to the counsel the experts give us,
> and we scratch our heads and wonder how we
> ended up here. One by one men and women are
> making their moves, beginning to move against
> the stream, refusing to be contemporary pastors,
> our lives trivialized by the contemporary, and

are embarking on the recovery of the contemplative. There are not great crowds of us, but minorities have been known to make a difference ... we are looking for ... what I am learning to call vocational holiness. Contemplation is the way (Peterson, *Under the Unpredictable_ Plant*, p. 112).

Contemplative prayer, then, offers an alternative to prayers that bombard heaven with requests from persons who assume that their passion and "faith" will somehow cause God to act according to their will. Instead of give me prayers, contemplatives learn to pray "Lord, give me yourself, and make me yours."

Difficulties in Prayer

I hope that the paragraphs above raised some questions for you. Most Christian leaders and the people they work with have encountered a variety of hindrances to prayer. Some of those hindrances, often found in the form of questions, are: Is it appropriate to try to persuade God? Why does God seem to answer some prayers, but not all? If God is omniscient, do we need to ask a loving God for what we need? Often we hear people say, "I have trouble with prayer because nothing much happens when I pray; I just don't have the time; I've had some negative experiences with prayer meetings; I can't know the will of God."

A whole book might not address adequately all these issues, but I would like to offer just two clues. Perhaps it would help to revise our definition of prayer and to change the content of our prayers.

Revising our definition of prayer—Can prayer become a whole-life conversation with God, seeking to know and be known by God through listening, scripture, meditation, discernment, spiritual direction, and other disciplines, and only secondarily an expression of human need? Could it be that God values these contemplative times, in communion with him, more than those moments when we make our petitions for ourselves and others?

Quite possibly, the more we commune with God the more we see God's will being worked out in our lives. The more we learn to trust God, the less we need to ask God to work out things our way. If our goal in prayer is to live in uninterrupted communion with God—rather than only getting "answers"—then, when our requests are not granted, we won't feel abandoned. An awareness of the awesome dependability and the unconditional love of God will emerge as the essential "benefits" of prayer rather than "answers."

Changing the content of our prayers—As we mature, then, we seek fewer "answers" and seek more of God. If our desire is to know and to be known by God, that is, to live in the Presence, "unanswered prayers" become less of an issue. "God with us" is, by faith, a reality. You can count on it!

It is essential that pastors and other leaders explore issues related to difficulties in prayer for their own development and satisfaction before they seek to teach and counsel others. That leads us to consider the context in which the minister's life of prayer occurs.

Ministry and Prayer

It is true that much of our prayer life is a lonely, personal struggle of the soul. But we need not pray alone. We have the church, spiritual leaders, and congregations to provide direction, strength, and fellowship. The word is community, meaning "in communion with." Believers are in community with one another when they are in communion with God.

Consider these questions:

> Does the pastor-leader need a small praying community?
> Can the congregation become a larger praying community?
> What about accountability in one's prayer life?

A discussion question of the minister's life of prayer begs for serious reflection upon the interface of private spiritual patterns and public spiritual leadership. The former sustains the latter; the latter cannot rise above the former. I believe that prayer is the first priority for pastors and leaders. No ministerial activity is more important, no program or ministry is more essential to congregational life and health than its life of prayer. Do you agree or disagree? Why?

First Steps to Ministry

Does the pastor-leader need a small praying community? Others have written helpfully and persuasively of the importance of a pastor finding or forming a small group for the purpose of united prayer. I take this as a given for the minister, but let me add this caution. This need not be a therapy group, a study group, or an intercessory group. Perhaps bits of each, occasionally, but primarily what is needed is a prayer group. The group (perhaps 4–7 persons) agrees to pray and learn how to pray *together*. Their agenda is an encounter with God. They are seeking personal renewal at the deepest levels. They are practicing communal holiness. They are sharing their walk with God—as much as they trust each other to share—the ecstasies and the hopes as well as the agonies and the hurts.

This kind of praying heals and helps wounded healers. It prepares them to pray, prayers of intercession with confidence and vigor and with other groups in other settings. I have observed that whenever ministers get together to pray, they immediately begin praying for renewal in the church, for a righteous city, for peace in the world, or for unevangelized peoples. I want to ask, when do they pray for themselves? Who prays for them?

Maybe the issue is this: can we who are leaders admit our needs and faults to someone or a small group, or must we project this image of "total victory"? We specialize in meeting needs, but have none! Can our human-ness become part of the content of our prayers? Can these prayers be shared with a few people who love us and love God?

Can the congregation become a larger praying community? A pastor-leader who prays in faith, with vulnerability, can lead a congregation in becoming a praying community, where people gladly gather to pray. Corporate prayer that includes the contemplative approach will meet needs, nourish, enable, cleanse, equip, and heal the congregation. Out of their own health and joy, then, they can do the work of intercession that is less motivated by fear, guilt, or selfish interests.

Jesus said, "my house shall be called a house of prayer" (Matt 21:13). A house or home ought to be a safe and happy place for living, loving, and praying. A church building ought to be primarily a place where people pray. A Sunday morning worship service has been described as prayer with a few additions. Why, then, do we sometimes pray so casually and

96

so briefly? When our pastors and leaders experience genuine renewal in their personal prayer lives, will our congregational life and worship be any different?

What about accountability in one's prayer life? Who calls us to give an account? Who asks, how is it with you and God? Who cares about our prayer life? If not the church, who? If not pastors and Christian leaders, who? Shouldn't there be several kinds of intentional congregational efforts designed to encourage and direct believers in their life of prayer? Shouldn't this be what the church does? Oh, of course we do this, but sometimes these spiritual growth opportunities get covered over or squeezed out by the more exciting, popular programs.

The next chapter in this book is about accountability in one's spiritual life. I hope that you will read it carefully in light of this chapter on prayer. If you wish to do further reading, I suggest my book, in which I have a chapter on spiritual direction (or spiritual friendship) and voluntary spiritual accountability (Grubbs, 1994, pp. 59–114).

The bottom line is that your life of prayer will shape and largely determine your effectiveness in ministry. If your life and ministry are focused around your walk with God, then the people you lead will have a similar focus. Your vocation will be pointing people to God and helping them to get connected with the Source. You may use many methods; your goal will never change. Our task as we "go into all the world" is to make disciples, and prayer is at the heart of disciple-making.

A Practical Plan for Prayer

We come to the place in this chapter where we will be very practical. Using all I've said thus far as introductory, I invite you now to create your own response. We will seek to formulate a practical plan for personal prayer. If this is new to you, I'll provide guidance. Others may only find ideas for revising an already workable plan, but I think most *pray-ers* benefit from a simple, usable prayer plan (ritual) to structure your personal prayer times.

Gordon T. Smith identifies essential components of a Christian spiritual life:

The call to renewal of the mind
The call to a patterned form of prayer and worship
The call to vocation
The call to accountability
The call to recreation

Smith makes it clear that these components must be developed and
practiced in a balanced rhythm of solitude and community (Smith,
1994, pp. 78–146).

It is Smith's second component that we will now consider. In a culture
characterized by individualism and spontaneity, many of us find patterns and ritual difficult. Eugene H. Peterson provides a helpful discussion on the importance of adopting a Rule (system or pattern) for our
praying (Peterson, 1992, pp.105–108). He says historical consensus provides this three-phased system to structure our prayer lives:

Lord's Day worship with the church – rooted in revelation, community,
and service.
Daily praying the Psalms – providing us vocabulary and companions
for praying.
Recollected praying through the day – extends our prayer into the
details of daily living.

This system is cyclical and interlocking. It provides wholeness and
helps to lift our prayers above the subjective expression of feelings. (For
further guidance on this Rule, see Peterson, 1989, Bruggeman, 1982,
and Gallagher, 1983.)

Let me now offer a ritual for regularized prayer that I have found helpful. The length of time for each segment is flexible, depending upon
need, temperament, and circumstances. But let's assume a 30 minutes
time block and six phases of five minutes each.

Relaxing—Take a few minutes to reorient your mind, body, and spirit.
Clear out and center down. Get comfortable. Remove distractions.
Breathe deeply. Repeat a familiar affirmation, perhaps, "Jesus is Lord,
Lord have mercy." Consciously move from "doing things" to "being
with." Give praise!
Reading—Preface this phase with a prayer to the Holy Spirit for illumi

nation and guidance. Turn first to the Psalms. (Devise a plan that gets you through the book several times a year). As time permits, use the Lectionary Readings for the Sunday following, especially if they are used in worship planning and preaching. (I use *The Book of Common Prayer,* Oxford, 1979, because it contains the Psalter, lectionary references, and other useful worship aids.) In addition to Bible reading, you may want to use a devotional book (see the Bibliography for recommendations) or listen to music. One suggestion: avoid the tendency to read only informationally. Instead, seek to read transformationally. (See Mulholland, 1985, pp. 47–60). The idea is to let scripture speak to you personally.

Reflecting—In a meditative, receptive mood, listen for what God might be saying to you. Do a fearless soul-life inventory. (The Alcoholics Anonymous Twelve Steps or John Wesley's *Examination of Conscience* may be adapted and used here). Confess. Renew your vocational vows and intentions. This is supplication — getting honest with God and seeking help for your personal needs.

Recording—Writing down our encounters with God and life is a time-honored discipline of spiritual growth. Write letters to God and make notes for further prayer, study, or reflection. Journaling may not be helpful for everyone, but give it a try if you haven't already.

Recalling—After you have prayed for yourself, you are ready to do intercession for others. Name and pray for those who have requested your prayers and for those persons, issues, and circumstances that concern you. Pray locally and globally.

Reviewing—This is wrap-up and conclusion time. Maybe a tad of evaluation is needed. Did I touch on each phase, perhaps too much time on one? Did I get a "word" from God and did I experience God's presence? What about next time? Anything I need to "do" now that I've prayed? Did I learn anything? What do I have to be thankful for? Express it by singing the *Doxology,* the *Gloria Patri,* or other songs of praise.

By now you may be thinking, "Wow! I'm well into my third hour already!" Maybe so, but do you have anything more important to do than to cultivate your relationship with God? Of course, three hours every day may be unreasonable for most of us. But every once in a while? And couldn't most sincere believers find a half-hour each day to follow a rule similar to the one outlined above?

Conclusion

In this chapter, I have asked you to define prayer more in contemplative ways and less in activist ways. To reduce prayer to a results-producing religious activity is a prostitution of God's invitation to "seek me with your whole heart" (Jeremiah 29:11–13). I suggested that "answers" are not the main objectives of prayer, *but a "relationship" is.* I challenged you to make prayer the integrating center and the consuming passion of your life and ministry. I outlined a possible ritual for your personal life of prayer. It may seem intimidating and complicated. If so, simplify and adapt it for your use.

Finally, I hope this chapter may cause you to want to devote yourself more fully to prayer, without compulsion or guilt. It matters less how you pray and more that you pray. Remember, prayer begins with relaxation.

Come, let us pray!

If you want to go further:

- Take a course on spiritual formation or prayer at a Bible college or seminary.
- Reserve an hour or so about every other day for serious study, reflection, and engagement in prayer.
- Try to get beyond a typical fifteen-minute routine. Several times a year schedule a twenty-four-hour prayer retreat as part of your ministerial work but not as vacation time.
- Once every few years, do a three- to five-day retreat with qualified spiritual direction.
- Take the Meyers-Briggs Type inventory. Using your four-letter code, seek to develop the spiritual disciplines appropriate for your type. See especially Chester P. Michael and Marie C. Norrisey, *Prayer and Temperament* (Charlotteville, VA: OpenDoor, 1984).
- Prepare a prayer room at your church or secure a house of prayer that is comfortable, safe, and offers solitude. Make this a part of your congregational prayer ministry; see *Face to Face With God: Establishing a Prayer Ministry*, Bjorn Pedersen (Minneapolis: Augsberg Press, 1995).

For a directory of retreat centers in the United States and Canada, write to:

Retreats International
1112 Memorial Library
Notre Dame, IN 46556
(219) 283-2764

Reference List

Edwards, Tilden. *Sabbath Time*. Nashville: Upper Room. 1992.

Foster, Richard J. *Celebration of Discipline*. San Francisco: Harper. 1978.

———. *Prayer: Finding the Heart's True Home*. San Francisco: Harper. 1998.

Grubbs, Dwight L. *Beginnings: Spiritual Formation for Leaders*. Lima: Fairway Press. 1994.

Hinson, Glenn. *A Serious Call to a Contemplative Life Style*. Philadelphia: Westminster. 1974.

Houston, James. *The Transforming Power of Prayer: Deepening your Friendship with God*. Colorado Springs: Navpress. 1996.

Howard, Evan B. *Praying the Scriptures*. Downers Grove: InterVarsity Press. 1999.

Mulholland, M. Robert. *Invitation to the Journey: A Road Map for Spiritual Formation*. Downers' Grove: InterVarsity Press.1993.

———. *Shaped by the Word: The Power of Scripture in Spiritual Formation*. Nashville: Upper Room. 1985.

Peterson, Eugene H. *The Contemplative Pastor*. Grand Rapids: Eerdmans.1986.

———. *Working the Angles: The Shape of Pastoral Integrity*. Grand Rapids: Eerdmans. 1992.

Vest, Norvene. *Gathered in the Word: Praying the Scripture in Small Groups*. Nashville: The Upper Room. 1996.

Chapter Eight:
Lori Salierno, *A Life of Accountability*

When I think about the mentors who have helped me along life's journey, Dr. Marie Strong always comes to mind. I like to compare her influence on my ministry to that of Elijah's role in Elisha's life (2 Kings 2). While I don't claim to inherit a double portion of Dr. Strong's spirit, I do believe her mantle touched my life.

As a new student in her class, I did not expect Dr. Strong to play an important role in my life. While I recognized her as a good Bible professor, her somewhat austere manner made me uncomfortable. When she requested I stay after class, I became even more uncomfortable.

"You have a problem I want corrected in my class," she said.
"What's that?"
"You're consistently late."
"Only two or three minutes," I said.
"Late is late. I want you here on time. Do you have a problem with that?"

In my heart I vowed to drop her class. While my mind entertained such thoughts, Professor Strong flashed me a rare smile. She continued, "I have good news, too. If you will apply yourself, you will receive the highest grade in this class, and you will go farther than any of the other students."

Excerpted from Lori Salierno, *When Roosters Crow; a fresh approach to accountability and integrity* (Anderson, IN: Warner Press, 1999). This book may be purchased by calling 800-741-7721; stock # 9781593171810.

Shocked, I said, "How do you know that?"
"Because I know you. You're dismissed."

From that day forward I arrived early to class, sat on the front row, and got the highest grade on every test. By the end of the semester Dr. Strong looked beautiful to me, and I decided to take every course she taught.

Accountability: The Rooster Concept

On the final night of Jesus' life, the Apostle Peter followed in the shadows as Jesus was moved from one temple leader to another. Each time Peter was asked whether he was one of the disciples of Jesus, he denied the connection and widened the distance between himself and his Lord. After the third denial a rooster crowed, calling Peter to accountability for his failure (John 18:15-27). The rooster brought Peter face to face with himself, his sin, and his Lord. A rooster represents a signal sent from God to warn you when your soul is in danger. With your cooperation the Holy Spirit can work to preserve integrity and spiritual vitality that will last a lifetime.

The Primary Accountability Partner: The Bible

Although I tend to resist following rules dictated by others, I can be quite rigid in demands I make of myself. After attending a seminar on prayer I decided to spend an hour a day praying and reading the Bible. Like the Apostle Paul I was determined to "punish my body and enslave it, so that after proclaiming to others I myself should not be disqualified" (1 Cor. 9:27 NRSV).

During a four-year period from mid-high school to mid-college I held to a rigid schedule. Nothing could keep me from my hour of power. The problem was that my devotions turned into an obsession to follow a ritual instead of an act of worship. When I made comments such as, "So-and-so must not be a very good Christian. She doesn't even have regular devotions," my dad got concerned.

"Lori, you're getting too legalistic," Dad said. "I want you to go four days without opening your Bible or spending time in prayer."

"But, Dad, I don't think I'd even feel saved if I did that," I protested.

"That's just the point. You're basing salvation on works rather than on God's grace. Take a break for four days, loosen up and just let God love you. Your prayer time will actually become richer if it's less regimented."

For four days my Bible lay closed, and I thought I'd go to hell for sure. I couldn't quite give up my prayer time, although I did change my routine. Instead of bowing before the Lord, I prayed on the run while walking, biking, or listening to inspirational music.

Of course I didn't need to change what I did; I just needed to change why I did it. The Pharisees did right in giving a tenth of their income to God. Jesus told them they should continue to tithe, but the motive from their hearts should be governed by love and justice (Luke 11:42). In my case I needed to eradicate my harsh judgment of others who failed to follow my example.

Even though my devotional life was less than ideal during those four years of college, I believe God honored my faithfulness. The insight I gained from Scripture continues to have value for me today, especially those passages committed to memory. Scripture stored in memory becomes a permanent resource available for instruction and correction. The psalmist wrote, "I have hidden your word in my heart that I might not sin against you" (Psalm 119:11, NIV). When I'm disturbed about something, I pull a related biblical passage from memory and replay it over and over in my mind. As I stay tuned to God's voice, I tend to keep a more spiritual focus.

The different versions and paraphrases of the Bible provide excellent help for in-depth study, but they play havoc with memorization. For the most part I memorize from only one version to avoid confusion. Unless I want to preserve a particularly beautiful expression, I avoid paraphrases because the authors are using their own words instead of translating the original manuscript.

Sometimes a verse of Scripture strikes me with such force that I can instantly recall every word of the text. When that happens I make it a point to memorize the reference. Just as I can't direct anyone to the church without an address, I can't recommend a verse to meet some-one's need without the biblical reference. To reinforce my memory I repeat the reference before and after the text each time I quote the verse. For example: "2 Timothy 2:15, 'Do your best to present yourself to God as one approved, a workman who does not need to be ashamed and who correctly handles the word of truth.' 2 Timothy 2:15."

As the premier accountability partner, the Bible provides a variety of signals to keep us on track spiritually. In fact, all other forms of accountability must be measured against the Bible for authenticity. Human counsel can be beneficial if it corroborates Scripture. Any advice that contradicts Scripture must be rejected no matter how wise it may seem.

Intentional Accountability

Persons we enlist to help us keep our ministry on track function in much the same way as the offensive linemen on a football team. If the quarterback makes a successful play, it is likely because of the protec-tion of the linemen.

The idea of being accountable to others makes some people nervous. They feel their reputation is threatened if anyone suggests a system of checks and balances. That is how the treasurer of one church felt when the board of trustees voted to have a yearly audit of the books. Rather than be subject to scrutiny, the treasurer resigned and left the church.

In contrast, a lady in another church became concerned when the board over her ceased to function. The bylaws called for an appointment to her position every year. "I feel I'm operating unofficially," she said. "It bothers me that I'm accountable to no one."

If anyone was ever above the need for supervision, this godly woman was, but she would have preferred to include others in the decision-making process.

Taking intentional steps to become accountable is a sign of strength, not weakness. We consider our ministry and our relationship with the Lord too precious to take lightly. "Let the wise also hear and gain in learning, the discerning acquire skill" (Proverbs 1:5 NRSV).

Biblical accountability provides for our inherent need for support, encouragement and fellowship; it also keeps us connected, helping us to avoid isolation—a state that is highly dangerous because it leads to the mistaken conclusion that no one will be harmed by what I do. "Two are better than one, / because they have a good return for their work: / If one falls down, / his friend can help him up. / But pity the man who falls / and has no one to help him up! / Also, if two lie down together, they will keep warm. / But how can one keep warm alone? / Though one may be overpowered, two can defend themselves. / A cord of three strands is not quickly broken" (Ecc 4:9-12 NIV).

Biblical accountability cultivates our relationship with God, a relationship that enhances our intimacy with him that in turn results in growth and increased effectiveness (see, for example, John 21:15-17). The goal of accountability is to keep you strong in the Lord so that you can go the distance and stay effective in ministry. It does so by providing an ongoing context for confession, integrity, and restoration.

Profile of a Confidant

If we base our selection process on the calling of Christ's disciples, we will not expect to find perfect people. Jesus was perfect, but his support people were not.

As a tax collector, Matthew did nothing to enhance the popularity of Jesus. Even if Matthew had conducted his business according to ethical standards, he would have been perceived as a ruthless bureaucrat like others who increased taxes and pocketed the difference. Besides, the Jews considered anyone aligned with Rome to be a traitor.

Peter, referred to as the Rock, sometimes behaved like Peter the Pebble. Nevertheless, this impetuous man, a mixture of courage and cowardice, left us a spiritual legacy—including how to handle failure.

Of course, Judas Iscariot may have been Christ's biggest disappointment. Yet even in his betrayal, Judas provided a measure of hope to Christian leaders who lean on others. If Jesus' ministry survived the setback inflicted by Judas (and it did), our ministry can continue even after someone betrays our confidence. The resurrection of Jesus proves that we can rise above any damage done by someone who violates a trust. Even though we shouldn't expect always to find "perfect" people, we will want to exercise extreme caution in choosing those who will participate in our ministry. I consider the first criterion to be a fervent commitment to Jesus Christ that extends beyond the church walls. "Let the righteous strike me; let the faithful correct me" (Psalm 141:5 NRSV). Only godly people with a consistent Christian lifestyle qualify. That means living the gospel at home, at work, and at play.

The ability to keep secrets is an essential quality for those who would serve in partnership with leaders. I actually have two groups working with me—a large group of prayer warriors to support me when I'm on the road and a core group to help me with more intimate details. Especially in the core group I look for those who can be trusted with confidential material.

The Prayer Warriors

When I first started to take my ministry on the road, I asked a few close friends and family members to pray for me during my travel time and speaking engagements. Although my ministry got off to a good start, I soon felt the need for more of the power that comes through prayer. Satan enjoys a stronghold in schools and universities, and he declares all-out warfare any time his position is threatened. Only through the power of the Holy Spirit, released during fervent prayer, can we defeat the devil.

As the names of people who might help me battle the enemy came to mind, I wrote letters inviting their participation and requested a reply in writing if they wanted to support me for a specified period—usually a year. Somehow a written commitment is more binding than one made verbally. Also, the indirect approach allowed individuals more freedom to decline if they so chose.

My prayer warriors are like the seventy leaders Jesus appointed to go ahead of him into the towns he intended to visit (Luke 10). My prayer warriors receive a copy of my schedule, and I ask them to cover me with prayer from the time I leave home until my return.

Enlisting Prayer Warriors

Identify the prayer warrior: Prayer warriors are persons who already have a clear and recognized personal relationship with God; they are persons who will make an intentional commitment to pray specifically for you, your family, and your vocation; and they are willing to attend prayer warrior events.

Establish the relationship: Do a formal recruitment; it is a way of saying how important this request is and how seriously you are in making it. First, send an invitation letter to become a prayer warrior. Then, encourage them to attend a prayer warrior event.

Give consistent, intentional attention: You want them to take this responsibility seriously, then you must take it even more seriously. This may be accomplished by planning a quarterly event and have that event be a big deal. Provide food—dinner, dessert, or breakfast. Provide childcare and invite the spouses. Use this occasion both to show appreciation and to train and equip in the area of prayer. A regular "Prayer Update" is essential. Send a monthly or quarterly memo, letter, or newsletter that shows the results of their prayers.

Because of my prayer warriors, dramatic results have taken place. When I arrived at one college, the chaplain was extremely distraught because a woman on campus had been raped by her date the night before. He asked me to speak to the student body about sexuality.

After my talk I went to the women's dorm for further discussion. The tough questions asked by the girls challenged me to depend on the Holy Spirit as never before. Within myself I had no easy answers to restore wholeness to women whose lives had been broken. At the close of the last chapel service more than one hundred students and many faculty members bowed at the altar to receive healing that only God can bring.

When Christian faculty members ask for the secret of effective ministry, I tell them about my prayer warriors. If my talks cause students to commit their lives to Christ or pledge to stay sexually pure or decide to go into full-time ministry, I know it is the result of people who pray for me.

My Core Group

On several occasions Jesus singled out three of his disciples as a support team. Peter, James, and John accompanied Jesus to the mountain where the transfiguration took place. Only those three men were present when Jesus raised the daughter of Jairus from the dead. In Gethsemane, though, they slept when Jesus needed them most.

For the last year I lived in Phoenix six women formed my core group. We held weekly meetings and were mutually accountable to each other. Areas of accountability included: Bible reading and application, Bible memorization, physical exercise, habits pertaining to use of one's language, and relationships in key arenas of living. Each person kept a daily record of progress in specified areas. Sometimes we shared reports with the entire group. At other times we split up into two or three groups.

Choosing individuals who will share intimate secrets requires the utmost care. Although I seldom choose close friends, because they tend to be less objective, I usually favor people I know well. Trust builds over a period of time. As a test, I might pass on a bit of confidential but innocuous information to see if it comes back to me. After two or three experiences with no feedback, I consider the individual to be a good candidate for a long-term relationship.

I change accountability partners every year or so. The strong bonds that develop within an accountability group sometimes create a feeling of "ownership" that stifles individual freedom. Without meaning to, an accountability partner can become so possessive that she does not want to relinquish control. Setting a time limit in the beginning will avoid misunderstanding later.

Covenant to Serve as Rooster

To the best of my ability I commit to serve as a Rooster during the next year. I agree to spend time in prayer and reading the Bible on a daily basis, and to record my spiritual progress each day on a weekly accoutability sheet, which has been provided. Instead of excusing or glossing over my failures, I will honestly admit my faults and make efforts to

correct them. To be an example to others. I will not partake of drugs or alcohol during the time this covenant is in effect.
Unless an emergency arises, I will faithfully attend meetings on a week-ly basis.
Furthermore, I promise to keep confidential everything revealed by any member of the group.

Signature

Finding the Right Persons to Serve as Roosters

First things first—someone said, "The time you invest on the outset will reap rich dividends on the back end." Intentionality is the key; even though the steps stated below seem obvious, practice each one. Do it consciously and with care. Do not rush in the selection of your account-ability partners:

• Acknowledge the need for accountability in your life.
• Admit the issues where you need to be accountable.
• Renounce rationalization and lies.
• Seek the truth.

Steps to finding the right person(s) include the following:

Identify the people. The job description for Roosters will look unlike any other kind of description. This is not just another job; it is a call-ing and you must look for persons who: have a heart hungry for God's Word and a sensitivity to his spirit; have a servant mind-set, an "others first" philosophy; are trustworthy and will take this position in your life and ministry seriously; are loyal, that is, they respect and support you; are close-mouthed and understand the principle of confidentiality; are teachable, willing to let you develop and train them; are committed, willing to sacrifice time and energy for you in this area; and are mature, that is, growing as persons in relation to others and to God.

Establish the relationship. You are asking persons to make a seri-ous and long-term commitment to your support. You are asking them to have a relationship with you that is direct, supportive, loving, and critical. The manner in which you establish the relationship with your accountability partners needs to reflect these qualities. Remember, you are also making a serious and long-term commitment to them.

Go about recruitment in a formal and methodical manner. Here are critical steps. You should, of course, personalize these, but you do not want to leave any step out.

Recruitment: Face-to-face contact is best. If you cannot sit down with them, then, send a letter outlining the role and follow up with a telephone call.

First meeting—first impressions can only happen once, so these items need to be very clear the first time through: why you need Roosters in your life, why you decided to recruit them, and what you expect out of this reciprocal relationship.

Define the details of commitment as to when, where, and how often (weekly/bi-weekly) you will meet. Length of commitment must be defined, beginning with smaller increments (3 months, then 6 months, then 9 months, and then 1 year), and recovenant together at the end of each term or at least once a year. The rooster job description should define your expectation of the relationship including, but not limited to practical help and spiritual guidance.

Ongoing activities should be defined regarding the format and nature of meetings (structure of gatherings and topics of discussion), reading materials to be used and assignments within them, the use of daily accountability sheets, and any retreat or other special event that the group will do together.

Decision making process should not be rushed. Pray and process the commitment for two weeks. Discuss it with your spouse (if married). Look over your schedule and see if it is realistic at this time. Decide if you will accept this position.

Follow-up begins with a phone call to find out what they want to do: If no—that is fine, no guilt, no manipulation; it means that it is not God's timing. If yes—confirm for them the details of your beginning activity or retreat. Pray and give thanks that God has provided you with such a unique person.

Give consistent, intentional attention. Accountability groups will need intentional, continuing nurture. Consider the following as essential to their ministry to you—and part of their commitment to you.

A Rooster Retreat for a 24 to 48 hour period somewhere away from the church will provide a wonderful setting to establish your covenant. This will grant an opportunity to review your mutual commitments, cast vision for the group, bond with one another, discuss materials to be used, and establish regular meeting dates. In sum, pray, plan, play.

Regular meetings: Meeting weekly will assure a high level of active, continuous support and accountability. You will need to work out what is possible with your schedule and the Roosters' schedule. A meeting place that is not public and where interruptions will not occur is required. Establishing a regular agenda for your meetings allows everyone to arrive each time expecting and knowing what will happen.

Always be on the look out for ways to thank the Roosters for serving as your volunteer accountability group. Verbalize thanks to individuals and to the group. Take them to dinner. Give them an appropriate gift, but remember you are not buying their support, you are thanking them for their support.

Mobilizing Your Team

We have discussed how to recruit and train people to be Prayer Warriors and Roosters in your life and ministry. These, however, are two key elements of an even larger circle of support and accountability. This larger team may serve as a hedge of protection around you. Who is on your team? Who is the group of persons including yourself who serve as a hedge of protection around you?

This accountability model provides: protection for you and others, effectiveness that sharpens and focuses your ministry, and encouragement that we are called to be together in ministry and in fellowship—a confessional lifestyle.

You, with all the assets that you possess, are at the center of this accountability model. Your assets include anything that you value and want to preserve throughout your lifetime. What are your strengths? What gifts do you bring to your calling?

Your spouse and your family are the people who are the people you love the most, who constitute the number one priority over your work or ministry, and who represent God's provision for you. God sets people into families for a reason. If you are married, identify the characteristics of this person who is so central to your safety and your integrity. Who is your family? List the names of all those you name as family. What are the characteristics of each of these whom God gave to you for safety, comfort, and accountability?

Lifers are the significant others in your life, other than your spouse, with whom you have a long lasting relationship. They know you very well and continue to care about you. They are your best friends. You value them second only to family relationships but the friendship is basically informal. Informal means that they are available when you need them even though you might not see them on a regular basis. Lifers have a history with you; accept you unconditionally, even while they are honest with you; and possess personal and objective points of view that you will listen to—no matter how difficult.

Roosters make a commitment to you before God that they will love you, pray for you, ask you tough questions, be intentional about accountability, and meet with you in a formal, structured meeting on a regular basis.

Prayer Warriors are persons who covenant to pray specifically for you. They agree to meet with you regularly, keep in touch so that they know the needs and concerns of your life, and pray over your schedule.

The Body of Christ is a key New Testament concept that describes the connectedness of all believers. It applies to all believers around the world; it also applies to a local congregation of believers where you worship.

There is, of course, a basic assumption here that is vital to your calling: you are a member of a worshiping community of believers. It is the place where you exercise your spiritual gifts. These believers are persons whom you can call on to pray for you; they are your brothers and sisters in Christ. They are faithful in their attendance, and they worship with you.

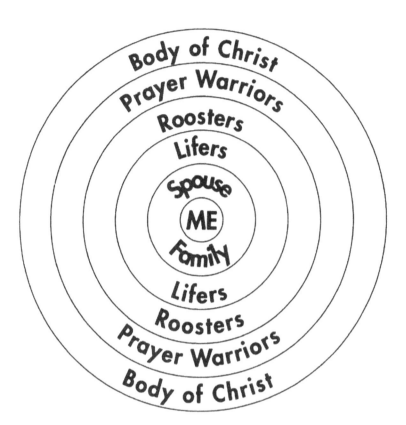

III.

𝔇oing–

discovering what we will do

Frederick Buechner defines vocation as "the place where your deep gladness meets the world's deep need" (Buechner, 119). We do not presume to tell you in the following pages the precise dimensions of your unique contribution to the Christian movement. Nor do we assume that you, today, need to know each dimension of that unique contribution. Self-in-Christ as gift to God is enhanced by the discovery, exercise, and empowerment of giftedness from the Holy Spirit. We are gifted to serve the church and the world by God's Spirit. What kind of life-giving persons shall we become? The shape of our giftedness contours our service and gives personal expression to a life in Christian ministry. "To each is given the manifestation of the Spirit for the common good" (1 Corinthians 12:7 NRSV).

Our prayer is that your life experience will give flesh-and-blood expression to Buechner's apt definition!

Buechner, Frederick. 1993. *Wishful Thinking: A Seeker's ABC.* San Francisco: Harper San Francisco.

The New Oxford *Annotated Bible: New Revised Standard Version.* 1994. New York: Oxford University Press.

Chapter Nine:

Timothy Dwyer, *Feeding the Sheep*

When they had finished breakfast, Jesus said to Simon
Peter, "Simon son of John, do you love me more than
these?" He said to him, "Yes, Lord; you know that I
love you." Jesus said to him, "Feed my lambs." A second time he said to him, "Simon son of John, do you
love me?" He said to him, "Yes Lord; you know that I
love you." Jesus said to him, "Tend my sheep." He said
to him the third time, "Simon son of John, do you love
me?" Peter felt hurt because he said to him the third
time, "Do you love me?" And he said to him, "Lord,
you know everything; you know that I love you." Jesus
said to him, "Feed my sheep. Very truly, I tell you,
when you were younger, you used to fasten your own
belt and to go wherever you wished. But when you
grow old, you will stretch out your hands, and someone
else will fasten a belt around you and take you where
you do not wish to go." (He said this to indicate the
kind of death by which he would glorify God.) After
this he said to him, "Follow me." —John 21:15–19

*Laura Baumeister was in way over her head at Smith College, and
had failed. Laura grew up on the West Coast, near Portland, and as
a little girl her greatest hope was that her mother would stop drinking. More than once she came home from school to a silent house,
her mother passed out on a bed. Her father was long gone by the
time Laura was a teenager, and her schooling was checkered. She*

This sermon was originally preached by Dr. Dwyer at the annual ordination
service of Indiana Ministries of the Church of God, October 1, 2000.

attended three high schools, and then, when Laura was sixteen, her mother committed suicide. She became a ward of the state, and soon became pregnant. After her son was born, she moved to the Los Angeles area, and then to Mendocino, California, where she worked in an emergency room, and attended College of the Redwoods, a junior college. It was there a professor told her about the Ada Comstock Program at Smith College.

Smith is an old and venerable New England college, in Northhampton, Mass. The Ada Comstock program was a special scholarship for older, non-traditional female students. Laura applied, was accepted, and with $600 (her life savings), her son, and a frying pan under the seat of the car, drove across the country to Smith. She loved the beauty of New England, and enjoyed her classes, but was in way over her head. Nothing she had done or studied prepared her for Smith. She kept quiet in class, had no midterms, and asked for extensions on her papers during her first semester. By Thanksgiving, she realized how far behind she really was, and in a panic, stopped going to class. The work was simply too much. She retreated into her apartment, didn't answer the phone or door, and knew she had been given her big chance, and had messed it up. She decided to go to Ellie Rothman, the administrator of the Comstock program, and face the facts.

Ms. Rothman was 60, a well-dressed and proper New England matron. Laura, however knew the drill. You fail and they kick you out, so Laura went in and said to her, "I didn't go to my finals. I know I didn't do the work. I know you have to kick me out." Ms. Rothman help up her hand and said, "Laura, you're going way too fast. If you give me permission, I will go before the academic cabinet and plead your case."

Laura began to weep. For the first time in her life someone was going to really help her. Ms. Rothman continued, "You're going to be on academic probation, and you will have to meet with me once a week." For Laura, it was a brilliant strategy. She knew she could be a student one week at a time.

When we meet Peter in John 21, he has failed because he, too, was in way over his head. After all, we are all in way over our heads with Jesus. But, Peter's failure was a massive, public, and humiliating failure. He had told Jesus, "Even though all the others fall away, I will never fall away" (Matt. 26:33). Then, however, it happened. When Jesus was arrested, a slave girl asked Peter if he was one of Jesus' disciples. He said he wasn't. Someone around the fire also asked him if he was one of the disciples. He again said he wasn't. Then, a slave thought he had seen Peter in the garden with Jesus, and for a third time, Peter denied Jesus.

Does someone who is a failure have a future? Any future with Jesus? Any future in Jesus' ministry?

John 21 is Peter's ordination day, the day in which Jesus will tell Peter five things he wants him to do-five things which will set the agenda for Peter's ministry forever. On this your ordination day, Jesus says the same five things to you. From here on, these five things are to set the agenda for your ministry. But it is of great significance that Peter's ordination day comes after a massive, public, and humiliating failure. Failure, however, is not the end of the story. In fact, it may be the beginning of the story, the prerequisite of the story. Brokenness and failure may shape the humility that alone can prepare us to hear the agenda of Jesus for our ministries. After all, "Unless a grain of wheat falls to the earth and dies, it abides alone, but if it dies, it shall bear much fruit" (John 12: 24).

Jesus tells Peter five things that are to set the agenda for his ministry. These five things are also to set the agenda for your ministry. No matter what particular shape it may take: chaplaincy, youth work, Christian education, music, teaching, or the glorious crown of the pulpit, these five things set the agenda for all ministry. What are they?

Feed the lambs

First, feed the lambs. In John 21:15 we read, "When they had finished breakfast, Jesus said to Simon Peter, 'Simon, son of John, do you love me more than these?' He said to him, 'Yes Lord; you know that I love you.' Jesus said to him, *"Feed my lambs."'*

The Greek word here, *boskein*, is used in the Greek text of Ezra 34:2 for the task of a shepherd feeding lambs. Why is feeding so necessary?

J. I. Packer once put it this way, "The outside observer sees us as staggering from gimmick to gimmick and stunt to stunt like so many drunks in a fog, not knowing at all where we are or which way we should be going.... The truth is that we have grieved the Spirit and God has withheld the Spirit ... for two generations and more, our churches have suffered from a famine of hearing the words of the Lord."

Let us be honest here. For far too often in the contemporary church, glibness of tongue, smoothness of speech and personal charisma have taken the place of the bread of life and the living water. The result is that the flock has gone hungry. Jesus says, "Feed the lambs."

My younger brother is a chef out on the West Coast. On our vacation trips there, we sometimes visit, and he likes to make a meal for us. When he does, I have learned that the chopping and slicing and grinding, the hours of preparation which he puts in are necessary to great food. Food needs preparation. For feeding the flock, preparation means study.

Lewis Sperry Chafer once told students in Dallas, "Don't study for a class; study for a lifetime of ministry." Billy Graham told six hundred ministers in London that in his ministry he has preached too much and studied too little. Donald Gray Barnhouse, who had an eminent ministry for decades at Tenth Presbyterian Church in Philadelphia, once said that if he had only three years to serve the Lord, he would devote the first two to study and preparation. Over three hundred years ago, Richard Baxter wrote of ministers and study, "Some take only an hour now and then as an unwanted task they are forced to undergo. Should there not be a desire to know God and divine things.... Many ministers study only to compose their sermons or little more." To feed the lambs, however, once must first prepare the food, and that means study.

What are the lambs to be fed with? It seems to me that, first of all, you feed the lambs with the message of the Lamb: the Lamb that Abraham said God would provide in Genesis 22. The Passover lamb which was slaughtered, and whose blood was placed on the doors so the death angel would pass by in Ex 12. The Lamb that was a sin offering in Leviticus 4:32. The lamb which was to be sacrificed each day, day after day, according to Numbers 28. The lamb which

Isaiah spoke of when he said there would be one who would go "like a lamb to the slaughter" in Is. 53:7. The Lamb that John the Baptist spoke of when one day he pointed to Jesus and said, "Behold the lamb of God who takes away the sins of the world" (John 1:29). The Lamb that was crucified the very hour when Passover lambs were slaughtered in John's gospel, and whose last word was tetelestai, "It is finished." The lambs need the message of the Lamb because that secures their forgiveness, removes guilt and makes them forever free. Not only that, but the lamb now sits on the throne in heaven in Rev. 5. Feed the lambs with the message of the Lamb.

What is the motive for feeding the lambs? Jesus asks Peter, "Do you love me?" He doesn't ask Peter that to shame him, to belittle his love as insufficient, or to point out that Peter doesn't have the right kind of love. No, I think Jesus asks Peter that question because love for Jesus is the reason we feed the lambs.

After all, when we feed the lambs, we stand in for God, who "makes us to lie down in green pastures and leads us beside still waters" (Ps 23:2). Jesus says to you in your ministry: "Feed my lambs."

Tend my sheep

There is a second thing Jesus says to Peter, and to you. He not only says "Feed my lambs," but He also says, "Tend my sheep" (John 21 :16). Why is it necessary to tend the flock, to shepherd the flock? Because Jesus knew that people are "like sheep without a shepherd" (Matt. 9:36).

When we lived in Auburn, in northern California, my wife and I rented a house from a landlord who had a back pasture. The two houses were on seven acres, and when we went to see the house, he took us into the back pasture with our dog Lacey. There were about six or seven sheep in the pasture, and Lacey thought she should play with them. She began to chase them, and though we called her back, the sheep ran from her, even though they really had nothing to fear, rushing straight into the barb wire fence at the other end of the pasture. People are like that, will frighten easily, and run straight into trouble. People are like sheep without a shepherd.

I am not much of a fan of Jim Carrey. He is a little too manic for me, a little too wild. However, I read a while back about his childhood in Toronto. When his dad lost his job as an accountant, the whole family had to work nights in a tire factory to make ends meet. For a while, they lived in a Volkswagen van together. Who knows what scars those experiences left? "Like sheep without a shepherd."

Henry Kissinger once said of Richard Nixon, after Watergate and the fall, noting how much potential and ability Nixon had, "Could you imagine what he would have been had somebody really loved him." "Like sheep without a shepherd."

In Scott Lasser's great novel, *Battle Creek*, there is a character by the name of Luke James. Luke is in his early twenties, a great baseball player who is hoping to be drafted. He is haunted, though, by a tragic mistake he made as a teenager and the years he spent in prison. His upbringing was rough, as his mom struggled to make ends meet, and his dad was mostly gone. At one point, Luke thinks back to when he was a little leaguer, after a game when he was sitting in the parking lot of the ball field, waiting for his mom to come and pick him up, and watching the other kids get into their parents' cars. Luke sees a teammate, a kid who is not very good, who struck out a couple of times that day. The kid is walking with his father who has his arm around the kid. They are talking and smiling, and the kid is drinking a pop his dad bought him. Luke wonders to himself, are there really fathers who love you even if you strike out? "Like sheep without a shepherd."

Since people are "like sheep without a shepherd," Jesus tells Peter to tend his flock. This is something Peter would remember, for years later as an old man he would write to church elders that they should do the same thing. "Shepherd the flock," he would say in 1 Peter 5:2. Paul would tell the leaders at Ephesus the same thing in Acts 20:28, "Shepherd the flock of God that is among you." These words naturally remind us of Jesus, who once said, "I am the good shepherd" (John 10:11).

This is very timely for us, because in recent years there have been quite a few voices telling us what to do and be as ministers of the gospel. Some have told us to be managers, others vision-casters, others to be purpose-driven. But, if you look at yourself primarily as a manager, you may be tempted to manipulate. If you look at yourself primarily as a vision-caster, you may forget that "your young people shall see visions, and your old people shall dream dreams" also (Acts 2:17). If you act in a way that is purpose-driven, you can forget to be love-driven. Instead, I call the church back to a revival of shepherd-ology, where we develop the heart of a shepherd, and skillful hands with which to tend the flock.

Kofi Annan, perhaps in good African fashion, is a shepherd. On a visit to East Timor in 1999, a man ran up to him and began recounting everything that had happened to him in the troubles of that country. Annan was already over-booked and running late, but he stayed with the man and comforted him for over an hour. In Kosovo, he sat with a 100 year old woman who could only say again and again, "How could this happen to me at my age?" He held the woman's hand and listened to her without moving. A few years back, in New York city, while walking with his wife, he noticed a man by a telephone booth, off to the side who seemed to be troubled. He went over to the man, listened to him talk about some family problems. For a long time, the man would come to see Annan in his office, once or twice a week, talking to him about his family. Now, Kofi Annan is a busy man (being secretary-general of the United Nations will do that to you), but he is also a shepherd.

Don Bergstrom is a shepherd. He is now pastor of Clairemont Church of God, near San Diego, but in the 1980's he pastored my home church in San Jose, California. There, he noticed my dad sitting near the back of the congregation every Sunday. My dad grew up a Catholic, stopped attending church as a young man, but when my mother died in 1981, he told me, "Tim, I am going to go to church with you next Sunday." So, he began to go, sitting near the back quietly. He wasn't a big giver, didn't serve on boards, and just quietly came to church. Don carefully built a relationship with my dad, not pushing him, just skillfully connecting. When my dad came down with cancer in 1986, Don and his wife Debbie began visiting my dad at his condo, once every week or two. They would have tea and talk. Don knew my dad was a private person, and not one to be pushed, but Don was a master at touching people, and he touched my dad. As my dad's strength weakened, the conversation deepened, until the day my dad went in the hospital for the last time, and was able to tell Don that he had made his peace with God. Jesus says, "Tend the flock."

What is it that hinders shepherding or tending the flock? I think there are three things. First, if you are a careerist, you will never be a good shepherd. If your eye is always on the next career move, always trying to network with the "right" people, always trying to serve on the "right" boards, always trying to make the "right" contacts, you will have your focus on the next place, not the people in front of you, and will never be a good shepherd.

Then, second, if you are a user or taker, you will not be a good shepherd. In the Anthony Hopkins-Cuba Gooding Jr. movie *Instinct*, Gooding plays a psychologist who is determined to make his career on Hopkins, who is an anthropologist who has lived among the apes in Africa and then killed some poachers. Gooding comes to see Hopkins a couple of times, and finally Hopkins says to him, "Taker." If you are a taker you will not be a good shepherd.

Jack Hayford tells about his early days at Church on the Way, when a young attractive bright family visited the church. The church was small, in desperate need of people, and so when Hayford and his wife were driving home, he said to her, "What a wonderful family. It would be great to get them. We could sure use them." The Spirit deeply convicted him at that point, for Jesus is not in the business of getting and using people. Jesus is not a user, nor are shepherds. Takers and *Users* of people are not shepherds.

Then, third, if you are too busy, you cannot be a good shepherd. Read the gospels sometime and notice that Jesus spends a great deal of time just hanging around. He does it at a well, in the fields, in houses. He always seems to be just sort of hanging around. If you are too busy to hang around and notice how God is working in unexpected ways in people's lives, you will not be a good shepherd.

What is the motivation for tending and shepherding the flock God gives you? Again, note how Jesus asks Peter, "Do you love me?" Love for Jesus is why we shepherd the flock. Jesus says, "Tend my sheep." Feed my lambs and tend my sheep.

Feed the sheep

Third, Jesus says to Peter in v 17, "'Simon, son of John, do you love me?' Peter felt hurt because he said to him the third time, 'Do you love me?' And he said to him, 'Lord, you know everything; you know that I love you.' Jesus said to him, 'Feed my sheep.'" The third agenda for all ministry, whatever form it might to take, is to feed the sheep. The question arises right away, how is this different from what was said in v. 15? The answer is that in v. 15, Jesus said to feed the *lambs*, the Greek word *arnia* is used. However, here in v. 17, Jesus says to feed the *sheep*, using the Greek word *probaba*. Lambs are the young, the new-born, the babes, the immature. The sheep are those who have grown, who have a modicum of maturity, the veterans of the faith. I think that Jesus is saying that the agenda for ministry is not only to feed the new-born, who are immature in the faith, but also to feed the veterans, who have matured and yet still need to be fed. Milk is for the new-born (see 1 Peter 2:1–3), while the mature need solid food (see Hebrews 5:14).

Why is this important? Perhaps because in our attempts to be relevant, to speak the language of the unbeliever, to make connections, we have actually spoken below the mature who need solid food. We have often undershot the mark and not fed those who have grown some already. In the book *Exit Interviews*, William Hendricks interviews a number of people who have left evangelical churches. It is interesting to note a recurring theme. It is not that they have left the faith, or are leaving God. Many are tired of simplistic messages, stale old cliches, worn out slogans. They want to be intellectually challenged, stimulated, to have their minds respected, to move to a higher level of understanding, to leave the kindergarten of the faith.

Part of our problem is that whole swaths of the Bible have gone untouched. Remember the temptation of Jesus? Three times Jesus quotes Deuteronomy in response to the temptation, from chapters 8, 6 and 6 again. You can bet that if Jesus needed Deuteronomy to combat temptation, your people do also! Not only Deuteronomy is needed, but also Isaiah and Jeremiah and Job and the book of Revelation. Feed the lambs!

I received an email not long ago from a youth minister whose young people were being confused by the *Left-Behind* series of books, who worried about the rapture. He wanted some suggestions on how to combat the anxiety, to get into the book of Revelation. It is the kind of message I receive regularly, to do some damage control based on popular teaching. The thing I always want to say is, teach the book of Revelation! The problem is not that we do not know Church of God doctrine, the problem is that we do not know and teach the book of Revelation. You see, if you feed the lambs solid food, they will not need to wander off and feed among the weeds.

Hebrews 5:14 says solid food is for the mature. Feed the veterans of the faith, the ones who have been through the wars, those grizzled with spiritual experience, the solid food they need. I was teaching a summer class on the book of Mark at church and one young man, about to start law school, was speaking one day of how understanding the culture from which the Bible emerged has given him a whole new view, a deeper and richer view of the Bible. Then, he said, "I feel like I have been cheated all these years." Don't cheat people! Feed the lambs, but not the lambs only, feed the sheep also.

Where you do not wish to go...

Fourth, in verses 18–19a, Jesus tells Peter that he will go down. "'Very truly, I tell you, when you were younger, you used to fasten your own belt and to go wherever you wished. But when you grow old, you will stretch out your hands and someone else will fasten a belt around you and take you where you do not wish to go.' He said this to indicate the kind of death by which he would glorify God." This is almost certainly a reference to crucifixion, that Peter would have his hands stretched out on a crossbeam and be led to a place where he would be crucified. For Peter, there would be no retirement condo in Florida, sipping daiquiris on the veranda with his pension checks in the mailbox. No, for Peter, it meant that he would face the terror and anguish of a cruel death. He would go down.

In the mysterious, sovereign will of God, some of you who are being ordained today will walk into disaster and anguish. It may not be martyrdom, like it was for Peter, but it may be times of great pain and darkness. In my own seminary experience, no one told me that this was possible in ministry, but Jesus told Peter that it was, and now I am also telling you. Please be aware also that it is not about shrewdness to avoid disaster, because each of us is more or less shrewd at different times. No, even the shrewdest person can sometimes in the mysterious sovereign will of God walk into disaster. For even the wisest and most godly and sincere person, sometimes anguish awaits.

Jonathan Edwards saw the hand of God on his ministry perhaps like no other in American history. He pastored at Northhampton, Massachusetts, the church which his grandfather had pastored. In 1734–1735, the First Great Awakening fell upon Northhampton, and hundreds were converted without a single altar call or appeal. The Awakening spread throughout New England and literally changed colonial America. Jonathan Edwards continued to pastor, and God blessed his ministry tremendously. Many consider him to be the greatest thinker in early America. Then, however, in 1750, after twenty-three faithful years at Northhampton, the church threw him out. It wasn't that he had really done anything wrong, just confronted some young people about their lifestyles, and the parents of those young people were "important," but after twenty-three years, he went down. In his farewell sermon, he said he had been cast "into an abyss of trouble and sorrow." Sometimes, in the mysterious sovereign will of God, even the best and wisest and most godly of us will go down.

Trouble sometimes seems to sneak up on us. But, then again, it doesn't sneak up on us. Remember these words: "In the world you have tribulation" (John 16:33)? How about these: "Through many tribulations we must enter the kingdom of God" (Acts 14:22)? How about these: "Humans are born for trouble as sparks fly upward" (Job 5:7)?

Now some of us are master-survivalists. We will kick and claw and scratch and gouge the eyes out of anyone who threatens our survival. Perhaps Peter faced that struggle also, for the apocryphal Acts of Peter tells the legend about the experience of Peter in Rome late in his life, when it was heard that there was a persecution and they were looking for him. Some of the brothers and sisters encouraged him to sneak out of town, so he could minister again in the future. While he was doing so, Peter met Jesus coming into town carrying a cross again. Jesus tells Peter that he is going to be crucified afresh, and Peter realizes that it is because he is denying Jesus once more. So, he returns to suffer the crucifixion that the Lord had told him he would face so many years before.

So, why go through with it? Why face ministry if there is a possibility that you will go down? Note that our verse says that Jesus was telling Peter of the death he would die "to glorify God." Isn't that what we want above all, to glorify God, even if it means anguish? "To him be honor and glory forever and ever."

The agenda Jesus sets for all of Peter's ministry, and all of our ministry, no matter the particular form it may take, is to feed the lambs, to tend the flock, to feed the sheep, and if it comes about in the mysterious sovereign will of God, to walk into moments of anguish.

Follow me

Finally, the fifth part of the agenda is to simply follow Jesus. Notice verse 19b, "After this, He said to him, 'Follow me.' " Follow Jesus. It was probably the first thing Peter ever heard Jesus say (Matt 4: 19). It was something Peter heard Jesus say to others (John 1:43). It was something that Peter heard people promise to do (Luke 9:61). And now again, it is one of the last things Peter hears Jesus say: "Follow me."

Why is it so important? Perhaps because in the midst of the pressures of life and ministry, it is so easy to get mixed up, confused, turned around, and be doing the work of the ministry, but to slowly have slipped away from following Jesus. Whatever else you do in ministry, do it by following Jesus and follow Jesus when you are doing it.

William Rainey Harper lost his way. Oh, he didn't run off with the offering plate, didn't run off with a secretary, didn't get arrested for some misdeed, but nevertheless, he lost his way. Harper was a renowned preacher and minister, perhaps the most famous churchman in his day. He was born in 1856, completed his Ph.D. when he was 18 years old, was a pastor in Chicago and elsewhere, and was able to form a friendship with John D. Rockefeller. Harper knew all the right people, and was one of the movers and shakers himself. When Rockefeller wanted to endow a new college, Harper was Rockefeller's choice for its first president, so in 1891, Harper became the first president of the University of Chicago. He worked sixteen-hour days, built buildings, built a faculty. In 1905, however, he was diagnosed with cancer. He made a final pilgrimage to Rockefeller, and then in January of 1906, he called to his bedside two close friends, Albion Small and Ernest Burton. He told them on his death-bed, "I have not followed Jesus Christ as closely as I ought to have done. I have come down from the plane on which I ought to have lived. I have justified it to myself at times as necessary because I was carrying so heavy loads. But I see now that it was all wrong." On January 10th, 1906, William Rainey Harper died at age fifty.

What a tragedy to come to the end of your life, when all of the illusions and pretenses are stripped away, and to have to admit to yourself that you have not followed Jesus as closely as you should have. What a tragedy to be working in ministry, but not following Jesus. What a tragedy to know all the right people, have all the right connections, but not be following Jesus. So, Jesus tells Peter, "Follow me."

What does it mean to follow Jesus? There are a couple of times where Jesus described himself and the way he operated. "I came not to be served, but to serve" (Mark 10:45). "For I am gentle and humble in heart" (Matt. 11:29). "I have loved you" (John 13:34). To follow Jesus means to operate with the same humility and gentleness and love that Jesus operated with.

It is an axiom: God's work must be done God's way. When it ceases to be done God's way, it ceases to be God's work. And, to do God's work God's way means to do it with the humility and gentleness and love of Jesus. In fact, God may be more concerned with how we do His work than what we do.

Perhaps like you and me, Peter was naturally distracted at this point. He notices another one of the apostles, the "beloved disciple," and asks Jesus, "What about him?" Jesus answers that if that disciple remains and is not to suffer a martyr's death, what is that to Peter? Then, again in v. 22, Jesus says again to Peter, "Follow me." Whatever else we do, whatever our ministry might be, Jesus says, "Follow me."

The express *Samina* left Athens on the evening of Sept. 26, 2000, for its regular run to a variety of the Aegean Islands, with over 500 people on board, including tourists, locals, military men and women. The people on the ship had entrusted themselves and their safety to the captain and crew. However, the captain and a number of the crew were so engrossed in watching a soccer game, that they stopped paying attention to the drift of the ship. The ship struck an outcropping of rocks near Paros and began to break up. Though many local fishermen came to the rescue with their boats, in the dark waters some 66 people were lost, pronounced dead by drowning. Ironically, on that shore was a lighthouse whose beam was visible for seven miles.

There will be people who will entrust themselves to your care. These are people God will appoint you to watch over. Never become so distracted that you forget their well-being. No matter what form your ministry may take in years to come, whether it be youth work or music or teaching or counseling or preaching, follow the agenda of Jesus for all ministry. Feed the lambs God gives you. Tend the flock. Feed not only the lambs, but the sheep also. And wherever the mysterious, sovereign will of God takes you, follow Jesus.

Sources:

Laura Baumeister's story is told in Tracy Kidder, *Hometown* (New York: Random House, 1999), pp. 117–131; J.I. Packer quote is from *God Has Spoken* (Downers Grove: IVP, 1979), p. 20; Lewis Sperry Chafer quote from Howard Hendricks, *Say It With Love* (Wheaton: Victor Books, 1976); Graham and Barnhouse quotes are from John Stott, *Your Mind Matters* (Downers Grove: IVP, 1972), p. 55; Richard Baxter (1615–1691) quote is from *The Reformed Pastor* (reprinted :Richmond: John Knox, 1956); Jim Carrey story is from *Time Magazine*, June 1, 1998, p. 82; Scott Lasser, Battle Creek (New York: Morrow, 1999); Kofi Annan story is from *Time*, Sept. 4, 2000, p. 40; Jack Hayford's story is from *Church on the Way* (Lincoln, VA: Chosen Books, 1982, p. 37; for Jonathan Edwards dismissal, see Iain Murray, *Jonathan Edwards: A New Biography* (Carlisle, PA: Banner of Truth, 1987), pp. 313–329; William Rainey Harper's story is from Ron Chernow, *Titan: The Life of John D. Rockefeller, Sr.* (New York: Random House, 1998), pp. 323–329, 494–495.

Chapter Ten:

David Sebastian, *Discovering the Gift*

The person God calls to ministry, God equips for ministry. It is a comforting thought to realize that our effectiveness in ministry is not born of our own strength, but is according to God's divine grace. There are many passages in the New Testament on the gifts of the Holy Spirit. The doctrine of spiritual gifts is not located in a mere isolated verse of scripture but is supported by major portions of New Testament texts.

> *For by the grace given to me I say to everyone among you not to think of yourself more highly than you ought to think, but to think with sober judgment, each according to the measure of faith that God has assigned. For as in one body we have many members, and not all the members have the same function, so we, who are many, are one body in Christ, and individually we are members one of another. We have gifts that differ according to the grace given to us; prophecy, in proportion to faith; ministry in ministering; the teacher, in teaching; the exhorter, in exhortation; the giver, in generosity; the leader, in diligence; the compassionate, in cheerfulness.*
> *—Romans 12:3–8*

> *So that you are not lacking in any spiritual gift as you wait for the revealing of our Lord Jesus Christ.*
> *—1 Corinthians 1:7*

> *I wish that all were as I myself am. But each has a particular gift from God, one having one kind and another a different kind.*
> *—1 Corinthians 7:7*

*And there are varieties of services, but the same Lord;
and there are varieties of activities, but it is the same
God who activates all of them in everyone. To each is
given the manifestation of the Spirit for the common
good. To one is given through the Spirit the utterance
of wisdom, and to another the utterance of knowledge
according to the same Spirit, to another faith by the
same Spirit, to another gifts of healing by the one Spirit,
to another the working of miracles, to another prophecy, to another the discernment of spirits, to another
various kinds of tongues, to another the interpretation
of tongues. All these are activated by one and the same
Spirit, who allots to each one individually just as the
Spirit chooses.*

—1 Corinthians 12:5–11

*And God has appointed in the church first apostles, sec-
ond prophets, third teachers; then deeds of power, then
gifts of healing, forms of assistance, forms of leadership, various kinds of tongues.*

—1 Corinthians 12:28

*But each of us was given grace according to the mea-
sure of Christ's gift. Therefore it is said, "When he
ascended on high he made captivity itself a captive
He gave gifts to his people."*

*(When it says, "He ascended," What does it mean,
but that he had also descended into the lower parts
of the earth? He who descended is the same one who
ascended far above all the heavens, so that he might fill
all things.) The gifts he gave were that some would be
apostles, some prophets, some evangelists, some pastors and teachers, to equip the saints for the work of
ministry, for building up the body of Christ, until all of
us come to the unity of the faith and of the knowledge of
the Son of God, to maturity, to the measure of the full
stature of Christ. We must no longer be children, tossed
to and fro and blown about by every wind of doctrine,
by people's trickery, by their craftiness in deceitful
scheming. But speaking the truth in love, we must grow*

up in every way into him who is the head, into Christ,
from whom the whole body, joined and knit together by
every ligament with which it is equipped, as each part
is working properly, promotes the body's growth in
building itself up in love.
—Ephesians 4:7–16

The end of all things is near; therefore be serious and
discipline yourselves for the sake of your prayers.
Above all, maintain constant love for one another, for
love covers a multitude of sins. Be hospitable to one
another without complaining, like good stewards of the
manifold grace of God, serve one another with whatev-
er gift each of you has received. Whoever speaks must
do so as one speaking the very words of God; whoever
serves must do so with the strength that God supplies,
so that God may be glorified in all things through
Jesus Christ. To him belong the glory and the power
forever and ever. Amen.
—1 Peter 4:7–11

While the Bible does not define a spiritual gift, the preceding scriptures
help us begin to understand that spiritual gifts are special abilities God
gives to every member of the body of Christ (Ephesians 4:7). Gifts are
given without regard to gender, ethnicity, or status. The prophet Joel
foresaw the day when the Spirit would empower all people, young and
old, male and female in acts of service marking the last days. Today,
ministers are serving in the latter days, the era of the Spirit, and receive
the good gifts of God for effective service (Acts 2). All believers are
given gifts for ministry, including those persons called to the set apart
ministry in order to accomplish the task to which they are called.
Ministers of the Gospel are given gifts, not for their own exaltation,
but for the edification of the Church. "Paul argued that the gifts differ
according to the grace given to us (Romans 12:6) and are intended for
the benefit of the whole Christian Community (1 Corinthians 12:7).
None gives grounds for individual boasting. If one is missing a particular gift, there is no reason to despair over it. For the Spirit is nurturing
that gift somewhere else in the community, a cause for celebration"
(Oden 1983, 74).

It is essential that ministers not only discover their own giftedness, but in turn help others unwrap their spiritual gifts as well. Ministers of the Gospel are stewards, that is, managers of God's gifts. When servant leaders realize gifts are received and not achieved, then there is great freedom from pride or self-deprivation and proper credit can be given to the Creator who is the giver of all good gifts. God has gifted ministers. Whether a gift is large or small, public or private, it is to be used to the glory of God (1 Peter 4:11). When people's gifts match their call to service, the results are fulfillment and effectiveness in the work of the kingdom.

Discerning God's will

Many persons considering ministry are interested to know whether they are in the will of God. One of the ways we can discover the will of God for our lives is through the discovery, development, and use of our spiritual gifts. The crucial question is "how do we realistically determine whether we are accurately discerning God's direction for ministry?"

Romans 12 is often quoted by those who are sensing a call to service. The call to ministry is a call to the surrendered life. Saint Paul reminds us "to present your bodies as a living sacrifice, holy and acceptable to God, which is your spiritual worship" (Romans 12:1b). The call to ministry embraces a willingness to consecrate all that we are to God. The text informs us that formation needs to take place so that we are not "conformed to this world, but… transformed by the renewing of your minds" (Romans 12:2a). The surrendered and reformed life are foundational for helping a person "discern what is the will of God—what is good acceptable and perfect" (Romans 12:2b).

The consecration theology prescribed in Romans 12:1–2, however, must be connected to the gift theology described in Romans 12:3–8. The writer continues to develop the theme of discerning God's direction for the surrendered life. The surrendered life is not to be an isolated life but an involved life which becomes a living sacrifice through acts of gifted service.

The surrendered, reformed, and gifted life is also an examined life. Paul reminds the servant to think soberly about oneself "not to think of yourself more highly than you ought to think" (Romans 12:3a). Sober thinking encourages us to realize that we have strengths and weaknesses. When we understand that all have strengths and weaknesses, great freedom is released for ministry.

Paul reminds us that each servant is given "a measure of faith that God has assigned" (Romans 12:3b). Each person has been given a measure of faith that is unique for that person. The analogy of the human body is given so that we may understand how important it is to allow differing gifts to become complimentary rather than competitive. "For as in one body we have many members, and not all members have the same function, so, we who are many, are one body in Christ, and individually we are members one of another" (Romans 12:4–5).

When properly understood this passage helps us to understand that one way the will of God can be discerned is when we discover our purpose within the body. Giftedness differs "according to the grace given to us" (Romans 12:6). Since God has created us and gifted us according to divine will then our quest is to discover that gift(s) and consecrate it to Kingdom service.

As a student associate I began sensing a spiritual leading to move into a preaching ministry. Part of this urging came not only from the prompting of the Holy Spirit but also from a careful observation of a senior pastor who took seriously the preaching of the word of God. His preaching was inspiring, but it was also intimidating to one just beginning ministry.

On a weekly basis we had a conversation about preaching. My mentor asked, "Is preaching something you feel you must do? Is there an urgency to preach?" Yes, there was an urgency but at the same time a sense of inadequacy to accomplish the task. My senior pastor talked about the negative aspect of gift comparison. Wisdom recognizes there will always be stronger and weaker preachers, teachers, and administrators because people and gifts vary. The issue is not the outcome or the effectiveness of our gifts. Rather it is the faithful exercise of the gift. The outcome belongs to God.

Since gifts are given according to the pleasure of God, servants must use gifts to the glory of God and the building up of the church. The discernment of the will of God seems best understood not in some abstract theory but in concrete discovery, development and use of spiritual gifts. If we are placed in the body by God and use our gifts, then perhaps we can say with confidence, we have discovered the will of God for this particular time and place.

Practical steps toward gift discovery

Preparation for ministry involves many things. One crucial dimension of preparation is to discover spiritual giftedness. "Nothing would delight the heart of the Giver of life more than a huge unwrapping party. We determine our gifts, not by just trying to be a clairvoyant with God, but by examining our heritage, our situation, and our individuality" (Hubbard 1985,19).

STEP 1 EXAMINE THE SCRIPTURES—The first step in unwrapping your spiritual gift is to examine the numerous biblical texts on spiritual gifts. What follows is a partial list (taken from the manual *Discover your Gifts*, Shumate and Hayes, 1990; Section III) of spiritual gifts. Do you recognize yourself in any of these listed gifts? As you read through the following working definitions and scripture references, circle the response that is most true of you:

Leadership: the ability to lead members of a group with carrying concern and foresight. "The exhorter, in exhortation; the giver, in generosity; the leader, in diligence; the compassionate, in cheerfulness" (Romans 12:8).

(1)	(2)	(3)	(4)	(5)
Very little	Little	Some	Much	Very much

Shepherding: the ability to oversee the spiritual lives of others and care for their spiritual needs by teaching and guiding them toward maturity. "The gifts he gave were that some would be apostles, some prophets, some evangelists, some pastors and teachers" (Ephesians 4:11).

(1)	(2)	(3)	(4)	(5)
Very little	Little	Some	Much	Very much

* *Discover Your Gifts* (student and leader) may be ordered by calling Warner Press 1-800-741-7721 and asking for BCDE006 and BCDE007

Teaching: the ability to communicate knowledge to others for the purpose of building them up. "The gifts he gave were that some would be apostles, some prophets, some evangelist, some pastors and **teachers**" (Ephesians 4:11).

(1)	(2)	(3)	(4)	(5)
Very little	Little	Some	Much	Very much

Evangelism: the ability to present the gospel to unbelievers in a clear and meaningful way which calls for response. "The gifts he gave were that some would be apostles, some prophets, some **evangelists**, some pastors and teachers" (Ephesians 4:11).

(1)	(2)	(3)	(4)	(5)
Very little	Little	Some	Much	Very much

Discernment: the ability to distinguish between truth and error, to know when a person or act is of God. "To another the working of miracles, to another prophecy, to another the **discernment** of spirits, to another various kinds of tongues, to another the interpretation of tongues" (1 Corinthians 12:10).

(1)	(2)	(3)	(4)	(5)
Very little	Little	Some	Much	Very much

Encouragement: the ability to motivate people through encouraging words to live practical Christian lives. "The exhorter, in exhortation; the giver, in generosity; the leader, in diligence; the compassionate, in cheerfulness" (Romans 12:8).

(1)	(2)	(3)	(4)	(5)
Very little	Little	Some	Much	Very much

Faith: the ability to envision what God wants to happen and to be certain the Lord is going to do it in response to prayer, even when there is not concrete evidence. "And if I have prophetic powers, and understand all mysteries and all knowledge, and if I have all **faith**, so as to remove mountains, but do not have love, I am nothing" (1 Corinthians 13:2).

(1)	(2)	(3)	(4)	(5)
Very little	Little	Some	Much	Very much

Mercy: the ability to empathize with hurting people-that is, feel and sense their suffering-and to translate that into cheerful acts of service. "The exhorter, in exhortation; the giver, in generosity; the leader, in diligence; the compassionate, in cheerfulness" (Romans 12:8).

(1)	(2)	(3)	(4)	(5)
Very little	Little	Some	Much	Very much

Healing: the ability to serve as God's channel in curing sickness and renewing health (physical, spiritual, emotional) through God's healing power. "To another faith by the same Spirit, to another gifts of healing by the one Spirit" (1 Corinthians 12:9).

(1)	(2)	(3)	(4)	(5)
Very little	Little	Some	Much	Very much

Prophecy: the ability to proclaim and apply God's truth so that believers may be edified, encouraged, and consoled, and so that non-believers may be convinced. "To another the working of miracles, to another prophecy, other various kinds of tongues, to another the interpretation of tongues. And God has appointed in the church first apostles, second prophets, third teachers; then deeds of power, then gifts of healing, forms of assistance, forms of leadership, various kinds of tongues" (1 Corinthians 12:10, 28).

(1)	(2)	(3)	(4)	(5)
Very little	Little	Some	Much	Very much

Administration: the ability to organize and guide human activities so that Christ's purpose is carried out. "And God has appointed in the church first apostles, second prophets, third teachers; then deeds of power, then gifts of healing, forms of assistance, forms of **leadership**, various kinds of tongues" (1 Corinthians 12:28).

(1)	(2)	(3)	(4)	(5)
Very little	Little	Some	Much	Very much

This listing is only a partial list of the New Testament gifts. Some authors would identify as many as 19 (Flynn 1978); others list 27 gifts of the Spirit (Wagner 1985). While no single list in the New Testament is exhaustive, neither is any book written about the number of gifts. Gift discovery begins, however, with a thorough biblical investigation.

STEP 2 EXPLORE WITH OTHERS—The second step in gift discovery is to talk with others (especially with ministers) who have discovered their spiritual gifts. One of the crucial elements in effective ministry is to establish connections with other ministerial colleagues. What better way to begin those connections than by initiating a conversation about spiritual gifts? Schedule an appointment with several ministers you would like to get to know and ask the following questions:

How did you sense your call to ministry? What were the internal and external validations of that call?

What are your spiritual gifts?

How did you discover your giftedness?

How have you developed your gifts?

How and where do you use your gifts?

As you listen to the stories of others, your own gift discovery will begin to develop. In turn, it is appropriate to share your story with others. One of the most effective ways to pass on our faith tradition is through shared stories.

STEP 3 EXPERIMENT WITH GIFTS—The third step in discovering your gift is through exploration and experimentation. Pray that God will reveal to you your area of giftedness. Through prayer and fasting, for example, you may sense teaching is a special ability God has given to you. If so, then volunteer to teach a Sunday school class. Possibly you have received a blessing by helping others accomplish a task or goal. If such is the case, then volunteer to be someone's assistant. Support them in their ministry and perhaps you may discover that you have the gift of helps. After prayer and study you may recognize you have an ability to organize and guide. In this instance you could volunteer for an administrative assignment in vacation Bible school or some other ministry opportunity. Generally speaking, God does not write our spiritual gift in the sky, but invites us to pray, study, and experiment with different gifts and ministries.

STEP 4 DETERMINE EFFECTIVENESS—Over a period of time determine your effectiveness, and do not be tempted to quit too quickly. Simply because you have a spiritual gift does not mean that times of frustration are behind you. If God has given you a gift, you will be able to accomplish the ministry. In addition to accomplishing the task, there will be a sense of satisfaction in exercising your gift. If, for example, God has given you a gift of teaching, then people will learn and fulfillment will come through such a gifted ministry.

STEP 5 EXPECT VERIFICATION—The last step of gifts discovery is to listen to others who recognize and affirm your giftedness. Gift recognition requires mature listening skills. We must not rush around asking everybody if they think that we are gifted in this or that. This could sound egocentric and boastful. Rather, over a period of time, we must listen for affirming words. Listen for confirmation such as " Thank you for organizing this event, everything went so smoothly."

If you are experimenting with a gift of teaching, watch for students to get excited about learning. Observe when they communicate, "what you taught really made sense and it had a life changing impact." When such observations are made, make a mental note. Often these affirmations come in order to confirm your spiritual gifts.

Spiritual Gift Development

After you have discovered your gift(s), begin to develop it. Most ministers grow in effectiveness over time. Gifts can be rough and in need of polishing. Giftedness must never lead to pride or spiritual smugness, but rather to humility that leads to effective service.

Often courses in college and seminary can help to develop spiritual gifts. Perhaps someone who has a spiritual gift of mercy would find that a course in mission education might be helpful to refine that gift. A person with a gift of discernment may allow that gift to be developed in a pastoral counseling class. Sometimes a spiritual gift of encouragement can develop in a class of preaching, teaching, or gospel singing. The development of spiritual gifts requires discipline and determination.

Spiritual gifts are to be used in the context of the body of Christ.
Therefore, ministers must seek accountability in ministry. The set apart

or ordained ministry recognizes the call and giftedness that comes from a gracious God; however, ordained ministry is also connected to the church. Through its ministry of ordination, the church is the human recognition of the call and the gifts that God has given to the minister within the context of the church. Thus, the minister has a dual accountability: first, to God the giver of gifts and ministry; second, to the church, which recognizes and holds accountable both the minister and the gifts.

The gifts of the Spirit are absolutely essential for the health and development of the church. It is a tragedy when gifts are neglected. The parable of the talents is a warning of missed opportunity (Mathew 25:14–30). "The gifts of God's Holy Spirit are precious and true. And the Lord of the church demandingly wants them treated as such. But they are neither like gold to be stored in Fort Knox nor like Rembrandt's painting to be hung in a well-guarded museum. They are fuel to be converted into spiritual power; they are seedlings, which will grow into fruitful trees; they are ore to be refined into useful tools. Any less profitable use of them will find the Master calling us to account" (Hubbard, 1985, 88).

As ministers begin to prepare themselves for service, the discovery, development, and use of spiritual gifts is imperative. Why should discovery come before development or use? Logic would determine that it is difficult to develop or use a non-existent gift. There are many gift inventories available (such as the Wagner-Houts and Shumate-Hayes) to help a person begin the discovery process. Colleges and seminaries exist to help persons called by God to do the hard work of developing spiritual gifts for effective kingdom service. Spiritual gifts must be unwrapped and used to the glory of God.

Reference List

Flynn, Leslie B., 19 Gifts of the Spirit, Victor Books: Fullerton, California, 1978.

Gifted and Called, Monograph Series, Church of God Ministries: Anderson, Indiana.

Hayes, Sherrill D., Charles R. Shumate, *Discover Your Gifts,* Board of Christian Education: Anderson, Indiana, 1992.

Hubbard, David Allen, *Unwrapping Your Spiritual Gifts,* Word Books: Waco, Texas 1985.

Oden, Thomas C., *Pastoral Theology*, Harper Collins: San Francisco, California 1983.

The Holy Bible, New Revised Standard Version, Zondervan Publishing House: Grand Rapids, Michigan1989.

Wagner, Peter C., *Your Spiritual Gifts Can Help Your Church Grow,* Regal Books: Ventura, California 1994.

Chapter Eleven:
Robert Edwards, *Empowering the Gift*

Have you ever prepared yourself for a new job or ministry, done everything that you thought you should have done to equip and motivate yourself to do it right and well, and then at the very beginning find out that you had more, so much more, to learn? I have found this to be true in my life over and over again.

Early in our ministry, Jan and I took an assignment with a missionary board to be the principal of a small, Swahili Bible school. As we entered the rural community of Mbulu, Tanzania I felt confident that I was prepared for the task at hand. We had previously spent two years teaching in an African Secondary School, and I had then entered the School of Theology completing a three year Master of Divinity program. In preparation we also had completed three months of intense language school learning Swahili in Nairobi, Kenya. I felt prepared and motivated for whatever was to fly my way. Little did I know that I was merely entering a long, wonderfully exhausting corridor of continued development, learning, and maturing of the gifts that God had granted me. I was like a young, apprentice carpenter who had all the tools in my tool box; now I needed to get them out, one by one, and actually begin to use them.

When I met with the Mbulu area pastors I would be working with for the next ten years, we were sitting on long wooden, backless benches in the church that stood beside our home. I asked them what they expected from me? At first they seemed befuddled by the question. When they found out that I really did wish to know what they thought, they began to give me a list of what they thought should be my priorities. I had thought they would mention classes to be taught in the school, after all

First Steps to Ministry

I was the new principal. As they talked one by one, I was stunned by their remarks. To a person they skipped lightly over what I had been trained to do and informed me that along with work at the Bible school, I was expected to start new churches throughout the region. Church planting! I had had classes and training in everything but church planting.

I recall stumbling the fifty yards back to our new home in a bit of a daze after that meeting. As I looked at the dry, brown grass and the puffs of dust that were created by the stomping of my feet, I was angry that they had not recognized my training and preparations to lead this school. Then the Holy Spirit put his arm of comfort and correction around my shoulder and whispered in my ear, "Now is the time you really begin your studies." Right there at the beginning of my ministry in a cross-cultural setting, I realized that I was not yet done. Not yet complete. If I were to succeed I needed further training—and softening—even as I began to minister.

Throughout the years since those days in the early 70s, I have watched and participated in the introduction to ministry of dozens of men and women entering cross cultural ministry. Most had spent years in seminary. Others had come from pastorates where they had been the senior pastor or associate. All were faced with, and had to go through, the inevitable misery of adjustment and change: loneliness, questioning, language learning. Some thrived at the adjustment period. Others dropped out after only a short period of time. Still others entered their assignment being neither effective nor defeated. I do realize that much of what I have experienced and observed has to do with overseas cross-cultural ministry, but there is a cross-over value to these experiences that relates to men and women entering ministry for the first time whether in the West or in foreign lands.

As the years have passed and I have entered various cross-cultural ministries, I have found the need to sharpen the skills and knowledge God has given to me. I also have found that I must constantly focus and refocus my mind, will, and spirit on whatever it is that God is wanting me to be. It has been a direct and willful commitment to excellence within my field of ministry. It has been a wonderful journey that the Holy Spirit has taken me through, as he has taught, disciplined, and encouraged me to mature in Christ.

I would like to suggest to you that you may wish also to sharpen your skills and continually focus your heart on Christ as you mature in ministry.

> Calling the Twelve to him, he sent them out two by two and gave them authority over evil spirits. These were his instructions: "Take nothing for the journey except a staff—no bread, no bag, no money in your belts. Wear sandals but not an extra tunic. Whenever you enter a house, stay there until you leave that town. And if any place will not welcome you or listen to you, shake the dust off your feet when you leave, as a testimony against them." They went out and preached that people should repent. They drove out many demons and anointed many sick people with oil and healed them (Mark 6:7–12; Luke 10:1–24; Luke 9:1-6; Matt 10:9–15 NIV).

The writers of the Gospels give us a look into how Jesus discipled his disciples. He lived with them, teaching them through his words and his actions. They observed up close how he taught, healed, cast out demons, and communicated with the Father. Then he did a very unusual thing. In the middle of this act of discipling, Jesus sent them out into the world to apply the things they had been observing and hearing.

The fact that this scripture is recorded in three Gospel accounts shows that the experience of doing had burned itself on the disciples' memories because of its significance to them. Up to this point they had only been listening and watching; now Jesus sent them out two by two to strengthen their training through touch and action. He sent them out in pairs, so that they could discuss together what they were doing, to pray together, and to encourage each other. This practice of Jesus was not an isolated incident, some spur of the moment action on Jesus' part. In Luke 10 we again see him doing the same with the seventy-two select disciples. In the recording of this event we read of the incredible elation that the seventy-two had when they returned and reported to Jesus what had happened (Luke 10:17). It was a time of sharpening and focusing in their training.

SHARPENING: "As iron sharpens iron, so one man sharpens another" (Proverbs 27:17).

So how can I sharpen the gifts God grants to me? I have two suggestions that have been effective in my life: strive to do what you are gifted to do with a dedication to excellence; and enter ministries that you would not normally do.

Do what you are trained for with excellence. My first experience at using a sharpening stone was a disaster. I had seen others use the grinding wheel, but I had never stood in front of the spinning stone, held a knife in my hands, and placed it to the stone. I was in a dirt floored workshop in Tanzania on the mission compound. As I turned the grinding stone on, the round, whirling stone appeared to be spinning in the wrong direction. Had I gone wrong already? As I placed the large blade of my red, Swiss Army knife against the stone I was surprised by the sparks and the noise. The drag of the stone seemed to be pulling the blade from my hand. My lack of experience as to how much pressure to apply turned my large blade into something more akin to a sharp toothpick. I had a general idea of what to do, but there was no substitute for actually doing the work.

As we enter the ministry, many of us are well schooled in theology, homiletics, leadership methods, and so on. As we step into the world of ministry, we find that great adjustment is needed as we move from the classroom to the pulpit. We have the tools of ministry, now we need to use them and hone them to a fine edge. I urge you as you enter your new ministry situation, develop and use those gifts that you know that God has given you to a point of excellence. Do not settle for less. If it is preaching, then do your very best in your preparation and delivery, looking for ways to improve the method. If it is in teaching, then use that skill to its fullest. Submerse yourself in the preparation and in the actual teaching. Immerse yourself into the lives of your students. If it is administration, then be the best administrator you possibly can be (Romans 12:6–8). Search for ways to use your gifts, and do it to the very best of your strength.

Do not be satisfied with mediocrity. There is no excuse to go into a situation unprepared. Many times, as leaders, we hide behind the guise of being "out of season," when in reality what happened was that we just didn't take the time to do the preparations. Make a conscious effort to hone the gifts that God has granted to you to a point of excellence.

At the urging of the Holy Spirit, enter ministries that you would not normally do. After ten years of ministry in an African rural setting as principal of a Bible School, Jan and I were asked to move to the neighboring country of Kenya to work with all of the urban congregations of the Church of God in Kenya. By that time we were very comfortable living and ministering in the bush, but we had no knowledge of how to live and minister in a major Third World Urban situation. The very thought of living in Nairobi, a city of over two million, was at first terrifying. As we sat around our kerosene lamp at night before the move, we wondered what we had gotten ourselves into.

When we expressed these doubts to our leaders, they responded in a very interesting way. They made arrangements to send me for three weeks to be with Dr. Samuel Hines at the Third Street Church of God in Washington D.C. It was a baptism of fire. I entered an apprenticeship with a master of the Word and of the urban setting. Sam involved me in every aspect of their vast and meaningful ministry at Third Street: the Wednesday Feeding Program for the homeless, driving the church bus, preaching behind that sacred pulpit, feasting together with the church at a large all church banquet at which he proclaimed a one week water only fast.

It was a hands on experience in ministry that I had never experienced before. In the three weeks I was in the capital, a country boy became comfortable in the city and took the first baby steps in learning how to minister to the urban dweller. Granted, when I returned to Nairobi, much of what I had learned in Washington was not the same. But through sensitivity to the Holy Spirit, I was able to adapt quickly what I had learned to the local situation of a large, world-class, African city. There is nothing like experiencing first hand areas of your life and ministry that stretch your mind, body, and belief systems.

I encourage you, therefore, to do ministries that push out your circle of security and comfort. Attempt ministries that are uncommon for you. These ministries may include prison ministries; emergency room and mental institution chaplaincies; accompanying police patrols in your city, going to pool halls, skate board parks, and extended care homes—all for the purpose of making yourself available to God and his children.

Do not hesitate to be sent out by Jesus into the highways and hedgerows of life, and learn from all that you do.

In working through these two suggestions, you will be sharpening the gifts that God has given to you.

FOCUS: internal empowerment, empowering of the soul

When I entered missionary service I had a great desire to not only communicate the Gospel simply and well, but also to live it in such a way that those I associated with would have a living example of how they, too, should live. I must admit that I have not always been the best example. In fact, over and again I found that I was the one learning how to live the Christian life from those who were young in the faith. The Swahili have a saying, *Elimu haina mwisho.* Roughly translated it means that there is no end to our need for education. The same is true with our maturing in Christ Jesus. We are ever reaching toward that better life in him. The author of Hebrews cheered us on in this maturation process when he wrote, "… let us throw off every thing that hinders and the sin that so easily entangles, and let us run with perseverance the race marked out for us. Let us fix our eyes on Jesus, the author and perfecter of our faith…" (Hebrews 12:1b –2a). Cast off the weight that hinders you. Fix your eyes on Jesus.

If I were completely honest with you, I know only too well what it would take for me to become the mature Christian that God wants me to be, but I am not willing to make the start. There are things that I know would bring me into a better relationship with Christ, but for lack of discipline I do not take that first step. It is as if there were a war raging within me crying for my attention. It is ever as Paul confides to us when he wrote the words, "I do not understand what I do. For what I want to do I do not do, but what I hate I do" (Romans 7:15).

Why is submission so difficult for us? One of the problem Biblical stories for me to read in the Old Testament is of the prophet who confronted King Jeroboam (1 Kings 13). The unnamed prophet was mightily used by God in his delivery of judgment, but he did not fully submit to God's requirements. As a result the message was delivered, but the prophet lost his life. How many of us has this happened to? We clearly hear the voice of God in our souls, but we do not submit fully to that will. We spend more time in front of the TV than we should. We do the immediate instead of the important. Thus we miss out on the true blessings that God wishes to give to us. We need to submit to the power that is greater than ourselves. If we call him Lord and wish to serve him, then we must be willing to fully submit to his directions for our lives.

In his wonderfully written book on spiritual disciplines titled, *The Life You've Always Wanted,* John Ortberg[1] urges readers to focus on the center of their spiritual life. He writes, "Instead of focusing on the boundaries, Jesus focused on the center, the heart of spiritual life" (p. 35). Too many times in our attempts to perform various Christian disciplines, our focus is on the acts, not on the spiritual center where Christ is trying to lead us.

I love the living parable that is related to us in Mark 8:22–26. A group of friends of a certain blind man, brought him to Jesus asking him to heal their friend. Jesus took the man by the hand and led him outside the city. After spitting on his eyes, Jesus placed his hands on the man and asked him, "Do you see anything?" As the blind man opened his eyes, squinting in the sun at those about him, he replied, "I see people; [but] they look like trees walking around." Once more Jesus put his hands on the man, as if he were fine tuning the man's eyes.

Many of us are like this man in our spiritual lives. We have spiritual eyes, but they are not yet as focused as God would wish them to be. As we listen to Christ's voice in our inner selves, we hear him saying, "Do you see anything?" And truly, what we see is not the sharply focused picture of relationship with God and his ministry, but a picture that seems somehow blurred and muted.

Very early in my career as a missionary I was challenged to deepen my walk with Christ. A missionary colleague, Stan Desjardine, threw me into a spiritual crisis with a small but probing question. As I look back on the situation now, I realize that it was the Holy Spirit who was urging me to draw closer to the Father. As we sat in my small, dusty office at the Bible school, Stan asked, "Bob, I know that you have finished seminary, but have you ever read the Bible from beginning to the end?" I tried to dismiss the question by answering about how I had studied all of the books of the Bible. That didn't satisfy him. "I know you have studied *about* the Bible," he continued, "but have you read it? Have you gone through it word for word, and let it speak to you?"

That question, for some reason, sent me into a three-week crisis. Why the crisis? Because whenever the Spirit of God urges us to move closer to our Lord, we find our flesh weak and limited. The war begins. I asked myself, what if I made a pact with God, a personal covenant, and could not or did not fulfill it? I could not dismiss the question and the many excuses I had developed. It weighed heavily on my mind. Then kneeling at my office chair, with tears in my eyes, I prayed, "Lord, Jesus. I know you want me to take this step with you. But I fear you ... oh God, for I know I am weak. If I make this pact, I want to forever complete it. With your help I will read every day your blessed Word, and I will systematically go through your Word, learning lessons that you wish to teach me, from this day forward." In doing so, I had taken a step of inner focus. I had taken a step toward God, making a Covenant with him. This was the first of many steps the Holy Spirit has addressed in my life in my quest to focus my soul on him.

Since that day I have been enabled by the Spirit of God to keep that personal covenant with him. Each year I read through the Bible systematically. Each year I choose a different version to read. A number of times I have gone through the Bible in my second language, Swahili. And his word speaks to me daily. Words and phrases come to life that I have read many times before, but that did not seem to speak to my situation. Stories and parables come to life as current events coincide with hidden meanings in the Word of God. I have never regretted that day of commitment, on a dusty floor in Tanzania.

How can we bring focus to our spiritual lives that will help us to give power to the gifts that God has granted to us? I would like to suggest a number of ways that have been helpful to me.

Christian Disciplines

It is a sad commentary on those of us who stand to represent God that many of us lack the basic spiritual disciplines in our lives that we expect from others whom we serve. As we work our way through seminary and into the ministry itself, we find ourselves so busy with studies, administration, sermon preparations, visitation, and committee meetings, that we drop into bed at night, almost too tired to whisper a prayer. We who preach about "grace verses works" are guilty of failing to come close to the one we are serving because we have no time to speak with the one who has sent us. We act as if we are punching God's time clock, with an 18 hour day before us ... seven days a week. Then after only a few short months of action, we feel like a thirsty man, stumbling in the desert sands, pulling a rope along behind him that is tied to a church bus full of parishioners. And we pull it right past the Master who is sitting by the well, longing for us to come sit beside him and drink from the ladle in his hand.

The truth of the matter is that if we don't take the time for our own personal walk with the Lord, we don't have the right to stand before our people. But when we do discipline our lives, we begin to find focus and power within ourselves as we minister.

Prayer, Intimacy with God—My daughter, Dontie, and I have had a very special relationship over the years. One day in her senior year in high school in Nairobi, Kenya, she came out to my office and sat down staring at me. I knew that she had something on her mind so I asked her what it was. She said that they had been studying at school about maturity in Christ and the need for young Christians to have a mentor. She then surprised me by asking me to be in a discipling relationship with her. I was pleased and a bit scared. Discipling other peoples' kids was fine, but how do you go about discipling your own child? I found some good materials from the Navigators, and the rest of that very special year for me, we met regularly to talk about spiritual matters. I must admit that I learned more from our talks than I think she did.

Even though Dontie has now graduated from University, we continue to discuss spiritual matters. We do this now via e-mail from a very long distance. She recently had some important career decisions to make and was looking for God's will in the matter. As the time for her decision was coming to a close I received the following e-message from her about her special time of talking with God. She wrote:

> ... Saturday morning I got up and went to the park for
> two hours to just pray, read the Bible, and be silent
> before God. I think I went expecting him to tell me def-
> initely if I was doing the right thing or not; like in the

Bible or in my prayers or quiet time. But I never heard
an answer. What I did feel was a great sense of peace.
I just listened to the trees, the birds and the squirrels.
And I listened to God saying, "Please hang out with me
more often, I like this." So more than anything I had
a deep hunger swell up inside me to just worship, and
spend devoted time more regularly with God.

As Christian leaders we need to recognize that God wants to hang out
with us. Not just to hear our needs and petitions, but also to spend time
with us in silence. That is when we give him a chance to speak and
minister to our souls.

I was talking with a mother of a boy who was a junior in my son's
high school. Both this young man and our son, Nathan, play on the var-
sity soccer team. She said that when her son hit the teen years, he just
stopped talking with her and her husband. With very moist eyes she said
that no matter how hard they tried to communicate with him, he just
would remain silent in their presence. He would only answer their questions with a grunt. She lamented how much she longed to hear his voice
and to know what was going on in his thinking.

In the same way, our Father desires to hear our inner voices. How can
we possibly be too busy to speak with our Lord? Prayer is our spirit
communicating with the very Spirit of God. Paul speaks of this as a
groaning of the spirit.

In the same way, the Spirit helps us in our weakness. We
do not know what we ought to pray for, but the Spirit
himself intercedes for us with groans that words cannot
express. And he who searches our hearts knows the mind
of the Spirit, because the Spirit intercedes for the saints
in accordance with God's will (Romans 8:26-27) .

It is through this intimacy—our talking with God—in our prayer life,
that we move closer to him and bring him into sharper focus. Our Father
in heaven longs to "hang out with us." He longs to hear our voice.

I find myself in continual communication with my Lord. After exercising in the morning, I stay on my knees for some time talking with Jesus

about the day. We discuss what is going to happen in the day, and I place before him my family and colleagues in ministry. Then as the day progresses I seek times of quiet to be with him in prayer: while the computer is booting up, as I am walking to the store, when I take the bike for a ride in the country. Frequently I will turn off the radio when I am alone in the car, so that I can talk with Christ as I drive. These are times that help me to focus on what is important in life, for as I seek his face, I also find my center in Christ.

Fasting, voluntarily doing without—My first attempt at a somewhat longer fast of only water was a disaster. I was doing a short internship in Washington D.C. with Dr. Sam Hines in an attempt to understand urban ministry to the large city. On the second Saturday evening of my three weeks with the Third Street Church of God, the church held a sumptuous banquet where they recognized the many of volunteers in the church. It was absolutely wonderful. Great food, tremendous entertainment, and one of Sam's delightful speeches. At the conclusion of his remarks, he declared a church-wide water only fast for the following week. We were to be in prayer for the church and its many ministries.

Sam explained what he meant by the fast. It would go from the next day, which was Sunday, through the following Sunday. The fast was voluntary, not mandatory. Those with medical reasons were exempt, but he explained that even they may wish to do without some food or other luxury in their lives during this concentrated prayer time. Others may wish to do without food, but take a glass of fruit juice once or twice during the day. For those who were healthy, and who felt the call of God on their lives to give up food for the full time, however, this would be a special period of drawing near to God.

I recall the battle that gently took place in my mind. I was indeed healthy and loved challenges. But I had never gone eight days without food, only drinking water during that period. After putting off the decision for several hours, I finally decided to take the plunge, that this was something that I wished to do.

During those eight days, the battle really never stopped in my mind. After the first day, the hunger pains subsided, but my thoughts about food never ceased. I recall making a calendar of the days that needed to pass until I could eat once again, and then marking them off slowly: one

line at noon and then the crossed line in the evening before bed. Then as
if that were not enough, I would color in the square as I lay down.
I found that I indeed had more time not having to plan about where the
next meal was to be. My prayer life increased and so did my Bible reading time. But my mind continually looked to the hour and the day, 6:00
p.m., Sunday night, when I could break the fast. I chided myself for the
Pharisee that I saw within myself. I was keeping the outward law, but
my inward spirit was not at peace with God. Was I really that shackled
by food?

With Sunday morning came a sense of accomplishment and excitement
was in my soul. Tonight, I thought, I eat again. As six o'clock neared
I began to make plans for the meal. When the hour struck, I found
myself in a Pizza Parlor, ordering a large All You Can Put On The Top
Pizza, extra large Coke, and an all you can eat Salad Bar. As the food
lay before me, I breathed what had to have been one of the shortest
and quickest prayers every offered to the Father, and I dug in with both
paws. It was indeed delicious, but as the evening advanced I realized
only too well, that a hot bowl of soup and a glass of fruit juice would
have been the preferred choice. My digestive system that had adapted to
"less" rebelled at what I was stuffing into it. The stomach cramps were
much similar to that which my wife has described when she gave birth
to our first child.

Of all the spiritual disciplines the act of fasting is perhaps the most difficult for those of us in the West. I can pray and read my Bible, but I
do not like the idea of abstinence. The voluntary act of doing without
something when it is in my power to have it, is just not one of the values of our capitalistic culture. Indeed it is exactly the opposite of all
that we are brought up to value and expect. Many congregations have
bought into this idea of not doing without.

A quick perusal through the Bible reveals that fasting had many purposes and facets. Fasting was expected, and the religious people did it
as part of their normal religious routine (Matthew 6:16–17, "when you
fast..."). Fasting was used as a means of showing one's sincerity for
repentance (Jonah 3:5), and one's humility in presenting supplications
for help (Esther 4:16 and 2 Samuel 12:16). Fasting could also be part of
the process of searching for the mind of God in times of decision-making (Acts 9:8-9). It may be done to commemorate an important event

in someone's life (Matt 4:2). Unfortunately, it was also abused. Some persons would use it in order to attempt to manipulate God, attempting to force God to do something for them (Luke 18:11–12). Jeremiah was quick to remind us that if it is done with the wrong heart, God will not listen (Jeremiah 14:12). One thing spiritual fasting is not, it is not a religious means of losing weight.

Although fasting is normally associated with abstinence from all foods and drink, fasting can also be a person's refraining from anything that he has control over: not eating meat, not eating foods with sugar or caffeine, refraining from intimate relations with your spouse for a time (1 Corinthians 7:5), not watching TV or listening to radio for a period of time.

The benefits of fasting are numerous.

• When we fast, we bring our bodies and minds under the subjection of the Lord, for we are doing this unto him. It is being done for spiritual reasons and for spiritual focus.
• When we fast, it helps break the bondage that time, events, media, and our internal desire for foods have over us.
• It is a spiritual sacrifice we are presenting to God our Father. When done properly, it is pleasing to him.
• Because we are doing it voluntarily, fasting helps to remind us of who we are and who God is.

Contrary to how it may appear, fasting is more a state of the mind and soul than it is of the physical being. When done properly we are not attempting to manipulate God. It is a cleaning and a clearing of the mind and soul so that we can hear God's voice more distinctly. Fasting is something that we do intentionally, specifically drawing ourselves under the authority of the rule of God. Instead of being controlled by the clock, by hunger, or by the media, we give control of our physical and spiritual lives over to God.

For some of us, we may wish to begin slowly and feel our way into this new discipline. We may wish to give up soft drinks for a week, drinking only water instead. We may wish to fast all foods from sun rise to sun set on one specific day each week. Perhaps we may wish to refrain from watching TV for a week, substituting instead the reading of a good religious book during the time you would have sat and watched. Whatever you fast, it will be the beginning of an experience that will bring your relationship with God into finer focus.

Systematic reading and study of the Word—I have been guilty of the sin of nonchalance in knowing and using the Word of God. Soon after graduation from seminary and moved to Tanzania, I was anxious to try out some of my experimental theology on the "older" missionaries. I recall talking with the late Dennis Habel, then the Principal of the Kima Theological College in Kenya. I loved and admired him deeply as a friend and colleague. Jan and I were staying at Dennis and Elaine's home over-night, sitting in their lovely living room drinking steaming Earl Gray Tea, and discussing our two Bible schools. I then made some remarks about my search for the "historical Jesus" and what that meant to me theologically.

I can still see Dennis leaning forward in his easy chair, silently staring at me, and stroking his mustache. He then, very kindly, began to tear me apart, beginning with the questions, "What right do you have to say that sort of thing, Bob? On what do you base those kind of assumptions, for they are found no where in the Bible? Are you going to teach that sort of thing to your students in Tanzania who are then going to go out and teach them to their people? How will that kind of seed take root in the soil of young hearts? Where will they stand? " *Where will they stand?* It still rings in my ears today.

I had nothing to answer, for in truth I had no foundation on which to stand. I was driven back by the Holy Spirit to the Bible, to reading systematically the Word of God, and searching for its voice to me. I knew that I needed to know what the Bible said, and not so much about what others said about the Bible. There started my love affair with the Word. The Word of God is foundational to all that we do. It is central to what we think, teach and preach. It is the only anchor onto which our faith holds. If we attempt to base our faith on anything other than the Word itself, it is like placing all that we own on a peg loosely fit into a mud wall. The Word is our compass in life by which we find our direction, for it always points toward the Father. If we are not focused on the Word, then we are focused on the wrong thing, for we are people of the Book.

Recently I was in the home of a missionary family who had previously lived and ministered in Belgium. On their dining room wall was a picture that stole my attention. The picture was from the era of the 1600s, done mainly in browns. It showed a bearded, older man sitting in front of a desk with a large book spread out in front of him. To his left was a young woman, probably his daughter, who was standing but leaning across the book with her hand on the outer cover as if she were about to close the book in a hurry. Both the man and the woman were looking back at the viewer; the young woman with a look of surprise and fear on her face. The older man had the look of surprise, but not that of fear. The title of the picture was *De Verboden Lectuur* (Flemish for "The Forbidden Literature") by Karel Ooms.

My host told me that almost every Protestant home in Belgium has a picture similar to this one on their walls. It is a reminder to them of their Christian heritage and of their love and strong belief in the Bible. During the early years of the Reformation, there came a Counter Reformation where the Catholic Church persecuted those who left the established church for the truths as taught by the Protestant reformers. One way that the religious authorities could tell who the Protestant were was to come unexpectedly to suspected homes, and search for a Bible in the home. The open Book was a sure sign of those who believed. I now have one of these pictures on my study wall, for I am a believer and wish to be identified with this Book that changes lives. We are people of the Book and the persecution of those who read the Word continues to this very day.

Recently I was informed of a group of Christians, one with whom I am acquainted, in one of the Middle Eastern nations being hauled off to jail and interrogated. As the five men were finishing their weekly Bible Study in their church hall, plain-clothes police came in and arrested them. The police took all of the Bibles in the church building, along with hymnals and the computer in the office. At the police station they were separated and questioned. My friend, who was taken into a room by himself, was hit several times in the face and stomach each time he would ask why they were being held. The police chief finally replied, "You never learn do you?" What was the charge? The charge was terrorism. These five men were being held because they were having a Bible study in their church, which was officially registered, as was their weekly meeting.

This story is repeated over and over again in nations that are closed to the Gospel of Christ. But why? It is because the Word of God is life changing and powerful. It unchains the mind and soul, and thus threatens those who would wish to imprison the thoughts and hearts of their people. We are people of the Word, and if we do not know that Word, if we are not immersed in that Word, then we are doing disservice to those who have suffered because of it.

How can we as God's men and women be more interested in other books that talk *about* the Word, and systematic theologies coming out of that Word, and not be into the very Word itself? If we wish our gifts from God to be empowered, then we must bring into sharp focus his very Word.

It is interesting that I have trouble finding time for the study of the Word of God. And yet I find time for other things that I deem important to me, such as time to watch my favorite programs on TV; time to read magazines; time to eat out in my favorite restaurant; time to find quality moments with my family; time to check my stocks and attempt to make them profitable; time to listen to the questionable words of political leaders. We always find time for those things that are important to us.

In 1994 I was diagnosed with a melanoma on my back. Although the doctor had already removed the spot in his office, I needed to go in to the hospital to have the spot widely excised so that there would be no malignancy reaching deep into my body. I can recall standing in his examining room by myself as he arranged a time for the operation to take place. As I waited, I went from wall to wall reading the certificates and citations that he had placed there from the various schools he had attended. I realized that I wanted to be sure that this man who held the difference between my life and my death in his hands, had thorough knowledge of what he was doing.

Is it no different with the people under our care? What do they expect from us? They expect for us to know the Word of God and for it to be the passion of our lives. They expect that we know intimately the One of the Word. It is good for us to know about the politics of our time, that we are good in sports, and to have a good sense of humor and delivery. But primarily our people want to know that we are persons focused on God, that we are shaped by his Word, and that we serve in the name of the One whom we know.

There are two great lies of the Enemy of the soul:
God does not hear or care about your prayers.
The Bible is just one book among many other books.

Do you wish to empower your gift of ministry? Then you must focus on God's Word.

Gradually making personal covenants with the Lord—I hesitate making the following suggestion, because I realize that it is not for everyone. I realize that this may even anger some of my readers. But I have found that one of the disciplines that has helped me to bring Christ into clearer focus, and that has empowered the gifts that God has granted to me, is that of gradually, through the quiet urging of the Holy Spirit, making personal covenants with my Lord. I have already discussed the crisis that I went through concerning my covenant with God to read his Word regularly and in an organized manner.

These personal covenants with God come over time. They are set into motion by the urging of the Holy Spirit to draw us into another level of our commitment to the Father. They are not made casually, but with much thought and prayer. Their significance may not be understood by others, even those who are close to us, but they are of supreme significance to us personally. They are never taken lightly. They are made between the individual and our Lord, and intimately kept and protected by that seeker.

Conclusion

In this chapter we have attempted to look at the process by which we can empower the gifting that God has granted to us. I have suggested that this empowerment takes place through the sharpening of those gifts, and through our personal Christian discipline. I have suggested that we sharpen our God-given gifts through the use of our gifts to a point of excellence. And we also sharpen those gifts through doing ministries and tasks that take us out of our normal ministries we are comfortable doing, and into ministries that will stretch us spiritually.

We then discussed the notion of bringing into focus those gifts through Christian disciplines. Those disciplines included our intimate prayer life, exercising the discipline of fasting, systematically reading God's holy word, and making personal Covenants with our Lord. These disciplines have helped to shape and focus my life personally throughout my ministry, and I pray that as the Holy Spirit speaks to your soul, they will also become a part of your life

End Note

[1]John Ortberg, *The Life You've Always Wanted,* Zondervan Publishing House, Grand Rapids, 1997.

Chapter Twelve:
James W. Lewis, *Balancing the Gift with Building a Life*

Should the life of a minister be assessed *primarily* on what we designate as "ministry"? What then would guide the "other" areas of a minister's life? On what basis can we or should we even attempt to address this issue? The church, I suspect, has contributed to the ambiguity ministers often experience in this area. Yet the seed of the problem cannot be reduced to assigning blame to the church. I will promote the claim that what we do in ministry cannot and should not be separated from who we are in the totality of our lives. This chapter explores how our unique calling to ministry infuses every dimension of our lives.

Something's Wrong, But What?

The contemporary landscape of Christian ministry reveals embarrassing cases of failed witness in the wider world. How often have we celebrated gifted preaching and teaching, and lamented in the next breath failed character and integrity? Why are we seeing comparable percentages of failed marriages in both the church and the wider society? Why does it appear that more and more ministers and their ministry leave a distasteful residue in the mouths of the immediate community? I hope to offer some reasons for such diagnoses, along with offering a perspective for a more fruitful witness in the world. Many of us believe something is wrong with this picture described above, but are at a loss to say just what.

Nearly five centuries ago the Reformer Martin Luther transformed the understanding of Christian vocation inherited from the Medieval Period. In the Medieval Period the concept of "calling" applied to the monks who sought union with God in the monastic orders and also to the priests who ministered in the church. Luther believed that there is no more special dignity given to the priestly office than to the "ordinary" work of the world. The radical separation between clergy and laity (though this separation is suspect in some sense) could not then mean that clergy were called to live a life isolated from the everyday world.

Christian ministers therefore are called to live a life that spans any separation or distinction between one's "special" ministerial duties and one's duties in other areas of life. Christian ministers must reject the idea that "burying" themselves in "church" work excuses them from faithful living in other areas of their daily life. The fact is that we all live in multiple contexts. We are fathers and mothers, husbands and wives, brothers and sisters, citizens and volunteers, friends and neighbors, teachers and students, lenders and borrowers, and more. We even find ourselves moving in and out of various contexts on a daily basis. The minister's life in these areas ought to reflect one's fundamental calling to ministry and one's public witness, together which serve to authenticate the truth of the gospel of Jesus Christ. In refusing to compartmentalize our lives, we open our lives to the transforming power of God's spirit to bless our "ministry." I have assumed here that our ministerial call brings with it the corresponding obligation to live faithful to the call in all of life. So a focus on the God who calls and on the nature of that call as revealed in Scripture is where we rightly begin.

A Biblical/Theological View: God's Call to Build a Life

God created the world and called humans to exercise stewardship over the created order. God's stewardship of creation is shared with us in our relationship with one another and with other parts of God's creation. The God who created the world, who called Abraham into covenant, who delivered Israel out of Egyptian captivity, further affirmed the specialness of this calling at Mount Sinai.

Through Moses God conditioned God's ownership of Israel upon the peoples' obedience to the covenant. In the Exodus passage, God indicated that God's calling of a particular people derived from God's ownership over *all* the earth:

> Now if you will obey me and keep my covenant, you
> will be my own special treasure from among all the

nations of the earth; for all the earth belongs to me. And
you will be to me a kingdom of priests, my holy nation.
(Exodus 19:5–6 NLT).

The great King David echoes this claim in Psalm 24:1: "The earth is the
LORD's, and everything in it. The world and all its people belong to him."

The scriptures above promote the belief that God does call a *particular*
people. Yet the calling must be viewed from a context that is universal in scope. Certainly the particular calling is not the result of special
merit on Israel's part that somehow earns them God's special favor. The
particular calling instead emerges from God's election of them. While
the calling is not wholly arbitrary, as human choices often are, it is still
God's sovereign act. There is a particular calling. Yet this particular
calling is in service to God's universal purpose and will: That all people
and nations come to worship and fellowship with God. This cosmic purpose continues in the life, death, and resurrection of Jesus.

The gospels provide the fundamental account of Jesus' life, death, and
resurrection. The gospel writers tell the story in their own specific voices. Matthew's gospel describes Jesus as the One who fulfills the Law of
God through a radical obedience displayed in the Sermon on the Mount
(5–7). Luke continues his story begun in the book of Acts by claiming
that Jesus ushers forth Good News, Joyous News, to *all* people—especially to the marginalized. Mark emphasizes the paradox of a victory
won through suffering. John's gospel seeks to prove that Jesus is the
Christ and there is life in his name.

The brevity of the above discussion should not minimize the power of
these gospel accounts to reveal the nature of God's kingdom revealed
through the particular ministry of Jesus of Nazareth. The growth or
expansion of God's kingdom is aptly illustrated in Jesus' parables. For
example, in Matthew's gospel, the parables of the mustard seed (13:31-
32) and of the yeast (13:33) depict the nature of God's kingdom as
growing from the very small to the very large. This portrait of God's
kingdom goes far in describing the nature and will of God for the whole
world. The salvation God offers in Jesus opens the redeemed to both
privilege and responsibility.

The privileges of salvation are well rehearsed in our churches today.

First Steps to Ministry

Forgiveness, joy, blessings of every kind are all consequences of the life of faith. The challenge to many believers today is the tendency to forget the corresponding obligations that come with salvation. In Jesus' temptation narrative in Matthew 4:1–11, Jesus demonstrates how faithfulness to the calling comes in the face of tests and worldly seductions which threaten to undermine one's ministry. Henri Nouwen has written provocatively about these challenges confronting the Christian leader (Nouwen 1989). Those of us called to ministry in the path of Jesus must be transformed in order to follow his leading *into* the world.

The Apostle Paul highlights this commitment in his letter to the Corinthians. In the face of his detractors Paul responds that he tries to live his life in such a way that no one would be hindered from finding the Lord. In this way God's calling on Paul's life required not less sacrifice but more, not the path of least resistance but the way of faithfulness:

> In *everything* we do we try to show that we are true ministers of God. We patiently endure troubles and hardships and calamities of every kind....We have proved ourselves by our purity, our understanding, our patience, our kindness, our sincere love, and the power of the Holy Spirit. We have faithfully preached the truth. God's power has been working in us. We have righteousness as our weapon, both to attack and to defend ourselves (2 Corinthians 6:4–7).

Further in Thessalonica, Paul also urges the believers there to live in a way that pleases God—more and more (1 Thessalonians 4:1). The writer of Colossians admonishes all believers with these words: "Live wisely among those who are not Christians, and make the most of every opportunity. Let your conversation be gracious and effective so that you will have the right answer for everyone" (4:5–6).

The calling to ministry therefore is a calling to faithful living in all of life. This is particularly true because the God who calls us is a God of all life. Yet there are obstacles to the effort of building a life that fits the life of God. Building a life is inseparable from the gift of our calling.

Obstacles to Building a Life

A Distorted View of the "Balanced Life"

At no time does building a life require a casual approach to the ministry. Developing a balanced life is not a license to short-circuit whole-hearted devotion to Jesus. We live in a society that does not look well on "fanaticism." While no one should advocate unreflective extremes, one must be careful about embracing a view of the balanced life that undermines faithfulness and passion in all of one's life.

Philip Kenneson suggests that we scrutinize those times when the maxim "moderation in all things" is invoked by us. According to Kenneson,

> Often [moderation] is not with reference to food, drink or work but with reference to our deepest convictions. In our society few epithets sting as deeply as being labeled a 'fanatic,' and so many people have adopted as a kind of general principle this maxim written six centuries before Christ by a pagan named Theognis: 'moderation in all things' (Kenneson 1999, 232)

A life worthy of the kingdom cannot be constructed on a spiritual foundation strengthened only by the stubble of mediocrity and lukewarmness. Be careful when tempted to invoke the *balanced life* as the goal of your life. For what you receive may be only an antidote to a life lived passionately in the kingdom.

In our country, living obedient lives will hardly appear "balanced." In fact, the form the Christian life takes will look ironically like fanaticism to many people, including many Christians. In the arena called life, we are called to be fan(atic)s.

Fragmentation of Life

In the United States, we face the challenge of living our lives in a fragmented manner. Obviously we all must live and operate in multiple contexts. You will exercise your gift of ministry in congregational life. Some persons will pastor and others will assist in the pastoral function.

Some will be worship leaders and others will minister with children and youth. Yet if one's life consists only of these activities, then life indeed would be both truncated and boring.

Those who serve as professional ministers also will realize that they live in many contexts. This is a given in the complexities of modern life. The concern instead is how does one live in these varied contexts with integrity. That is, "Am I the *same* person at home, in the mall, on the highway, at the bank, that I am in my ministerial vocation?" The desired response hopefully is in the affirmative. One's vocation of ministry must pervade all of life. The organizing vision for your life emerges from the calling placed on your life by the Lord of the Church.

Beware of the obstacle that threatens to make you "legion." The obstacle is how our society shapes us to accept the logic of multiple identities, or a splitting of the self into different selves for different contexts. The division of the self is made to appear as the only reasonable approach to living in a liberal democratic society. To risk oversimplification the division I am suggesting is between so-called "public" and "private" dimensions of our lives. While such a division appears legitimate in our country, it renders our lives somewhat ambivalent. Those of us who carry the banner of Christian ministry are particularly challenged in this respect. We are called to embrace the passion and purpose of our calling. Our society frequently resists attempts, however, to transfer such spiritual passion and purpose directly into the "public" arena where people live out their everyday lives.

Our society exerts enormous pressure on us to limit the expression of our fundamental convictions and beliefs to the realm of the "private." That is, we are perfectly justified to exercise our calling in our congregational settings. But our guiding Christian commitments generally will not be given identical status once we move within other areas of our life. We must not surrender to this way of thinking. Yet, do not think that I am suggesting that you actively seek to evangelize the store clerk at every visit, or genuinely expect your banker to grant a loan solely on the basis of your Christian confession. What *is* problematic is giving in to the belief that life in the world will require us to live from a perspective undergirded by assumptions vastly different from our fundamental calling to be disciples of Jesus.

A distorted view of the balanced life and the consequences of a fragmented life present obstacles to one's efforts at building a whole life in service to God and the world. How might one overcome these obstacles? The worship of God provides access and divine resources for shaping a whole life, nourished by the divine call. Corporate worship becomes the pivotal place for beginning and continuing the quest of building a life.

The Role of Corporate Worship in Building a Life

Encountering God's Divine Presence with Others: Corporate Worship

In corporate worship we are called to the true worship of God. Being in God's presence with others reminds us of God's sovereignty and love. The God who called Abraham, Isaac, Jacob, and others, has called us into a relationship of intimacy. As we gather to worship, we gather in the name of Jesus of Nazareth. We gather from the North, South, East, and West. We gather from diverse places, occupations, and other particularities. Yet the God we worship is the God of the whole world. Gathering in the name of Jesus reminds us of the particular God who calls us to worship and praise. This is a God not limited by any human barrier. In gathering together for worship as the "people" of God, we are finally sent forth into the world. Encountering God as God's servants will turn us outward to be servants to the whole world. The gift of ministry is indeed a calling to build a life in the world.

Encountering God's Presence Among Others: Service

There is a "gathering" and a "sending forth." There is an "invocation" and a "benediction." There is a "behold" and an "amen." The worship of the Trinitarian God continues in the wider world. This is the place where the completeness of our lives is on display. In a society where individualism and self-sufficiency is as natural to our national landscape as the air we breathe, those who would be disciples of Jesus are called to acknowledge their whole life as a praise offering to God.

Building a life makes sense only as we consider the kind of life worthy of building. The life worthy of building is a life that participates fully in the life of Christ (Philippians 3:10–11). It is a life fundamentally shaped within the worshiping community. We have discussed this dimension above. We are urged in scripture to resist being conformed to the world, but rather to be transformed by the renewing of our mind—all for the purpose of discerning the will of God (Romans 12:1–2).

Thus, the dominant culture (world) also possesses a real power to shape people in some rather definite ways. That is why corporate worship is so integral to our lives, since it offers us those opportunities to experience the Trinitarian God and the reality of being a part of the body of Christ. The participation in the life of God continues in the world in the form of loving service both to God and the neighbor. What an ongoing challenge this is! Our real life in the body of Christ—in all its dimensions— represents embodied faith. Can we model a life any less faithful in other dimensions of our individual and corporate existence? We are still members of the body of Christ as we move out in *every* area of life. We still operate and function as a minister of the gospel and of Jesus Christ in all dimensions of human interactions. The life being built for witness in the world is the same life imprinted with the divine call to ministry. We are not our own any longer (as if we ever were), we have been purchased with a price (1 Corinthians 6:19–20). What are some faithful ways, with God's help, to build a life that honors God in all dimensions of one's life? Let's reflect on this a bit more.

Reflection on Building a Life Within God's Call

No one can prescribe exactly the program for building your life. I do want to offer for your reflection, however, some ideas or questions to start you thinking about this whole area of building a life. This is a short list and is not intended to be exhaustive. Your intimate relationship with God will do much more to direct and shape your life. Here are a few suggestions for your consideration:

1. Consider becoming a part of an accountability group of other ministers who view faithfulness in all of life as part of their calling. The group should be persons who are willing to be truthful about their victories and struggles. Being with others in this way can help you avoid the tendency to self-sufficiency and idolatry. In all of this there is no substitute for gathering for corporate worship with other believers.

2. Devote time for self-development that builds you up that you might be able to build others up: Read a variety of books and literature to stimulate your imagination and to give you an expanded view of the world; travel different places to meet other people groups and cultures, to inspire your soul and to break your heart; cherish opportunities to appreciate a beautiful sunrise or a breathtaking sunset, the singing of the birds and the smell of the flowers, the growth of the crops along a winding rural highway, and even the cry of newborn baby (new life). **Always be a learner, be apt to teach. Enjoy the gift of life within you and within others!**

3. Discover ways to make love concrete in the places right around you. Start by asking the Lord to help you love your spouse and your children, as you should (if you do have spouse and/or children). What are some ways you might nurture these primary relationships? Practice gestures of love, forgiveness, encouragement, and truth telling in the midst of everyday life experiences.

4. Devote some time in your life and "schedule" to volunteer in a food pantry, a rescue mission, a homeless shelter, a local school classroom, etc., or to attend meetings, when you can, of the local school board, civic organizations, and so on. Are there places like this where you live that would welcome your presence?

5. Maintain a log over a period of time (say a month) for the purpose of identifying where you spend (devote) your time. What will this reveal to you about your priorities? How does your calling as a disciple and as a minister help you to know how to order your life? Be alert to the needed changes that are called for and ask God and others for help in making these changes.

6. What are some other ways you can think of to build a life that honors God. Stay on the journey. God is not through with you yet. Praise God!

A Final Word: Be Patient

If you have not discerned it so far, the call to live faithfully in all of life is a call to every believer. However, we have been addressing those with the special calling to serve the church and local congregations in special ways. In this chapter, we are reminded of who God is, God's purpose for the world, and God's election of particular people like yourself to be a sign of God's will to redeem the world. Also the God who calls us and sets us apart desires that we live our lives as faithful witnesses in everyday life. Therefore, the calling to ministry is not simply a call to exercise certain "churchly" duties at the prescribed times of the week in just the prescribed ways. These concerns are important, too. Our calling rather extends to all areas of life because the God who calls us cares for the whole world. We are called likewise to imitate God in everything we do (Ephesians 5:1–2).

As we live out our calling in the world, keep in mind the character of our God as revealed in scripture. God's love is always "other-directed" (Kenneson 1999, 41). God could have compelled compliance from Israel, or certainly permitted Israel's total destruction. Yet God's patient love made space for Israel's disobedience. In some sense, God was willing to give up control for the purpose of building a people who would worship God faithfully (Kenneson 1999, 110).

In your ministry within the community of faith, may God's love in you be a patient love for self and others. The Holy Spirit now sent for the Church's witness and life will be God's ever-present power in your life. The Holy Spirit will make the presence of Jesus real in you and among all believers as you seek to witness in the world (Acts 1:8). In your calling to ministry build a life with God's blueprint and direction. Open your heart and mind to learn from God and from whomever God sends your way.

Building a life accompanies the quest to live a very human life among the peoples of the world. Building a life is a process though. It will not happen overnight or next week. Just as building anything of value and permanence takes time, building a life *out of the call to ministry* will be an ongoing process for you. It will also be a process for the men, women, boys, and girls you will serve in the name of Jesus. So look at the faces of your neighbors—the waitress at the local restaurant, the teller at the community bank, the young person hanging out on the street corner, the anxious patient in the hospital, the dutiful postal employee who brings your mail, your spouse or very close friend, and the numberless other faces around you. Realize that in living among them and interacting with them you are honoring God's call on your life of ministry.

GO FORTH BY GOD'S MERCY AND GRACE, AND BUILD A
LIFE THAT HONORS GOD AND SERVES YOUR FELLOW
HUMAN BEINGS IN THE WORLD!

Reference List

Kenneson, Philip D. 1999. *Life on the Vine: Cultivating the Fruit of the Spirit in Christian Community.* Downers Grove, Il: InterVarsity Press.

Nouwen, J. M. 1989. *In the Name of Jesus: Reflections on Christian Leadership.* New York: The Crossroad Publishing Company.

IV.

Overcoming–

skills for winning the war

"Let anyone who has an ear listen to what the Spirit is saying to the churches. To everyone who conquers, I will give permission to eat from the tree of life that is in the paradise of God" (Revelation 2:7 NRSV).

The rate of attrition from a life in Christian ministry in recent decades has been staggering. The number of persons leaving vocational ministry in North America has consistently dwarfed the number of those beginning that same pathway. No church has escaped denomination or movement.

The person who perseveres in the faith and endures is considered an overcomer. Robert Mounce comments upon the use of the term in the book of Revelation: "The overcomer in Revelation is not one who has conquered an earthly foe by force, but one who has remained faithful in Christ to the very end" (Mounce, 90).

The pastoral wisdom in this section will not guarantee fruitfulness and health in your ministry. However, we believe that you will find here insights that will aid you in beginning well and in the establishment of solid principles for an enduring course of vocational Christian ministry. Pastoral ethics that reflect Christian values, understanding congregational culture, basic insights for financing ministry in the church, and learning how to restore the wounded provide a sound foundation on which to construct a life in Christian ministry.

Our Lord is an overcomer! With him, we discover wisdom and strength to overcome in our journey.

"Now to him who is able to keep you from falling, and to make you stand without blemish in the presence of his glory with rejoicing, to the only God our Savior, through Jesus Christ our Lord, be glory, majesty, power, and authority, before all time and now and forever. Amen" (Jude 24–25, NRSV).

Mounce, Robert H. 1977. *New International Commentary on the New Testament: The Book of Revelation.* Grand Rapids: Eerdmans.

Chapter Thirteen:
Fred and Kay Shively, *Pastoral Ethics*

The importance of ethics in a minister's life cannot be overrated. The system of moral values by which we live undergirds and informs every aspect of our lives. The word *ethics* derives from the Greek *ethos*, which means character. The minister's character is the basis of his or her ministry. Perhaps we might well paraphrase Paul to say, "If I speak in the tongues of *mortals* and of angels, but have not *character*, I am a noisy gong or a clanging cymbal."[1] In the final analysis, what really matters is not how well we preach, how strong our evangelistic charisma, or how well we administer the church's business. What it all comes down to at the end is what kind of persons we are.

One's ethics can be thought of as a set of principles of right conduct, a system of moral values, or the rules or standards governing one's behavior. It might be reasonable to think that ministers, above all persons, would live by an unshakable set of principles based on Scripture. After all, Christianity teaches that we have an infallible guide in Jesus. Every Christian is supposed to make Jesus Christ the Lord of his/her life. We are supposed to be able to say with Paul, "Be imitators of me as I am of Christ."[2] It might be reasonable to think that a minister's character would be above reproach, that he or she would never behave unethically or immorally. It might be reasonable—but it would also be naive. More ministers have shipwrecked because of unethical behavior

---

Note: The authors have chosen to address the gender problem inherent in referring to ministers, who will be both male and female, by alternating pronouns when using the plural seemed less satisfactory. They apologize for any inconvenience to the reader caused by this admittedly imperfect solution.

than have ever done so because of wrong theology or doctrine. We cannot assume that ministers, any more than anyone else, will automatically be persons of character.

What makes a person of character? It does not automatically happen once one becomes a Christian, studies for the ministry, or earns the approval of one's peers by ordination. In fact, being a person of character is not automatic at all. Developing an ethical framework that will help us steer through the perils of life requires a firm commitment and ever-vigilant attention. We will look in this chapter at several characteristics embodied by a person of character.

Integrity

The linchpin of character is integrity. We generally associate integrity with honesty, but it is more than honesty. The word originates from a Latin word meaning _whole_ or _complete_. A person of integrity possesses wholeness, a soundness of character. All of the parts of her life fit together. She is the same person wherever we see her, whatever the circumstance. To know her is to know basically how she will behave in important matters. Transparent is a word that describes her. She is the same with one person as with another. In fact, she is the same when no one is watching, because she knows who she is. Her behavior depends not on others, but on herself. Shakespeare's famous words, spoken by Polonius in _Hamlet_, are good advice about integrity:

> "To thine own self be true.
> And it must follow, as the night the day,
> Thou canst not then be false to any man." [3]

The minister who has integrity need not fear that his wife, or his children, will "give him away" by telling "what he's really like at home." He is the same person at home as in public. Who we really are, as a matter of fact, is who we are at home. When the person of integrity stands in the pulpit, he can look his family in the eye and know that the words of Scripture that he shares, the sermons that he preaches, will come through to them with no barriers. He need not fear that they will be thinking, "Why don't you preach it to yourself?" He has already preached it to himself before preaching it in the pulpit, and has made certain that his life measures up.

The minister of character practices financial integrity. Particularly in small towns, ministers seem to have historically had a reputation for not paying their bills on time. True, their salaries are often meager. But one dare not use an inadequate salary as an excuse for financial irresponsibility. Whether they fear that others will know or not, ministers must be scrupulously careful to leave clear financial records that they could show to anyone without shame. Most American people live today on credit. Doing so is precarious for anyone, but especially for a minister. Living within one's means is one mark of character.

Though rare in the past, an increasingly common occurrence today is a minister with a former marriage, and children by that marriage—children for whom the minister is financially responsible. For a minister to refuse to pay—or to be derelict in paying—child support is a scandal that must not be tolerated and might well be grounds for a credential review.

Truthfulness is a key aspect of integrity. Ministers have also had a reputation for exaggeration, for glossing over or stretching the truth in order to make themselves look better. As a professional group, ministers seem more than usually concerned about the impression they make on others, perhaps because of unrealistic expectations held for them by the entire religious community. They dare not appear less than successful or perfect. They sometimes feel much pressure, therefore, to claim that the church is experiencing greater numerical or spiritual growth than is true or that everything is rosy and problem-free, lest people think they are not doing a good job. Can we dare to tell the truth, even when we don't look so successful by the telling?

At the same time, truthfulness is a complex issue. When to speak and when to be silent requires sensitivity—and honesty with oneself. One may tell the truth with a variety of motives. Truth that should not be told can be more damaging than a lie. When we consider how much of the truth to tell, we should consider the purpose of the telling. The fact that someone will be inconvenienced, angered, or even hurt by the truth may not be reason enough for not telling, if another person will be injured by not knowing. "Who needs to know?" and "What will be gained—and

lost—by the telling?" are important questions to ask. Will the hearer
be given important information or just juicy news? Will another person
be unnecessarily hurt? Paul's admonition in Ephesians 4:15 offers an
excellent test: that we "speak the truth in love." In "The Fool's Prayer,"
Edward Rowland Sill has the court jester, in a moment of great seriousness, pray these words:

> The ill-timed truth we should have kept,
> Who knows how sharp it pierced and stung!
> The word we had not sense to say,
> Who knows how grandly it had rung! [4]

The question of truthfulness leads us to another aspect of integrity,
trustworthiness. That ministers are expected to keep confidences should
go without saying. Yet, ministers are sometimes less careful about
guarding confidences than they should be. People are often more willing to be vulnerable with ministers than with anyone else, baring their
souls, telling things they have never shared with another person, things
they may even regret telling in a later, more guarded moment. Imagine
their great shame to hear themselves referred to as "Exhibit A" in a
future sermon. They may not be mentioned by name, of course, but they
recognize themselves, and because they do, they assume that everyone
else will recognize them as well. A minister should never divulge even
what appears to be the most harmless information about another without
prior permission. This rule applies, perhaps especially applies, to one's
spouse and children. A minister's family should never be "broad-sided"
by hearing family stories told from the pulpit or reported back to them
from a meeting. No matter how innocuous the anecdote seems, a minister of integrity will ask permission before sharing it publicly. And if
permission is not given willingly, it will go untold.

Much of what we are saying can be summed up by the word respect.
A minister of character respects other persons—respects their privacy
and their personal boundaries. Of course, respect for others is dependent
first upon one's self-respect. Jesus said something similar to that when
he referred to the second commandment; we must love others as we
love ourselves. We can respect others only if we respect ourselves.

A minister's integrity may be compromised or even destroyed by any
number of temptations. Many of these lie in wait for ministers, but the

"big three" are the same for ministers as for everyone else: sex, money, and power. In his book by the same title, Richard Foster speaks of the great need for a disciplined Christian response to these temptations.[5] These three were recognized by the monastics of the Middle Ages as they took vows of poverty (confronting money), chastity (confronting sex), and obedience (confronting power).

In a symbolic way, Jesus was faced with the same challenges in the wilderness at the beginning of his ministry. The thought of turning the rock into a stone was a temptation to passion, to satisfy the desires of the flesh. The challenge to leap from the pinnacle of the temple was a temptation to pride, to demonstrate super-human abilities to all those watching. The offer for him to rule the nations of the world was the temptation to power, to have control over many people. The temptations to both power and pride are related closely to the mis-use of money, which has been in both Jesus' day and our own, a symbol of power.

It is also important to note that Jesus' temptations did not end with the wilderness experience. He had to rely upon the power of God his entire life to confront the temptation to turn away from the suffering that inevitably awaited him in Jerusalem. His prayer in the Garden of Gethsemane, "Not my will but yours be done," [6] was his final victory over these temptations.

How Important is Character to the Church?

Is the minister's character important to the person in the pew? What are the characteristics that the people in churches want to see most in persons called to serve as professional ministers? A study by the Association of Theological Schools in 1987 produced some interesting results.[7] All of the characteristics at the very top relate to personal qualities or virtues. Ranking number one are concerns that this person be willing to do "service without regard for acclaim." This includes the ability to recognize one's own emotional and physical limitations; to laugh easily, especially at oneself; and to believe the message that one preaches.

The second highest factor is maintaining personal integrity even in the face of pressure to compromise. This person is able to honor commitments and to keep promises. This virtue includes the ability to work independently without prodding and to relate non-defensively with others. Ironically, ministers join other professionals in sometimes scoring high on the Defensiveness Scale of the Minnesota Multiphasic Personality Inventory (MMPI).[8]

The third factor relates to living out a Christian example that calls forth respect from others, including such virtues as generosity and moral behavior that is above reproach. There is also congruence (oneness) between what one says and what one does. Only in the fourth and fifth highest virtues do we find a move from personal characteristics to ministry skills, and these also include personal qualities. The fourth describes responsible functioning, the demonstration of competence and personal responsibility in completing tasks. This includes the willingness to grow and develop pastoral skills, to accept differences, the ability not to be threatened by the "success" of others.

The fifth quality is community building—doing those things that bring people together. It includes taking time to get to know people well, learning traditions and customs before attempting to bring change, developing trust, helping people to know that they are needed, and seeking to understand those who may be discontented. This quality calls for honesty and the ability genuinely to appreciate people as they are.

After including two ministry skills (perceptive counseling—sixth, and the ability to think theologically—seventh), this study returns to a minister's ability to handle stress calmly while affirming others (eighth) and the ability to acknowledge one's own limitations and mistakes and to be open to continued growth and learning (ninth).

At the bottom end of the scale, describing characteristics least desired, people say they do *not* want a self-serving minister, a person who avoids intimacy by critical and demeaning behavior. This kind of minister exercises power by belittling or condemning others. The next most serious qualities involve illicit sexual behavior and actions that shock or offend. The third most serious set of problems centers on emotional immaturity and actions that demonstrate insensitivity. These responses suggest that persons today are looking for ministers who acknowledge their humanness while exhibiting Christian character.

The Unmarried Minister

In the Protestant world, an assumption seems to prevail that ministers are, or should be, married. A significant number of ministers, however, will be single for at least part of, if not their entire, professional lives. It should go without saying that the expectations of character and integrity discussed here apply regardless of one's marital state. Unmarried ministers will face many of the same challenges as their married colleagues, but some will be uniquely their own, whether they have never married or find themselves suddenly single as a result of divorce or death.

Particularly for younger ministers, some parishioners will be tempted to look upon them as if they were sons or daughters who haven't yet really settled down as mature adults. Parishioners may assume that they are "lonely." They may intrude on the minister's private life and even expect that the minister will welcome such intrusion. They may be ever vigilant for opportunities to lend help or advice. A particularly frustrating challenge is the assumption among many parishioners that everyone wants—or needs—to be married. Even more mature unmarried ministers will face the inevitable matchmaker whose mission is to find them a mate. With all of these challenges, the unmarried minister must have a strong sense of appropriate boundaries and graciously fend off attempts to violate those boundaries. Time, social life, home, and other aspects of the minister's personal life should be respected just as they should be for a minister with a spouse and children.

Some unmarried ministers will, indeed, wish to pursue romantic relationships, albeit without assistance from parishioners. They are entitled to date, to engage in mutually satisfying romantic relationships, and to seek for a life mate; however, they will need to exercise discretion and discipline. It is highly inadvisable for a minister to date persons with whom he or she has a pastoral relationship. If the minister wishes to pursue a serious relationship with a person under his/her pastoral care, the parties are encouraged to discuss the situation with a mentor whom they trust, They are further encouraged to make responsible adjustments such as a temporary change of worship location for the parishioner or change of employment for the minister. While such advice may seem restrictive, ministers should recognize the dual relationship inherent in such a situation (dual relationships will be discussed in a following section). They should also recognize the wisdom of being able to pursue one's personal relationships away from the scrutiny of an intensely interested congregation.

Sexuality is one of God's most delightful gifts. God created us from the beginning as sexual beings and declared that creation to be good. Used responsibly, our sexuality brings great joy and fulfillment into relationships. Misused, it wreaks unequaled emotional, psychological, and spiritual havoc. Just as sexual fidelity is required of married ministers, celibacy is expected of unmarried ministers. The minister of character will live with sexual integrity.

Marriage and Family . . . Ministry Style

Gone, hopefully, are the days when married ministers were expected to sacrifice their families on the altars of the church. In that era, the church was seen as synonymous with God. Since God's call on our lives takes priority, the reasoning went, so must God's work—the church. It was a conviction held not only by parishioners, but by ministers and their families as well. It was sincere, born of a desire to serve God faithfully with all that one was. But it wreaked a terrible destruction in many ministers' homes. Many a minister's wife bore her loneliness in silent bitterness, struggling with the guilt of resenting God and the church for demanding so much of her husband's time. While her husband was counseling and praying with parishioners, her own hurts went unnoticed. Ministers' sons and daughters walked away from the church in disappointment and anger, wishing they were not the pastor's own children so they could receive some of the attention they saw other children receive.

In recent years, thankfully, we have begun to recognize that God's call on us includes a call to love our families well. The Ephesians 5 passage in which Paul admonishes husbands to love their wives was meant for all husbands, including those who are ministers. When Paul encourages husbands and wives (1 Corinthians 7) to grant each other their "conjugal rights," he is, again, speaking to all married Christians. Indeed, we should read every scripture in which we are taught how to treat others as being meant not only for our neighbors or fellow church-goers, but for our own families. What would be the result if every minister applied Colossians 3:12–14 to his own family relationships: "As God's chosen ones, holy and beloved, clothe yourselves with compassion, kindness,

184

humility, meekness, and patience. Bear with one another and, if anyone has a complaint against another, forgive each other; just as the Lord has forgiven you, so you also must forgive. Above all, clothe yourselves with love, which binds everything together in perfect harmony"?

Likewise, the minister's relationship with his children must be loving and gentle. Paul's words in Ephesians are again important: "Fathers, do not provoke your children, or they may lose heart."[9] Children are to be disciplined, to be sure, but the correct definition of discipline is teaching, not punishment. The minister of character will be careful to discipline his children in the spirit of Christ. A minister who cannot practice self-control in disciplining his children is in serious spiritual trouble. It is inexcusable that he be physically, verbally, or emotionally abusive to his children. Such abuse is in reality spiritual abuse of the most damaging kind.

Just as we have noted that good character does not develop automatically, a good marriage also does not occur spontaneously. A good marital relationship requires a commitment of time—quantity time, not just "quality" time. The minister must make clear to a congregation that her family relationships are a priority. Each family must find a schedule that works for them. The important thing is that the minister's family recognize that they are a priority in her life. The truth is, of course, that male ministers may find balancing job and family more difficult than do female ministers. Our society still assumes that mothers are obligated to be available to their children and spouses; we do not excuse their neglecting their families for the job. However, the same is not true for men. Society still praises—and rewards—the man who leaves home before daybreak and doesn't return until sometime after the dinner hour. Male ministers who make a strong commitment to their families may face criticism from congregation and community alike. Nevertheless, it must be done.

A sound and happy marriage is the most effective defense against one of the most tragic sins to which anyone can succumb—infidelity. Reports of sexual misconduct among ministers have become increasingly common. Evangelical authors Stanley J. Grenz and Roy D. Bell note that sexual misconduct is so common among ministers that insurance companies are "limiting their coverage of abuse cases or excluding it altogether."[10] They claim that it has reached "epidemic proportions."[11]

Statistics are not easily obtained, but those that do exist indicate that ministers are unfaithful at least as frequently as secular counselors, if not more frequently.[12]

One of the first surveys on the subject was taken for a Ph.D. dissertation at Fuller Seminary in 1984. Of 300 ministers surveyed, 12.7% reported that they had had sexual intercourse with a parishioner, and 39% admitted to "sexual contact." Grenz and Bell also cite a report by Peter Rutter (*Sex in the Forbidden Zone*), as well as a 1987 survey by *Christianity Today* giving virtually the same figures.[13] And Jim and Sally Conway claim in *Sexual Harassment No More* that 37% of ministers surveyed admit to "inappropriate sexual behavior."[14] As Grenz and Bell point out, such statistics may indicate only the proverbial tip of the iceberg, since they usually cover only ministers willing to self-report such behavior.

On the one hand, infidelity in a minister seems unthinkable. Yet, we all know that it happens. How can this be? Of course, it begins, as does any sin, with a spiritual problem. Rarely do ministers who succumb to temptations to compromise set out to do so. In conversations of ministers concerning pastors who have fallen to sexual temptation, it is not unusual for at least one to respond, "I would never do that." The wise person will avoid such a statement, because he or she will realize that anyone is susceptible to such temptation. When one thinks oneself invulnerable, when one's guard is down, the possibility of such a tragedy is greatest. No one is exempt from the possibility of falling.

Warning: Danger Zones

The siren songs that ambush ministers come subtly and without apparent warning. In order to avoid them, one must be aware of everyday realities. As the philosopher Socrates urged, "Know yourself." How can we know who might be at risk for such behavior? A number of warning signs of vulnerability that may lead particularly to sexual misconduct have been identified by counselors. R. S. Epstein and R. I. Simon developed an "Exploitation Index"[15] to help identify persons who might be at risk of violating sexual boundaries. A practitioner (in this case, a minister) is at risk when she begins to drop her guard and grow lax in paying attention to warning signs. Epstein and Simon separated beginning signs from secondary violations. In the early stages, a person can be helped to avoid crossing the boundary. The boundaries they identified are general violations, eroticism, exhibitionism, dependency, power seeking, greed, enabling, and aberrant behaviors. It is important to note that crossing sexual boundaries is often accompanied by other dynamics involving power, greed, and pride.

Raymond Brock and Horace Lukens suggest that a minister who recognizes any of the following signs in his/her behavior should seek counseling or consultation.[15]

- Working late to avoid going home to one's spouse and/or children.
- Making pastoral calls on the way home and having unpredictable arrival times, frequently missing dinner or other "off-duty" times.
- Not taking days off. When days off are taken, the spouse is not included in plans.
- Being "always available" to parishioners.
- Excessive self-disclosure to a parishioner (especially about intimate issues).
- Unless counseling is a full-time assignment, the tendency to counsel more than 10 hours a week while trying to keep up with the other tasks of ministry.
- Unwillingness to refer parishioners to appropriate professionals.
- Beginning to dream or fantasize about colleagues, counselees, or parishioners.
- Finding oneself repeatedly attracted to other women or men.
- Needing the excitement of public exposure (the limelight) and congregational response to compensate for the lack of personal and family fulfillment.
- Fostering dependency of others upon oneself in order to feel important or powerful.
- Failing to maintain a personal devotional life beyond pulpit preparation.
- Believing that "I don't need" supervision, consultation, personal counseling, or professional support.

Other danger signs include the following:

- Turning to church members to meet emotional needs.
- Failure of prayer and personal spiritual nurture.
- Lack of intimacy with spouse.
- Behavioral problems with children.
- Financial problems, financial irresponsibility.
- Recurrent difficulty with authority figures.
- Fatigue and stress brought on by building campaigns and other totally absorbing projects.
- Lack of awareness of boundary issues in the minis ter/parishioner relationship.
- Ambivalence about power, refusal to acknowledge the
  power of a minister over others.
- Failure to understand the dynamic of transference and counter-transference.

Transference is a common psychological dynamic of the counseling relationship in which the counselee (parishioner) develops a dependence relationship upon the counselor (minister). The minister then becomes a vitally important person in the parishioner's life, someone they think they cannot live without. This dynamic is not unusual and is not, within itself, altogether harmful. A wise counselor/minister will help the parishioner to understand this dependency, along with its impact and potentially dangerous effects on both persons.

The problem comes when the minister begins to experience counter-transference, coming also to see the parishioner as a vital person, some-one he cannot do without. Ministers often have a strong need to be needed. This need makes the minister vulnerable to this co-dependent relationship. The parishioner idealizes the minister as, perhaps, the most gentle, understanding person in the world, "the only person who truly understands and cares about me." Such an idealized position is a heady experience for a minister who may feel otherwise unappreciated or mis-understood. As both of the dynamics of transference and counter-trans-ference go unchecked, they develop into mutual expressions of concern and intimacy. Words become actions. What began innocently as genu-ine concern has been gradually subverted into an emotionally devastat-ing relationship with the potential of hurting many other persons.

We should point out here that, while such relationships may evolve into sexual affairs, such does not have to be the case in order for the results to be devastating. The relationship may be described as "romantic" rather than explicitly sexual. Or it may be an emotional (even "spiritual") intimacy. Let us make no mistake: any degree of intimacy in which the minister abandons his/her own boundaries and enters into a mutually needy relationship with a parishioner is wrong and is a violation of the trust which has been placed in him/her. Ministers have a fiduciary responsibility for their parishioners. That is, they holds the spiritual and emotional well-being of the congregation in their hands as a trust from God and enjoy thereby a special relationship of confidence and trust among the people. Entering into a self-serving relationship not only betrays that trust but renders one incapable of fulfilling one's obligations to parishioners.

A study by David Richards in 1993[16] showed three types of inappropriate acting out, listed here in the order of increasing seriousness: 1) the temporary affair, 2) the extended relationship, and 3) the courtship/stepping stone relationship. The temporary affair usually happens to the person who has never had such a relationship and who has become vulnerable, perhaps by some crisis, and who reaches out for support. Although the relationship is temporary, if the causes are not addressed, the person may be vulnerable for other, even more devastating affairs.

An extended relationship creates more pain. The marriage of either party is at great risk, and extensive therapy may be necessary for healing. In the stepping stone relationship, the minister may be considered a sexual predator who intentionally sets out to establish the relationship. Persons like this have often learned to manipulate and use others for self-gratification. Obviously, this behavior needs to be identified, confronted, and disciplined.

How can a minister avoid falling to temptation? Being well educated in the dynamics of minister-parishioner relationships is critical. The minister must maintain a vital relationship of prayer and be willing to search her heart honestly. An open, loving relationship to one's spouse is essential. Marriage enrichment experiences (formal or informal) can nurture the marital relationship. An accountability relationship with a ministerial colleague or small group of colleagues can be an asset. The minister must also be aware of the signs of burnout and avoid it by paying attention to a balanced schedule and getting proper rest, recreation, relaxation, and renewal.

We must acknowledge that there are widely accepted practices in the church that place the minister in a precarious position. In the first place, ministers are generally handed an unquestioning trust. Second, they often have a good measure of discretionary time, being able to come and go with little accountability to anyone. Add to this the fact that they are expected to counsel parishioners, often in private, about the most intimate details of their lives. Finally, the church's "family" vocabulary encourages, if not demands, intimacy between pastor and parishioners. We exchange not only handshakes, but hugs, at the slightest provocation. A minister who does not warm to such displays may be criticized as cool, even unloving. A major adjustment in the mentality of both the church and the ministry might be advisable at this point. Warmth and caring can be displayed at the same time that one practices appropriate restraint. Cultural differences dictated by geographic and ethnic customs should, of course, be considered. Behavior thought obligatory in one congregation might be thought inappropriate in another. The minister will soon learn the local customs. Beyond that, a good rule might be to restrict any action beyond a handshake to the public arena, in full view of others, and to be careful never to display any affection that would cause embarrassment or pain to one's own or the other person's spouse.

The ministerial relationship requires great caution in maintaining friendships in the congregation. Friendships are mutual relationships. Friends share their vulnerabilities, their frustrations, even their doubts and angers with each other. Some would suggest that the fiduciary responsibility ministers carry for the spiritual well-being of their parishioners precludes engaging in intimate friendships with parishioners. At the same time, we must also recognize that dual relationships (filling two roles with the same person) are to some extent inevitable as well as not altogether undesirable. Ministers usually live and socialize in the communities in which they minister and therefore cannot avoid—particularly in small communities—being neighbors, associates in various organizations, perhaps "Little League parents," customers, clients, patients, and filling other roles in addition to minister. Marie Fortune, a leading expert on clergy sexual misconduct, has created a graph[18] which demonstrates her philosophy that the more one develops intimate relationships in the church, the less effective one is likely to be as a spiritual guide or pastor. While she does not believe effective ministry occurs when the pastor is completely aloof from parishioners, she believes that somewhere in the middle of the graph the minister crosses a boundary from effective to ineffective ministry. The mutual sharing of deep needs and emotions in intimate friendships can place the minister's effectiveness in jeopardy. It is the minister's responsibility to monitor carefully all relationships and keep them in perspective, remembering that one's pastoral responsibilities take priority. After all, one's parishioners have other friends; the minister is their only pastor.

As ministers, we must exercise personal control over our time and behavior. We must establish kindly, but firmly, that we, not the parishioner, are responsible for setting the policies and boundaries. Practically, we can beware of compromising situations. We should have no secretive meetings with parishioners. Counseling should occur at the church, preferably with an open door or another person nearby. This admittedly compromises the privacy that a parishioner may want, but it is a protection for both persons. The number of counseling sessions with any one parishioner should be limited. If an issue has not been resolved in four sessions, the minister should refer the parishioner to a counselor with greater expertise. The minister's personal guidelines should be communicated to the congregation and followed without exception.

Summary

A middle-aged man introduced his minister-father to a congregation with these words: "He lives what he preaches." No greater tribute can be given than this affirmation by the ones who know us best. The ministry is a high calling that requires an absolute commitment to a Christlike life. We have emphasized that this commitment is no easy path that may be followed automatically simply because one has made an initial decision to follow Christ but requires prayerful, thoughtful attention to the meaning of God's call on our lives. We have acknowledged at the same time that others may hold ministers to unreasonable expectations of super-human perfection. We are not advocating an unrealistic, even sanctimonious caricature of piety, but a genuine desire to live a transformed life which, Paul reminds us in 1 Corinthians 12, is the calling given to anyone who would follow Christ.

Ministry takes place in real life, not in some cloistered, sanctified Holy of Holies where we are protected from the frustrations and temptations of the world. We live in the same world as our parishioners, and if they are to see that the Christian life is possible for them, they must see their minister successfully living it out. It is not always easy, but it is possible.

Both Paul and John referred to the rewards of living a life of integrity. Paul urged Timothy to have "faith and a good conscience," warning him that by rejecting a good conscience, some had suffered "shipwreck in the faith" (1 Timothy 1:19). And John urged his readers to love "not in word or speech but in truth and action," promising that "if our hearts do not condemn us, we have boldness before God" (1 John 3:18, 21).

The writer of Hebrews reminded us of our primary model for ministry, when he suggested, "Consider that Jesus, the apostle and high priest of our confession, was faithful to the one who appointed him" (Hebrews 3:1–2). Jesus demonstrated the meaning of integrity by being in his person what he taught. A young minister who was struggling to maintain a Christian lifestyle was asked, "What is the relationship of your life to your ministry?" "Well," he pondered. "My life influences my ministry." "No," replied the questioner, "your life is your ministry."

End Notes

[1] 1 Corinthians 13:1 (NRSV).

[2] 1 Corinthians 11:1 (NRSV).

[3] *Hamlet*, William Shakespeare, ed. Thomas Marc Parrott (New York: Charles Scribner's Sons, 1953). Act I, Scene III, lines 78–80.

[4] "The Fool's Prayer," Edward Rowland Sill, *The New Home Book of Best Loved Poems*, ed. Richard Charlton MacKenzie (Garden City, NY: Garden City Publishing Co., 1946), 319–20.

[5] Richard J. Foster, *Money, Sex, and Power* (New York: Harper & Row, 1985).

[6] Luke 22:42b (NRSV).

[7] Adapted from "Affair Prevention in the Ministry," Raymond T. Brock and Horace C. Lukens in *Journal of Psychology and Christianity*, Vol. 8, 1989.

[8] William G. Dahlstrom and George S. Welsh, *An MMPI Handbook: A Guide to Use in Clinical Practice and Research* (Minneapolis: University of Minnesota Press, 1960), 269–73.

[9] Ephesians 6:4.

[10] Stanley J. Grenz and Roy D. Bell, *Betrayal of Trust: Sexual Misconduct in the Pastorate* (Downers Grove, IL: InterVarsity Press, 1995), 19.

[11] Grenz and Bell, 20.

[12] Grenz and Bell, 21.

[13] Grenz and Bell, 22–23.

[14] Peter Iadicola, "Criminology's Contributions to the Study of Religious Crime," in *Wolves Within the Fold: Religious Leadership and Abuses of Power*, ed. by Anson Shupe (New Brunswick, NJ: Rutgers U.P., 1998), 217.

[15] R. S. Epstein and R. I. Simon, "The Exploitation Index: An Early Warning Indicator of Boundary Violation in Psychotherapy." *Bulletin of the Menninger Clinic*, 54, 450–65.

[16] Adapted from "Affair Prevention in the Ministry," Brock and Lukens.

[17] Gary C. Augustin, "Factors Found with Clergy Involved in Sexual Misconduct," *American Journal of Pastoral Counseling*, Vol. 1, No. 1, 1997.

[18] Marie Fortune, Trainer's Manual for *Clergy Misconduct: Sexual Abuse in the Ministerial Relationship,* Seattle, WA: Center for the Prevention of Sexual and Domestic Violence.

Chapter Fourteen:
Joseph Cookston, *Understanding Congregational Culture*

To passersby, one of the identifying exterior marks of New Life Church was the sizeable bus that usually occupied a spot in the south parking lot under the mercury vapor light. Painted a royal blue with a striking band of silver-painted fish signs just below the passenger windows, the bus had been long-time dubbed the Blue Whale by at least two generations of riders.

Thought more or less roadworthy by most members of the congregation, the Blue Whale had become more of the latter in recent months. For starters, three months ago thirty-four retreatants had been stranded in a distant state while making their way to ski slopes. Recently, when weather conditions turned sultry with high humidity, two persons were kept busy wiping condensation from inside the windshield. With a high volume of outside air blowing in from fully open windows, two passengers barely avoided asthma attacks.

Youth pastor Dana was convinced the time was right to change the way New Life provided transportation for youth events: permanently park the Blue Whale and move toward contracting vehicles for specific uses.

In her first year of ministry, Dana was little less than shocked by the resistance she encountered. Most who heard of her suggestion reacted negatively. Board members bulked at the idea. Parents reeled at the thought of increased costs. Even some youth weren't sure about the prospect of not having their own bus.

What seemed to be a perfectly logical conclusion to Dana had met with surprising opposition from most persons in the congregation. Dana did well to step back and consider an important dimension of her congregation, what some have come to identify as a congregation's culture.

Understanding Congregational Culture

Thinking about congregations as organizations that possess something akin to a particular culture is relatively new. For some time, congregational analysts have looked at congregations through such helpful lenses as the need for clear articulation of mission, vision and purpose statements; leadership styles; organizational structures; systems relationships; and similar concerns. Applying the idea of culture to the congregational discussion is proving to be a productive way of understanding more clearly the intersection of ministry practice and congregational dynamics. Let's take a longer look at what the study of culture is.

What Is The Study of Culture?

For many years, studies of culture have been more or less confined to studies of larger people groups of the world. The preoccupation of the study of culture is to identify the differences among people groups. Cultural studies observe the visible aspects of a society—symbols, stories, social patterns—then analyze those aspects for shared values, norms, and meanings of the group members.

Aspects of culture specifically focus on the idea of how a group of people makes meaning for themselves, how they put their world together, how they come to understand their experiences, what has happened to them, and what their future actions will be. Important variables that stress those kinds of meanings are the values and goals of a particular culture.

Culture embodies notions of many levels of meaning. People who work in culture studies use these kinds of descriptions: thick descriptions of habitual and traditional ways of thinking, feeling, reacting (Kluckholm 1961), interactions among people (Ernest 1985), accumulated learning over a period of time (Kluckholm 1961/ Schein 1990), the way a group solves problems of survival—external and internal (Kluckholm 1961/ Schein 1990), a guide for new members (Ernest 1985), metaphor and images of order (Smircich 1983), complex group norms (Maehr and

Braskamp 1986), and shared understandings and values communicated through cultural forms (Beyer and Trice 1987).

In the past two decades the idea of culture has been borrowed to describe smaller collections of people who share some kinds of connectedness and history together: nations, regions, communities, organizations, corporations, schools and even congregations. Current researchers view culture as a critical variable within an organization, one necessary in understanding a particular group of people.

What Is Congregational Culture?

The definitions of culture are numerous. Organizational researcher Edgar Schein offers one of the more helpful descriptions—a six-part definition for organizational culture that encompasses many of the above descriptions:

> (a) a pattern of basic assumptions, (b) invented, discovered, or developed by a given group, (c) as it learns to cope with its problems of external adaptation and internal integration, (d) that has worked well enough to be considered valid and, therefore (e) is to be taught to new members as the (f) correct ways to perceive, think, feel in relation to those problems (Schein 1985).

Let's unpack that definition as it may apply to the congregation.

(a) A pattern of basic assumptions

Over time congregations forge a common sense of history, values, and purpose through a collective interpretation by its members. As people in congregations gain more history together, they move from a focus on the individual toward a focus more on the group. Patterns of thinking and behavior emerge as the group interprets and works through the realities that confront them. This pattern of basic assumptions makes up the context for the interpretation of an ordered system of meaning within which persons in the congregation relate to each other, their immediate communities, the environment, and the world.

(b) Invented, discovered, or developed by a given group

Congregational culture is the outcome of group learning (Schein 1985). Critical events, or marker events, give shape to a congregation's basic assumptions. Events like prolonged revival, death of a significant leader, natural disaster, survival against enormous odds, or physical healing give shape to the beliefs and assumptions of a congregation. The reconstruction and retelling of a congregation's history reveals that the formation of assumptions and beliefs happen around events that are experienced in hindsight as critical, in the sense that they involved high levels of emotionality and clear rethinking of those things that define the congregation.

Group norms often arise from these critical events. When a congregation eventually comes to recognize a particular feeling, experience, or activity as common, members embrace certain shared understandings about themselves. These understandings which become part of the cultural fiber of the congregation include group anxieties, emotional responses, overt actions, and emotional releases.

(c) As it learns to cope with its problems of external adaptation and internal integration

Congregations learn. Through critical events in congregational life, congregations take on perceptions and approaches to problem solving that arise from repeated attempts to resolve tension or bring understanding. Two mechanisms are helpful in describing how groups like congregations learn: (1) positive problem solving and (2) pain and anxiety reduction.

Positive problem solving

Learning outcomes are positive if they are rewarding—rewarding in the sense that they reflect the achievement of some goal or satisfy some felt need. Certain behavior, ways of thinking, sets of feelings or beliefs, or new assumptions can be positively reinforced if they simply solve the problem at hand.

Anxiety reduction

The goal in anxiety reduction learning is simply to reduce pain or to lessen anxiety. Learning comes from avoidance of what is thought to be undesirable. More or less trial-and-error, this learning mechanism is less predictable and more unfocused in that the cause of the anxiety is not always known.

(d) That has worked well enough to be considered valid

Congregations certainly can be practical. One of the first steps in problem solving is to review what worked in the past. What were the structures, the words from Scripture or behaviors that helped achieve resolution to a particular dilemma? What beliefs about God and his purposes for a congregation sustained its church leaders through financial difficulty or legal engagement? What were the emotional responses that brought healing to relationships during the uncertain times of great transition?

To the degree that these instruments sustain a congregation with meaning and resolution to the dilemmas of its life together, they become valid approaches with which to engage future challenges. They become the first line defense mechanisms of the congregation.

(e) Is to be taught to new members

The longer the history of a congregation the greater time period over which to test how well certain beliefs and assumptions make sense and give identity and meaning to the congregation. The layers of stories, testimonies, successful programs, and systems of decision making are sufficient to form a commonly agreed upon way of doing things. The congregation has formed a reservoir of interpretations, norms, values and beliefs which bind people together and explain and interpret their way of fulfilling God's mission for them.

Out of this reservoir flow the tangible forms which symbolize their commonly shared values. These forms then become the practices whereby these meanings are expressed, affirmed, and communicated to new members through teaching classes, congregational rituals, commonly used language, symbols on letterhead, in the narthex, and sanctuary.

**(f) Correct ways to perceive, think, feel in
relationship to those problems.**

Over time congregations form a certain the way we do things around
here. That majority viewpoint arises from a conviction that members
have voted, one way or another, to determine that which defines and
gives purpose to their way of doing ministry and of being together in
congregation. There is a correctness about this way of viewing the interactions of the congregation that plays into the idea of a congregation's
self-image.

Congregations represent more than the aggregate faith of assembled
individuals. In similar fashion, though they may be connected to a larger church denomination or collection of congregations, each particular
congregation maintains a culture more or less distinct from the wider
church group. Dudley and Johnson describe this congregational identity:
"congregations carry a corporate character that is developed in response
to their experience in ministry. . . . One pivotal element of identity is a
congregational self-image that provides coherence to the members and
direction for their activities" (Dudley and Johnson 1993, 1). For better
or worse, this congregational self-image becomes the dominant mode of
operation.

What Are the Layers of Congregational Culture?

*Youth Pastor Dana stepped back from the rising emotional battle over
the Blue Whale. With a flicker of insight, she decided to take careful
note of responses from different groups of the congregation, responses
that tended to occur repeatedly.*

*She noted several persons from the elder board placed heavy emphasis
upon the church bus itself. Their concern seemed centered on the fact of
the bus, "We have the bus, let's use it. Fix it if we have to, but let's keep
it on the road. We've always had a church bus." Some pointed out that
the use and maintenance of the church bus are prescribed in the church
by-laws. Besides the by-laws, the scheduling of the church bus is in the
written job description of the youth pastor. The emphasis seemed to be
on the bus itself and the structures surrounding its upkeep and use.*

Furthermore, Dana noted that parents voiced their expectations that the church provide transportation to and from certain kinds of youth functions. They valued the opportunity for their kids to tour and serve at a distance from their community. The church ought to support excursions to camps, conventions, and extended service projects.

Through the weeks as Dana continued to pay attention to persons' comments and concerns, she began to detect a level of concern beyond the obvious. She began thinking that perhaps the Blue Whale wasn't so much the issue but deeper concerns that persons did not actually voice, only implied. For example, evidently a former youth pastor had given reason for congregational distrust of a youth pastor's ability to handle money matters. Therefore, congregational leaders must be cautious when changes in the youth program might involve increased funds. A related implication had to do with the degree to which a youth pastor could really be responsible. Dana sensed an underlying suspicion that her point of view could not be wholly seen as credible. Additionally, several board members seemed to have an unspoken conviction that it is preferable for the church to own large capital items. Renting is always money thrown away. Furthermore, the church must be a good steward of its money; renting is not good stewardship.

By writing down what she was hearing and observing, Dana began to question what she was really hearing and to make helpful connections among the multiple levels of concern that ultimately fostered conflict in the Blue Whale controversy.

Benjamin Schein (1991) comes to the rescue in helping to abbreviate the levels of organizational culture. He presents a three-layered framework that unpacks separate but interrelated strata for understanding culture. (Schein's references to organization have been altered to correspond with congregational descriptions.)

Artifact
Visible
creations of
a congregation
that identify a
congregation
Stories, rituals, recognitions, language, structures,
symbols, logos, personal
address,
(The Blue Whale)

Values
Strategies, goals, vision statements,
What ought to be
(The church ought to provide transportation.
Youth ought to have opportunity to travel.)

Assumptions
Unconscious, taken-for-granted beliefs and habits of
perception, thought and feeling; self-image
What is—the way we do things around here
(Youth pastors cannot handle money well, nor can they be entirely
trusted. Renting is poor stewardship.)

The creations of a congregation are what you see when you enter the building or mix with the people. You notice the way people dress and the changes of dress dictated by function. You listen to how people address each other. You walk through the physical layout of the building and the placement of people and different ministry areas. You notice the way technology and art is used, visible and audible patterns of behavior. You encounter personal stories, narratives of the congregation, choices of language describing religious themes and gestures of friendship. You notice objects made by the people, young and old, which express their goals and beliefs about God and God's purposes. **These are the artifacts of a congregation that emanate from the substantive reservoir of collective values.**

The values of a congregation are expressed openly and may be condensed into particular value statements: "people find a place to belong," "Christ is central," or "service is a way of life." **Values for a congre-**

gation are what ought to be, those commonly held assents which
are testable in congregation by common agreement. Values are particularly noted in congregational mission and vision statements and the
goals that result from these statements. Expectations of congregational
members, organizational by-laws, guiding documents, slogans, logos,
publication headlines, sermon series titles give evidence of congregational values.

*Developing out of shared experiences over a period of time, congre-
gational assumptions describe what actually is—the way things are
around here.* They are habits of perception, thought, feeling and emo-
tion and serve as the ultimate sources of value and artifact. As unconscious and taken-for-granted beliefs, these basic assumptions encompass
belief about a congregation's relationship to the surrounding world, the
nature of present realities, time and space; the nature of human relationships, human nature and human activity. These assumptions determine
life perceptions, thought processes and feelings and behavior of the congregation as a whole.

The insightful use of the culture idea to describe the social aspects of
the congregation assumes a continuity among these three cultural levels, an interlocking of assumptions, values and artifacts into patterns
that make sense. The strength of a congregation's culture and identity
depends to a large degree upon patterns which find rootage in compatible and consistent sets of assumptions, values, and artifacts (Cookston
1995, 48).

What's So Important About Congregational Culture And Congregational Ministry?

Aspiring ministers and church leaders have dreams and goals for their
congregations. These dreams and goals usually cause change in the
ways a congregation has been doing what it does. To the extent that
what a congregation has been doing is tied up in a purpose, meaning,
and self-image that have proved effective in solving congregational
problems for a significant time period, these changes may threaten
certain congregational basic assumptions. Moran and Volkwein (1992)
offer insightful characteristics of organizational culture that make strong
connections between congregational culture and congregational ministry.

• **Congregational culture is highly enduring.**

Congregational life is stable and persistent across time. Persons in congregations tend to respond in predictable, persisting patterns that are based on past experiences and their understanding of the meaning of those experiences.

Wise church leaders recognize the existence of enduring patterns of a congregation's way of thinking about and interpreting their circumstances and their responses to those circumstances. Ministry necessarily takes place within the peculiarities of a congregation and is, to some extent, shaped by those collective patterns.

• **Congregational culture evolves slowly.**

Patterns of values and beliefs in congregations develop over longer periods of time. The contrast in the density of cultural layers between newer church plants and older congregations, for example, is to be expected because of the inherent differences in time and critical events that have been shared.

Congregational purpose and meaning emerge through the interlocking of multiple experiences and times of reflection on the meaning of those experiences. High levels of personal investment by congregational members have been expended in the formation of those common assumptions.

Investment, personal or congregational, directly affects the rate of change. In ministry terms, the aware minister finds ways to discover the degree to which church people are heavily invested in a particular point of view or practice before innocently stepping on some cultural landmine.

• **Congregational culture is altered slowly.**

Because existing congregational assumptions are learned, new assumptions can also be learned. The rate of relearning, however, will correspond to the length of time those values have been held and the critical nature of the events that gave them credence.

The good news is that most agree that congregational culture can be changed, but that change usually proceeds at a slower pace than most ministers would like. As current congregational habits were learned, so can new habits eventually replace those that have, over time, become less effective.

- **Congregational culture operates at levels deeply embedded in collective unconsciousness.**

If asked, most members of a congregation would be unable to identify basic values or beliefs that steer their congregation. They may point to beliefs that are more doctrinal or generally Christian in nature. But the basic assumptions from which the life of their congregation takes its cues are likely to be more difficult to identify.

What people say in meetings and the official tally of votes does not always convey the true consensus of the congregation. Minutes and votes tend to reflect what persons think should or ought to be. What they really think oftimes comes to play out in informal settings like parking lot conversations after the meeting. When they occur, these conversations emerge from imperceptible assumption levels of congregational expectations and suspicions.

- **Congregational culture is invisible**.

The reason those assumptions are difficult to identify is that for the most part they flow from a subterranean reservoir in which have been gathered congregational habits of perception, feeling, and thought. Though invisible, these assumptions describe what actually is: the way things are around here.

Though invisible, these assumptions are not blocked from the minister's view. Congregational life abounds with cues about its invisible patterns of operation. Attentive ministers utilize skills like observing repetitious behavior patterns, listening for recurring themes and values in congregational stories, noting frequently used words and the meanings they convey, and the reasons for celebrations and recognitions.

What Are Implications for Ministers?

Taking the culture of a congregation seriously identifies at least two primary tasks for the effective minister. Both tasks are highly engaging with people and require a certain degree of ability for observing and interpreting of human behavior. The tasks involve (1) discovering and (2) influencing congregational culture.

Discovering congregation culture

In many ways, effective ministers become readers of their congregations. They need to know the patterns of their congregations, the ways people think and respond. The central tasks of reading pivot around the collective meanings of the particular congregation. The minister seeks to discover how recurring themes and symbols are linked into a meaningful whole and how these relate to the behavior patterns of people in the congregation.

This discovery work can be an exciting process as a minister engages in some simple yet productive tasks.

Observing—On occasion, step out of leadership roles. Observe the actions, speech patterns, inferences, repeated phrases, words of personal address, seating arrangements, frequent visual contact. Observations can be both formal (meetings) and informal (conversation in the church narthex). Simply note what you see. Give attention to what appears to be repeated observations.

Interviews—Invite persons to share their stories with you. Use lead-in statements such as: tell me about a particularly joyful time for you in this congregation or a particularly difficult time. What seems to pull this congregation together? What do people around here think is important?

Sorts—This approach is somewhat more directive. From your observations and conversations with people, select a group of words—ten or so—that have some degree of importance. Write each word on a note card. Such words might include: vision, no debt, risk, learning, friendships, community, service, harmony, tradition and the like.

Utilize sorts in a variety of ways. Ask individuals to select a certain number of words that have meaning for them, then words that they perceive have meaning for their congregation. They may put the selected words in priority and share their reasoning. They may select words that do not have meaning for them or their congregation. Sorts give persons a chance to think about the values, even the assumptions, that provide meaning for them and their congregation.

Synthesize—Collect the words, behaviors, and congregational patterns that tend to be repeated. Reflect on the connections and allow common themes to generate from what you have noted. These themes provide a strong indication of the values and assumptions that direct congregational life.

Influencing congregational culture

Dana was ready to present to the elder board her proposal supporting the demise of the Blue Whale and seeking alternative modes of transportation. She decided to address what she had come to understand as the underlying issues of the Blue Whale controversy. For the assumption that owning is always preferred over renting and that the church leaders must be good financial stewards, she would demonstrate that, though the rental approach would have some additional costs, those costs would be outweighed by savings in insurance, maintenance, and licensing. Additional pluses would be vehicle dependability, road service, and driver experience.

She planned to tap into the desire of parents for the church to provide means for their youth to participate in a wider range of off-site ministry opportunities. The church can continue to provide; however, the provision just looks different now than in the past.

By her thoughtful presentation with accurate figures and fact-finding, she hoped to communicate her own trustworthiness. Also, her manner of presentation and poise would add to a perception of her ability to act responsibly even during controversy.

Dana knew the process might be slow, but she felt prepared to begin helping a congregation change its assumptions about transportation

provision and, in the process, make room for another parking spot in
the south parking lot by the mercury vapor light.

It is a tantalizing prospect that a congregation's culture may be a critical key by which ministers and church leaders can influence and direct the course of their congregation. The belief is that, as organizations, congregations that have internal cultures supportive of their mission and vision are more likely to be successful. The task of ministers and church leaders is to find ways to let the future direction of the congregation emerge from the stories and symbols, the values and assumptions already in place in the congregation.

Tasks that tend to influence the shaping of congregational culture, while not difficult, are strategic. Such tasks focus on exploring ways to:

- Define clearly the central ministry tasks of the congregation;

- Announce frequently and in a variety of ways mission and vision statements;

- Make available information, training and motivation aligned with primary ministry tasks;

- Encourage persons to tell their stories;

- Find venues for persons to describe personal benefits for being involved in congregational ministry;

- Communicate congregational expectations to new members; and

- Build trusting relationships.

Final Thoughts

Congregational researcher James Wind presents a significant challenge regarding the whole enterprise of preparing persons for ministry. He suggests that "the discovery of congregational culture poses an interpretive challenge as sizable as that presented by the scriptures themselves.

Think of how much we invest in preparing people to exegete the scriptures. We need to make an equal investment in preparing people to exegete congregational life" (1993, 105).

As vital as the discipline of extracting meaning from the scriptures for contemporary life, so is the discipline of understanding the dynamics of congregational life.

Reference List

Beyer, J.M. and H.M. Trice. 1987. How an organization's rites reveal its culture. *Organizational Dynamics* 15(4):5–24.

Cookston, J.L. 1995. *Congregation culture: Contours of organizational influence upon lay leadership investment.* Dissertation for degree requirements Trinity International University, Deerfield, Il.

Dudley, C.S. and S. Johnson. 1991. *Congregational self images for social ministry. In Carriers of the faith: Lessons from congregational studies,* eds. C.S. Dudley, J.W. Carroll, and J.P. Wind. Louisville, Ky.: Westminster/John Knox Press.

Ernest, R.C. 1985. Corporate cultures and effective planning. *Personnel Administrator* 30(3): 49–60.

Hopewell, J.F. 1987. *Congregation: Stories and structures.* Philadelphia, Pa.: Fortress Press.

Kluckholn, C. 1951. The concept of culture. In *The policy sciences,* eds. D. Lerner and H. Lassell. Palo Alto, Calif.: Stanford University Press.

Maehr, M.L. and L.A. Braskamp. 1986. *The motivation factor: A theory of personal investment.* Lexington, Mass.: D.C. Heath & Company.

Moran, E.T., and J. F. Volkwein. 1992. The cultural approach to the formation of organizational climate. *Human Relations* 45(1): 19–47.

Schein, E.H. 1985. Organizational culture and leadership. San Francisco, Calif: Jossey-Bass.

———. 1990. Organizational culture. *American Psychologist* 45(2): 109–19.

———. 1991. The role of the founder in the creation of organizational culture. In *Reframing organizational culture* eds. P. J. Frost, L.F. Moore, M.R. Louis, C.C. Lundberg, and J. Martin. Newbury Park, Calif.: Sage Publications, Inc.

Schwarts, H. and S. Davis. 1981. Matching corporate culture and business strategy. *Organizational Dynamics* Summer: 1048.

Smircich, L. 1983. Concepts of culture and organizational analysis. *Administrative Science Quarterly* 28: 339–58.

———. 1985. Is the concept of culture a paradigm for understanding organizations and ourselves? In *Organizational Culture,* eds. P.J. Frost, L.F. Moore, M.R. Louis, C.C. Lundberg, and J. Martin. Beverly Hills, Calif.: Saga Publications, Inc.

Tichy, N.M. 1982. Managing change strategically: The technical, political, and cultural keys. *Organizational Dynamics* Autumn: 59-80.

Wind, J.P. 1993. Leading congregation, discovering congregational cultures. Christian Century 110(4): 105–10.

Chapter Fifteen:
Stan Toler, *Financing Ministry in the Church*

There's an interesting story about a man who was hiking in a mountain region. Coming across an old fashioned pump, he stopped for a drink. A tin cup was tied to the pump handle. The traveler noticed a note in the cup as he untied it. He quickly took the note from the cup and read it, "It is safe to drink from this well. I fixed the pump and put a new sucker washer in it. The washer dries out and the pump needs to be primed. Under the large white rock west of the well, there is a bottle of water. There's enough water in it to prime the pump, but not enough if you take a drink first. Pour a little of the water into the pump to soak the leather washer. Then pour in the rest of the water and pump fast. You'll soon get water."

The note continued, "Have faith. This well won't run dry. After you've pumped all the water you want, fill the bottle back up and put it where you found it. Put this note back in the cup and tie the cup to the handle. Another thirsty traveler will soon be along."

"This well won't run dry"—what a beautiful portrait of God's supply! The prophet reflected on it, " 'I will satisfy the priests with abundance, and my people will be filled with my bounty,' declares the LORD" (Jeremiah 31:14 NIV).

Jesus taught a similar truth about heavenly resources, "Give, and it will be given to you. A good measure, pressed down, shaken together and running over, will be poured into your lap. For with the measure you use, it will be measured to you" (Luke 6:38).

Successful local church ministry is not only refreshed by the well of

God's grace, it is also concerned with the other passersby—with teaching parishioners how to keep the supply alive by passing the blessing along. Receiving and giving are vital links in the chain of discipleship.

Dreams of growing the church will quickly perish without the means for carrying them out. Those "means" not only include Spirit-enabled and trained workers, they also include a vision and plan for receiving and distributing donations.

This chapter will serve as a guide for developing a plan to financing the local church ministries. In my book, *Developing a Giving Church,* the results of an interesting survey done by the Christian Stewardship Association is noted. It revealed that "85 percent of pastors feel they haven't been taught or empowered to teach principles of biblical stewardship and finance. It was also revealed that 90 percent of churches have no program to teach stewardship principles."[1]

You may be asking, "How do I mobilize the laity to become channels of God's resources? Where do I begin?"

There are five basic principles that have been forged in the fires of my own ministerial career. They are workable principles. I know that they work because they have worked for me through several building programs, over many years of financial planning and budgeting, and in several years of teaching them to Christian leaders and lay persons across North America.

> **"There is no happiness in the Christian life until we acknowledge God's ownership and try to grow in our sense of stewardship."**
> **—Doug Carter**

Principle One: Develop A Philosophy Of Giving.

The latter part of the twentieth century brought us an emphasis on philosophy-driven church ministries. Suddenly we began to realize that the what (program) of ministry is built on the *why* (purpose) of ministry. Rick Warren, Bill Hybels and others caused us to focus on the motivations behind our ministries rather than on its mechanics.

Church Models Though many churches share some of the same wording in their mission statements, the dynamics of how that mission is fulfilled vary greatly. No two churches are identical, no matter how similar their statements of purpose are. Each local church is as unique as a Scandinavian snowflake. The fulfillment of its mission varies with the abilities and "availabilities" of its members.

However, there are some similarities in the way local churches receive and disburse their funds.

Some churches are *Mom & Pop spenders.* In our "discount store chain" environment, it's always interesting to run across a little "Mom & Pop" grocery or hardware store holding out against the mega-stores. Mom & Pop stores aren't usually advertised during the nightly news segments. They usually don't have a contract with the local newspaper for full-page ads in the Sunday supplement. They live on the edge of obsolescence. Sometimes they are only a few payments away from fore-closure.

There are churches just like that. "Thrifty is as thrifty was." Their entire church history has been one of cutting corners—from the paint on the wall to the pastor's salary. "Anything goes—as long as it doesn't cost much."

In direct contrast to the "Mom & Pop" church is the *Cathedral of No Tomorrow Church*. "Cathedral of No Tomorrow" churches wouldn't build a garage for the Sunday school bus if it didn't cost at least a million. "Money is no object," they say. But far too often, the "Cathedral of No Tomorrow" church becomes the "Temple of Doom" church. Careless spending is the culprit. Its leaders fail to heed the words of the Savior, "Suppose one of you wants to build a tower. Will he not first sit down and estimate the cost to see if he has enough money to complete it?" (Luke 14:28).

The *Corporate Church* is another interesting study in ecclesiastical receiving and spending. It's the practical church—to a fault. It suffers from what someone has called the "paralysis of analysis." It builds little bureaucratic fences around its dreams. It is awash in a sea of committee minutes on what "should be done" if only the "resources were available."

In the "Corporate Church," the *very few* make very many decisions. The tithes and offerings are brought to a little room, where little minds make tiny decisions on how few of the funds will be disbursed for the glory of God and the increase of the Kingdom.

Perhaps the *Team Church* offers the best hope for receiving and spending God's resources. The "coach" (pastor) envisions a "game plan" (stewardship ministries), communicates the "plan" to the "team" (laity), who then share the responsibilities of playing out the "game plan" in the outreach, education, worship, and fellowship activities of the church.

Giving is a shared opportunity. It comes from a "team spirit" that has been cultivated by the coach, and the coach/pastor has modeled obedience in his or her own stewardship of God's resources.

> **"The life worth living is giving for the good of others**
> **—Booker T. Washington**

Principle Two: Instill A Vision For Giving.

Church finance begins with a very basic view of money. Quite simply stated, money belongs to God. "The earth is the Lord's, and everything in it, the world, and all who live in it" (Psalm 24:1). The fundamental truth is this: You and I—and those we lead—are *managers* of God's money.

It is extremely important to both understand and teach that every cent collected in the offering plates came from God in the first place. It is equally important to understand and teach that it belongs to him in the final analysis.

> "*God's* money."
> "*God's* offering."
> "*God's* building."
> "*God's* people."

Those are among the key words that should be woven into the stewardship language of the local church. A little boy had two quarters, one for ice cream and one for the church offering. Unfortunately, he accidentally dropped one of the quarters into the storm sewer. "Well, Lord," the boy said, "there goes your quarter." Money problems in the local church are fed by wrong attitudes.

Unhealthy attitudes about earning, saving, and spending money will carry over into the local church ministry. While per-capita income over the past thirty years is up thirty-one percent, in most churches there has been no appreciable upswing in per-member giving. Only when that trend is reversed, will there be a steady flow of resources flowing through the church out into the community.

Church members must understand that God gives his resources for their use in evangelizing and discipling efforts.

Emphasize Tithing

Financing the local church ministry must include the practice and teaching of **tithing**. The prophet Malachi served as God's spokesperson, "'Bring the whole tithe into the storehouse, that there may be food in my house. Test me in this,' says the LORD Almighty, 'and see if I will not throw open the floodgates of heaven and pour out so much blessing that you will not have room enough for it'" (Malachi 3:10).

Three lessons can be learned from this fifth-century BC stewardship sermon:

First, when we tithe we get direct access to the capital of heaven. God promised to open the *floodgates of heaven* to those who tithe (10a). Since the "earth is the Lord's," he is the chief financial officer of the universe. And he continually makes heaven's reserves available to me, as I obey him in my giving.

Secondly, God's returns are compounded. God said, he would *pour out so much blessing that you will not have room enough for it* (10b). This promise has been fulfilled time and again. The old cliché that you can't out-give God is true!

A Texas oil tycoon went to a little bank to cash a personal check. The teller returned, "I'm sorry sir, we can't cash this." "What's the problem?" The surprised oil man asked. The clerk replied, "Insufficient funds, sir."

"That can't be!" The man bellowed. "I have plenty of money!"

"Oh no, sir," the clerk responded. "Not you. It's us!"
God's "bank" is never at risk. His returns are compounded from a bountiful supply. "Morning by morning new mercies I see."[2]

Third, paying tithe is an insured deposit. God's word says, "I will prevent pests from devouring your crops, and the vines in your fields will not cast their fruit" (v. 11). It's an "inheritance that doesn't fade away," Peter reiterated. "The money we give to God is not lost. We will see it again. God will return our investment here on earth and later in heaven."[3]

Just because people attend church each week doesn't mean they are wise in the ways of giving. Stewardship must be *taught* and stewardship must be *caught.*

The New Testament provides many examples of the need to go beyond foundational stewardship (tithing). Believers should be reminded of the Macedonian example of grace-giving in 2 Corinthians 9:1–9. Clearly, in this passage New Testament Christians are given an example of "over and above" giving.

Giving is a Discipleship Duty

Instilling a vision for giving means communicating that "giving" is one "part" that makes up the "whole" of discipleship. God is the supreme giver. It is rooted in his very heart and nature. "For God so loved the world that he gave his one and only son that whoever believes in him shall not perish but have eternal life" (John 3:16). His people must also be givers.

The spiritual health of a congregation is directly related to their spiritual exercises. If giving isn't as much a habit as prayer and Bible study, then spiritual atrophy will set in—and spiritual paralysis or death will soon result.

Jesus said, "Where your treasure is, there your heart will be also" (Matthew 6:21). Consider these current "treasure" statistics:

The average American has 10 credit cards (Average debt: $2,887).
The average household income (2.7 persons) is $41,000.
The average child spends $423 a year in the marketplace.

The average teen spends $3,400 per year in the marketplace.[4]

Whole-life stewardship is the critical message in today's church. Over my many years in the pastorate I have taught parishioners to be stewards of life in the following areas:

> Stewardship of relationships.
> Stewardship of health.
> Stewardship of money.
> Stewardship of gifts.

Strong biblical teaching in these important areas will help build "well-rounded" stewards.

Educate the Leaders

Obviously, the resources are there to finance the local church. The challenge is in turning "spenders" into "stewards." Church attendees must be taught that God's work is financed through the faithful and obedient gifts of his people.

Training begins with the church leadership.

Local church ministry is an outstanding place for disciples of Christ to develop leadership skills. Each child of God is given at least one ability that can be used in the overall ministry of the church. Obviously, some have leadership gifts, and persons with those skills are usually in leadership positions.

Along with the *recognition* of their leadership, they need to know they are entrusted with its *responsibility*. The Apostle Paul dared to say, "Follow my example, as I follow the example of Christ" (1 Corinthians 11:1). "Do as I do," the Apostle invited, and that would involve his devotions as well as his duties.

When Paul wrote to the church in Corinth, "On the first day of every week, each one of you should set aside a sum of money in keeping with his income" (1 Corinthians16:2a), he knew all eyes would be upon his own "setting aside." The people would want to know if Paul was tithing. His life would be their lesson. Church leaders must be taught that their personal stewardship prompts the stewardship attitudes and actions of the other members of their local church.

> Examine yourselves to see whether you are in the
> faith; test yourselves. Do you not realize that Christ
> Jesus is in you—unless, of course, you fail the test?"
> (2 Corinthians 13:5).
>
> Test me, O Lord, and try me, examine my heart and
> my mind (Psalm 26:2).

Principle Three: Organize A Giving Plan.

A program without a plan is usually just organized confusion. Too
many local church ministries have suffered the wounds of "shotgun
planning." The Shotgun Planner just aims and fires, hoping that one
of the "program pellets" will strike its mark. In contrast, the "Rifle
Marksman" planner "scopes" out the situation, looks for obstacles,
focuses attention on the target, and then fires slowly and cautiously. The
target is hit with fewer "bystander casualties."

Stewardship planning needs more of the latter. Careful and focused
implementation is absolutely necessary. There are definite steps that can
be taken to hit the "stewardship target." Here are a few: 1) Evaluate the
sources of income; 2) Project expenses for the coming year; 3) Factor
in the practical property, personnel, and people resources; 4) Compile a
workable annual budget; and then, 5) Implement a plan of action.

The Budget
Webster says a budget is a "statement of the financial position of an
administration for a definite period of time based on estimates of expen-
ditures during the period and proposals for financing them." What are
the characteristics of a good budget?

First, it must be realistically projected. The budget is based on the
expected income and expenses of the local church. What was the total
giving last year? What percentage increase do you expect for the coming year? What are the economic factors? Are layoffs in sight? Has
there been an increase or decrease in attendance?

Unrealistic budgets can have a negative impact on giving. A "Mega
City" budget, for example, should not be imposed on a "Rural" congregation. A people discouraged by not being able to meet weekly giving

projections can easily develop a "what's-the-use" attitude. Budgets must be within reach and yet also reflect faith in God's promise to give an increase for faithfulness.

Second, it must be carefully documented. Consideration should be given to record the projections that have been duly prayed over and discussed. A sloppily prepared paper, hastily run through the copier (with the pages wrinkling because they're still warm) conveys careless preparation. Scribbled figures on an overhead transparency will communicate a lack of planning.

The budget may be presented to the congregation in a printed format. The presentation should be neat, concise, and reflect the careful consideration that has gone into its compilation.

Third, it must be adequately communicated. A trusted church leader should take time to explain the "ins and outs" of the proposed budget. The presentation should be made at a church business meeting or stewardship banquet. Questions may be solicited, but the presenter should stay focused on the purpose of the budget, its ministry priorities and its expeditious approval.

The Stewardship Plan

An annual stewardship plan should include a strategy to "educate and motivate the people in the local church to spiritual faithfulness. Although finances are usually the focus, an effective stewardship campaign is not just limited to finances. It includes the broader purpose of educating people in the proper management of their time, talent, and treasure for the glory of God—the total stewardship of the believer."[5]

The goal of the annual stewardship emphasis is to create an awareness of our responsibility to God and to obey him in the giving of our tithes and offerings.

The Stewardship Plan may include:

Stewardship Month Emphasis
        Choosing a theme
        Preaching a series on biblical stewardship
        Sunday school and small group stewardship lessons

Direct mail
Drama
Testimonials
Presentation of an annual budget

"The measure of our giving must be the measure of God's giving."
—Steve Weber

Principle Four: Create A Climate Of Trust.

This is the "investigative journalism" age. Whenever the local news station wants to win a "May Ratings Sweep" it usually throws in several investigative reports. A climate of mistrust has pervaded our culture. Today's leaders are under serious scrutiny, and the church is no exception. Too many horror stories about money mismanagement in the church have broken through the headlines.

Church leaders should make every effort to keep the church finances transparent.

Financial reports should be printed and made available.
Regular reports should be given to the church board.
Extreme caution should be given in the counting, posting, and transporting of offerings.
The church treasurer should be bonded.
Funds should be counted with a "buddy system" approach.
Safes, bank bags, audits, and security should be considered.

Open financial practices create a climate that is conducive to giving. Financial leaders should be conscious of any attempt to "close" the finances from the gaze of the congregation. An open book policy should be the norm!

"Now it is required that those who have been given a trust must prove faithful."
—1 Corinthians 4:2

Principle Five: Find A Need And Fill It!

exciting is a carefully planned program for implementing the Master
Plan. That new sanctuary or educational wing could be the very project
that causes your "Temp" member to get permanently Most people are
results oriented. Church members are no different; they want their gifts
to make a difference!

Pastors who are successful in fund-raising are careful to put a "face on
a dollar." People give to projects that capture their imagination. When
your people see how their contributions are being multiplied in property
and personnel improvements, it will be an incentive for further giving.
For instance, there's something exciting about a property Master Plan
displayed in the foyer.

Further, parents concerned about the need for a vibrant youth ministry
will usually respond to the carefully considered addition of a youth minister. Also, the "find a need and fill it" principle will be realized when
the congregation understands its donations are reaching lost souls. The
Great Commission and the Great Commandment are both being fulfilled
when the church is giving toward the training and sending of missionaries. When those endeavors are presented to the church family, along
with an opportunity to share in the endeavor, excitement prevails.
Finally, taking the stewardship journey with the local church will
require a great deal of time and patience. I'm reminded of the pastor
who was conversing with a little girl before the Sunday evening service.
He asked how old the little girl was. She straightened out her little fin-
gers and held them before her face, "I'm four."

"Four!" the pastor replied, "Are you going to have a birthday soon?"

"Yep, and then I'll be five," she announced.

And then there was a long pause, accompanied by a serious look on
the little girl's countenance. She said, "And when I'm five, I'll learn to
share."

"And why is that," the pastor responded.

"Well," she added, "ya' know it takes a long time to learn to share."

It's true, it will take a long time to develop generous stewards in the local church. There is no quick fix to church finances. But, the rewards over the long haul of eternity will be worth the stewardship trip!

Passages that Preach

Scripture	Topic
1 Chronicles 28–29	King David's Building Program
Exodus 35	Moses and the Involvement of People
Nehemiah 1–4	Nehemiah's Rebuilding of the Walls
Acts 4:34–5:2	The Apostles and Benevolent Giving
Luke 8:2–3	Jesus and the Miracle of Giving
2 Corinthians 8–9	Paul and Grace Giving

Recommended Resources

Books:
A *Life Well Spent* by Russ Crosson (Thomas Nelson, 1994)
Generous Living by Ronald Blue (Zondervan, 1997)
Giving and Tithing by Larry Burkett (Moody Press, 1998)
The Millionaire Next Door by Thomas Stanley and William Dank (Longstreet Press, 1996)
Spiritual Investments by Gary Moore (Templet on Foundation Press, 1998)
Ten Golden Rules for Financial Success by Gary Moore (HarperCollins Publishers, 1997)
Wealthy and Wise by Claude Rosenberg (Little Brown, 1994)
Developing A Giving Church by Stan Toler and Elmer Towns (Beacon Hill Press, 1

Stewardship Agencies
INJOY Stewardship Services
P.O. Box 7700
Atlanta, GA 30357-0700
800-333-6509
www.Injoy.com

Christian Stewardship Association
3195 S. Superior
P.O. Box 07747
Milwaukee, WI 53207
414-483-1945
CSA@stewardship.org
www.stewardship.org

Raising Money for Your Church
Barna Research Group Ltd.
647 West Broadway
Glendale, CA 91204-6509

Virgil Hensley, Inc.
6116 East 32nd Street
Tulsa, OK 74135
918-664-8520

Church Growth Institute
Larry Gilbert, President
1-800-553-GROW
Phone for Stewardship Resource Packets by Elmer Towns, *Tithing Is Christian, God Is Able, Our Family Giving to God's Family, From Victory to Victory.*
These programs were written by Elmer Towns and used at Thomas Road Baptist Church, Lynchburg, Virginia.

Christian Financial Concepts
800-722-1976
www.cfcministry.org

Crown Ministries
407-331-6000
www.crown.org

Newtithing Group
415-274-2761
www.crown.org

The Philanthropic Initiative Inc.
617-338-2590
www.tpi.org

Ronald Blue & Co.
800-987-2987
www.ronblue.com

End Notes

[1] Toler, Stan, and Elmer Towns, 1999, *Developing a Giving Church,* Kansas City: Beacon Hill Press, 11.
[2] Chisholm, Thomas O., "Great Is Thy Faithfulness," *Sing to the Lord,* 1993, Kansas City: Lillenas Publishing.
[3] Toler and Towns, 48.
[4] *American Demographics Magazine,* April 1, 2000, 61.
[5] Toler and Towns, 48.

Chapter Sixteen:
James Lyon, *Restoring the Wounded*

"Brethren, if a man is caught in any trespass, you who are spiritual, restore such a one in a spirit of gentleness…" (Galatians 6:1 NASB).

All of us are engaged, consciously or not, in a contest for supremacy in this world. Two pervasive powers direct the conflict; two polar opposites are locked in combat all around us. Heaven and hell vie for our attention and allegiance. The stakes are high.

We have not been born by chance. Providence has designed our placement in this world, with purposes that often transcend our finite understanding. "He chose us in Him before the foundation of the world, that we should be holy and blameless before Him" (Ephesians 1:4 NASB). "For we are His workmanship, created in Christ Jesus for good works, which God prepared beforehand, that we should walk in them" (Ephesians 2:10 NASB).

Choosing to align ourselves with God's Son—and, consequently, choosing to renounce the claims of his adversary, the enemy of our souls—is the defining moment of human experience. Confession, repentance, baptism, sanctification: these are the tangible evidences of our choice and transformation. And, once enlisted in heaven's company for heaven's aims, the battle will be joined.

Victory is promised; victory is within our grasp. "Greater is He that is in you, than He that is in the world" (1 John 4:4b NASB). Spiritual empowerment to rise above the enemy's mischief, to not only endure but triumph for Jesus' sake, is at the core of holiness theology. "Now may the God of peace himself sanctify you entirely; and may your spirit and soul and body be preserved complete, without blame at the coming of our Lord Jesus Christ" (1 Thessalonians 5:23 NASB).

But what of the casualties along the way? Is it possible that some will fall by the wayside? Can even the elect, "redeemed by the Blood" and "sanctified by the Lamb," stumble into sin, betray the cause, and compromise their calling? Are those who are wounded in this way still "the Lord's?" Can the morally maimed be properly reintroduced into positions of command and leadership? What if the wounds are self-inflicted? What of those who fail by choice? Can these be restored? And, if so, restored to what?

First, it must be admitted that the history of God's people is sadly littered with moral failure. The debris of sin can be found along the "straight and narrow" highway as well as along the "broad way that leads to destruction." Samson failed. Saul failed. David failed. Solomon failed. Jonah failed. The Hebrews failed. All twelve of the disciples of Jesus failed. Peter, among these, failed spectacularly. Demas failed. Some in the Corinthian Church failed. All trafficked in willful, disobedient sin, aiding and abetting the enemy, after having once pledged fidelity to God. In both testaments, the evidence of failure is both overwhelming and sobering.

Second, it must be observed that God is in the restoration business. The Gospel is, in the main, a record of the Lord's effort to reclaim, to redeem, and to restore to its rightful place that which was originally his, but which, in time, was lost. Luke 15 famously outlines with compelling clarity the passion and focus for restoration in God's kingdom. The lost sheep, the lost coin, the lost son—and the intense efforts to redeem them—are at the core of this series of revealing parables.

Furthermore, while all those who stray (in the biblical narratives) are not restored, many are. The potential for restoration plainly exists for some and, we might safely assume, for all. "… God, our Savior, who desires all men to be saved and to come to the knowledge of the truth" (1 Timothy 2:3–4 NASB). Indeed, the Scripture commands "those who are spiritual" to "restore" any "caught in any trespass" (Galatians 1:6 NASB).

Third, there are common threads that herald restoration in the

Scriptures, threads which outline processes and responsibilities that, if embraced, release the backslidden from their bondage and restore them to the Lord's employ. Restoration is more than massaging broken hearts and bringing closure to sad chapters in life; restoration is refusing to surrender any of heaven's own to hell's work. Restoration is the effective redeployment of wounded soldiers (remade whole) into constructive ministry, for the glory of God.

Everyone knows of someone who has failed in ministry. Once anointed by God, the pastor is overcome by temptation and betrays his marriage vow. The otherwise prudent youth pastor allows his mind (and heart) to wander and sleeps with the needy teenager whose own home is in chaos. The music minister falsifies receipts and embarks on a pattern of embezzlement—not much money at first, but month-by-month, the pilfering grows. The missionary once consumed with passion for the spiritually lost in the foreign field is distracted by the ever-present sex trade and develops a passion for porn instead. The gifted church leader, impeccably dressed and always tender and kind, but stalked by unresolved pain from his childhood, finds himself self-medicating by smoking dope and dabbling with the edge of the law. The popular preacher wrestles with confusion deep inside his soul and finally announces that he is gay. Angry, hurt, and insecure, the middle-aged pastor loses credibility because he gossips destructively, tearing others down in a mad attempt to build himself up. The scenarios of failure are legion.

Samson at last surrenders to the machinations of his lover and squanders the God-given power he had used to defend Israel (Judges 13–16). Head and shoulders above his peers, Saul is chosen by God, but he collapses spiritually and emotionally in disobedience (1 Samuel 9–31). David's flesh reigns and the king not only commits adultery, but murder, as well (2 Samuel 11–12). Solomon's wisdom is no match for his lust (Nehemiah 13:26). Jonah's willful prejudice and contempt for his Assyrian neighbors drives him to abandon the prophetic office (Jonah 14). The Hebrews, blessed by the revelation and favor of God and custodians of the sacred writ, cannot seem to hold steady and blow with the world's wind, embracing the slavery of idolatry, after being freed from the slavery of Egypt (Genesis—Malachi).

James. John. Andrew. Nathanael. Matthew. And all the rest of the twelve disciples: after walking with Christ for three years, after witnessing the most extraordinary life in history, after listening to the heart of God and seeing his hand move supernaturally, all of them flee when Jesus is arrested, abandoning the One they professed to love, their faith in the Messiah they had claimed a sham.

And Peter? Simon Peter, "the rock?" He bravely declares his unfailing loyalty to Christ and then, within hours, broods in the dark shadows of cowardice, profanely refusing even to acknowledge that he knew Jesus (Matthew 26). Peter's devolution is rivaled only by his arrogance.

Demas walks with Paul across the face of the Empire, again a witness to the power of the living Christ, but, in the end, "having loved this present world," deserted him and, it seems, the Gospel (2 Timothy 4:10 NASB).

The Church of God at Corinth was plagued by "immorality of such a kind as does not exist even among the Gentiles, that someone has his father's wife" (1 Corinthians 6:1). This scourge was made all the worse by their "arrogance" and "boasting."

Still, Samson regains his strength, at the last. Saul, however, is lost and never reclaimed. Solomon fades, a melancholy figure. David, Jonah, and the Hebrews are given second chances. Judas ends his own life. The other disciples transform the world. Peter is wonderfully engaged, once again, by his Lord, at the seashore of Galilee (John 21). The Corinthian Church shines by the end of Paul's second letter. Demas disappears.

What separates the restored from the doomed? Five things:

1. Honest and Straightforward Acknowledgement of Failure

Restoration hinges on the honest and straightforward admission of the wayward soul's failure. Sin can never be addressed if it is not named. It cannot be purged if it is not identified. It cannot be cleansed if it cannot be seen.

Occasionally, we comprehend our sin alone. We, by the prompting of the Spirit and the channel of conscience, understand our failure, without the help of an outside voice. Guilt, shame, loss of peace, all creep into the soul and remind us of our error. Others may not be aware that we are lifting cash from the choir's offering, be we know. We fear discovery. We comprehend our sin.

More often than not, however, we rationalize our sin. We delude ourselves into believing that our behavior is acceptable or, at least, not reprehensible. We refuse to look at ourselves honestly; we ignore the silent stirring of our muted conscience; we avoid responsibility. We compartmentalize our routines, dividing our lives into sections, preferring to see just bits at a time, afraid of seeing the whole. We become defensive when questioned and find ourselves working harder to maintain the facade of propriety. The performance becomes exhausting, but we continue acting, day after day, postponing the inevitable.

In either case, confession must take place, either at the prompting of the Spirit in the sinner's heart or by the approach of another member of the Body of Christ, following the commands of Matthew 18:15 and Galatians 6:1.

Confession is the cleansing of the wound, the forcing to the surface of the infected pus that has festered and stained the soul. It can be excruciating, but there is no other way for restoration to begin. The prophet Nathan understood this when he confronted David, regarding the king's sin with Bathsheba. The Apostle Paul understood this when he confronted the Corinthian Church regarding its indulgence of sexual immorality. Jesus knew this, when he warned Peter of his impending failure, with a prophecy sure to bring the truth to the disciple's mind even at the moment of his betrayal.

Such confession must be clear and straightforward. It cannot be couched in exculpatory language or minimized by self-serving context. Such confession must be made to God, of course, but it should also be made to the Body of Christ (perhaps, by disclosing to a member of the Body on behalf of the whole); "… confess your sins to one another …" (James 5:16 NASB). As a general rule, confession should be made, also, to anyone directly injured by our sin.

Displaying our dirty laundry before the whole church is not usually necessary in confession. But owning our dirty laundry in the company of a representative of the larger church can be a powerful step towards restoration. Local congregations would do well to establish venues to facilitate healing in this way. Pastors, naturally, find themselves in the role of confessor, for parishioners, from time-to-time. But, carefully prepared Church Councils (where pledges of confidentiality are embraced) or specifically constituted confessional small groups can also play important roles, when the penitent needs more than a pastor can provide.

Revealing personal failure in an appropriate setting, allows the wounded soldier to begin to believe that the Body of Christ will recognize his or her restoration. Confession to God opens the door for the Lord's forgiveness. Confession to the church opens the door for the church's forgiveness.

2. Repentance.

To repent is to change course, to reverse direction. Once confession has been made (and forgiveness received), repentance must next be demonstrated. An unequivocal commitment to turn away from the offending behavior must be made. Jonah decided, finally, to obey God's call to Nineveh. The Hebrews embraced, once more, the law of God in Ezra's day, after fleeing from it generations before. Peter would never again deny Christ.

As with confession, the commitment to repent is most effectively made in the company of other members of the Body of Christ. Our promises, made in the hearing of others (and, if need be, in writing) bind and empower us in ways that private promises do not. In the same way that a marriage vow is made before witnesses, a renewed commitment to walk with Christ is best made before witnesses.

A definitive plan to help guarantee the success of our pledge to walk uprightly will maximize success. Accountability systems have great power to guard our steps. Identifying weaknesses and circumstances in which we feel most vulnerable to temptation can help steer a clear course. Engaging another member of the church to work with us in being faithful is wise. Such "repentance plans" may be necessary for months or years, depending on the nature of the infraction and personal history, but every effort at restoration needs such a plan.

3. Restitution.

Some sins require restitution. Restitution is the attempt to restore
the loss someone else has suffered by our hand. Restitution typically
involves a formal apology to the injured party and evidence of intent to
repent. It may involve a financial compensation or promise to perform
some service or good work. Restitution also has great power to help the
wounded soldier understand that restoration is possible. Once more, the
Body of Christ should play an instrumental role in the identification and
implementation of any restitution arrangement. The church, through its
appointed representatives, can fairly judge the propriety and satisfaction
of the restitution effort. Once authenticated by the church, the person
being restored can accept more readily closure with the injured party
than if no restitution takes place.

4. Loving Discipline.

Restoration time frames and authentication of repentance implemented
by the Body of Christ provide a covering of loving discipline that facili-
tates the long-term viability and success of future ministry. Examples of
loving discipline might include requirements for: (a) regular reporting
on restitution progress, (b) routine meetings with mentors or counselors,
(c) assigned reading materials, etc. Most local churches are ill equipped
to deliver loving discipline; we are loath to make formal judgments
about others or become involved in on-going, potentially awkward disciplinary relationships.

Still, by stepping up to the challenge, churches can holistically redeem
wounded soldiers and strengthen the ministry. Establishment of
accountability partnerships, accountability small groups (of three or four
persons, appointed by some church authority), and/or disciplinary policies for restoration in church life (embraced by the Church Council, for
instance) will deal the enemy a severe blow.

Humility on the part of those representing the church, in the face of the
offending sin, is absolutely essential. The proverbial "But for the grace
of God go I ..." should naturally fall from everyone's lips. The process
of discipline in restoration must never be punitive, but redemptive; it
must never be judgmental, but forgiving; it must never be born by pride,
but delivered with modesty.

Moral lapses generally require a two-year time-out from ministry, before restoration can be considered. Counseling and restitution regimens should also be enforced. Loving discipline requires a commitment on the part of the church's leadership to stand fast and consistently in the implementation of its policies.

5. Restoration Closure.

Once honest and straightforward confession has been made, once repentance has been owned and demonstrated, once restitution has been pursued and completed, and once a structure of loving discipline has been enforced, a signal moment of closure to the restoration process should be arranged once again, in the presence of the Body of Christ. A formal end to the process should be recognized by the church; the memory of the sin should be sealed and removed from all conversation; a celebration of the Lord's goodness and mercy should be enjoyed. The wounded soldier, now remade whole, should take his or her place back on the front line, free of the past and empowered spiritually to face the future.

No two circumstances are just alike. Universal principles are the province of Scripture alone. General rules, though, do have validity. Most wounded soldiers can be restored to their original rank in heaven's army, if the appropriate steps are taken over a sufficient period of time. David's stunning failures did not deny him the throne (although his effectiveness was diminished). Peter's lapses did not alter the Lord's profound apostolic call on his life. Jonah regained his prophetic gift, even after sailing from Joppa.

Failure brings its own reward, of course, even for those restored Our choices give birth to consequences. Samson's strength was ultimately restored, but he lost his life in its expression.

But, above the fractures in our own lives, the sovereign plan of God unfolds, through and beyond the restoration process. Miraculously, inexplicably, the hand of Providence moves and molds events in tandem with its own plans. When we cooperate with those plans, in Christ, we live abundantly. When we fail to do so, we step backwards into the darkness. And, when we come to our senses (as did the prodigal in Luke 15), we, by the grace of God and the restorative process of God's people, can step back into the purposes for which he originally created us. We can fight, once more, on the Lord's side.

Reference List

Jay Adams, *Handbook of Church Discipline* (Zondervan, 1987).
Building a framework for discipline and restoration on Matthew
18:15–17, Adams concisely and practically guides the reader, step-
by-step. Although relatively brief, Adams's Handbook is, nevertheless, an outstanding primer and reference; it should be included in
every church leader's library.

Berghoef, Gerard and Lester DeKoster, *The Elders Handbook:
A Practical Guide for Church Leaders* (Baker Book House,
Christian's Library Press, 1979). Firmly grounded in reformed theology, the authors view church leadership and discipline through
a lens that may vary from that of a congregational and Arminian
tradition. Still, amply illustrated with scripture, this nicely organized
resource provides solid insight on the parameters and possibilities of
restoration.

Gordon MacDonald, *Rebuilding Your Broken World* (Thomas Nelson,
1990). MacDonald's personal history gave birth to this excellent
examination of the issues and processes of restoration. The author's
own course (prominent ministry, failure, time out, and restoration)
have set the standard in the last decade for holistic rebuilding of
ministry. This is a must read for anyone exploring the subject.

BIOGRAPHIES

Stephen S. Carver is professor of biblical studies and the chair of the religion and Christian ministries department at Warner Pacific College, Portland, Oregon, where he has taught since the fall of 1995. Dr. Carver received his Ph.D. from Luther Seminary in St. Paul, Minnesota and his M. Div. from North American Baptist Seminary in Sioux Falls, SD. Before coming to Warner, Dr. Carver taught at North American Baptist Seminary as an adjunct instructor of New Testament and Greek for one year. Prior to that, he served as a minister of youth for several years, including two and half years at the Church of God in Brookings, South Dakota. While in college and in seminary, Dr. Carver also become involved in prison ministry, first at a county jail and later as a chaplain intern.

Joseph L. Cookston, Ph.D. (Trinity International University) in educational studies and congregational development, is pastor of education and families at Salem Church of God. He and Merry, his wife, live in Englewood, Ohio, and enjoy their two young adult children.

G. Samuel Dunbar currently serves as senior pastor of the First Church of God, St. Louis, Michigan. He received his BA and MA degrees from Anderson University and has served pastorates in Indiana and Oregon as well as serving eleven years as state executive ministers for the Churches of God in Oregon. Sam also served as adjunct faculty for Warner Pacific College in Portland, Oregon and Kima International School of Theology in Kenya, East Africa. He and his wife, Mary, are the parents of three children: Nathan, Jenny, and Benjamin.

Tim Dwyer is professor of Christian Scriptures at Roberts Wesleyan University, Rochester, New York. He has held pastorates in California and Indiana, and also served as youth minister and jail chaplain. His Ph.D. in New Testament Exegesis is from the University of Aberdeen in Scotland. Tim is married to Paula, and has two sons, Peter and Philip.

Robert Edwards is the last born of four children to long serving Church of God pastors, Harold and Vera Edwards. His early years were in Piqua, Ohio, before the family moved to Dayton, Ohio, for a new pastorate. Bob married Janet Blackwell in 1966 while attending Anderson University. In 1967 he received a BA with a major in mathematics. That same year they were commissioned as short term missionaries to teach in a rural Kenyan high school for two years, Bob teaching Mathematics and Jan teaching all of the sciences. During that period they felt a strong call from the Lord to enter full time missionary service, and returned for preparation to the School of Theology, Anderson University to work on an Master of Divinity Degree. Upon completion of that degree they were commissioned by the Missionary Board of the Church of God to be the Principal of a small, Swahili Bible School in the bush of Tanzania. After ten years of ministry in Tanzania, the Board asked them to go to the neighboring nation of Kenya to serve as the Director of Urban Development for the large and strong Church of God in Kenya. During this period of time Bob completed both a Masters of Theology in Missiology and a Doctor of Missiology from the School of World Missions, Fuller Theological Seminary. His study concerned the various aspects of the growth of urban congregations throughout the Church of God in Kenya. In 1989 Bob was asked to be the Regional Director for the Africa Region for the Missionary Board. From 1998–2002, Bob and Jan ministered as Regional Directors for Europe, the CIS, and the Middle East, while living in Germany. Since 2002, Bob has been coordinator of Global Missions, the successor to the Missionary Board. They have two children, Dontie and Nathan.

Jeannette Flynn currently serves the Church of God in North America as the leader of the Kingdom Ministry Team of Church of God Ministries, Anderson, Indiana. In this position she leads the church in meeting the needs of the local congregation in areas of Christian education, pastoral and church health and growth, leadership development, and credentials, to name a few. She was born in Ohio, was raised in the Church of God, Anderson, has earned undergraduate degrees in education and theology. She graduated from the School of Theology, Anderson University, with a M.Div. She has served local congregations as associate and senior pastor, and is married with two children and four grandchildren.

Lou Foltz and his wife, Myra, live on a small farm outside of Portland, Oregon. He serves as a professor of educational psychology at Warner Pacific College. He has taught courses in learning theory and human development to college students as well as public school and Sunday school teachers over the past twenty years. A student of cultures, he has visited over forty countries and has taken cultural history courses in The People's Republic of China, Ukraine, and, most recently, Costa Rica. He received his Ph.D. degree from the University of California at Berkeley. He states that the most important accomplishment in his life has been both the one most difficult and the most easy: opening his life to the unmerited saving grace of his Savior, Jesus Christ, and learning anew each day to walk after him.

Dwight L. Grubbs was born in the Church of God parsonage in Homestead, Florida in 1933. He grew up in Lamar, South Carolina and Monroe, Louisiana where his father, Reverend J.C. Grubbs served congregations of the Church of God. Dr. Grubbs received his bachelor's degree in education at Northeast Louisiana State University, the Master of Divinity and the Master of Religious Education degrees at the School of Theology, Anderson University (Anderson, Indiana) and the Doctor of Ministry degree at Texas Christian University (Fort Worth, Texas). He also completed one-year internships in marriage and family therapy at the Marriage and Family Consultation Center (Houston, Texas) and the Indiana Counseling and Pastoral Care Center (Indianapolis, Indiana).

After serving four years as a public school teacher and twelve years as a pastor, Grubbs was, from 1973 to 1978, Associate Professor of Applied Theology at Gulf-Coast Bible College in Houston, Texas. From 1978 to 1995, he served at the School of Theology, Anderson University, Anderson, Indiana as Professor of Applied Theology and Director of Spiritual Life. His areas of interest and specialization include pastoral ministry, marriage, and family living, Christian spirituality, pastoral counseling, church history, worship, and preaching. His book, *Beginnings: Spiritual Formation for Leaders*, was published by Fairway Press in 1994. Dwight lives with his wife Sylvia. Their home is in Anderson, Indiana.

James W. Lewis currently serves as associate dean and professor of theology and ethics at Anderson School of Theology, Anderson, Indiana. His academic and ministerial background reflects the surprising twists of a life committed to honoring God in all of one's life. From Texas A&M University, he received a BS degree in mathematics (1972) and an MBA in business finance (1964). He worked as a certified public accountant for several years afterwards. After confessing Jesus as Lord and Savior in 1976, his wife, Barbara, two daughters, Andrea and Kimberli, and he moved in August 1982 to Ft. Worth, Texas, to begin his M.Div. work at Southwestern Baptist Theological Seminary. With only twelve hours remaining, they moved to Durham, North Carolina, where he began Ph.D. studies in theology and ethics, under the supervision of Dr. Stanley Hauerwas. While in North Carolina, he was ordained into the ministry and pastored five and one-half years at the First Church of God, Raleigh, North Carolina. He is accountable to and presently attending Sherman Street Church of God, Anderson, Indiana. He loves the vocation of Christian ministry and rejoices in those additional opportunities to serve the church and the world outside the vocation of university teaching.

Jim Lyon is senior pastor of Madison Park Church of God in Anderson, Indiana. He attended Warner Pacific College, Portland, Oregon; Seattle Pacific University; and the University of Washington Law School, Seattle, Washington, before entering the pastoral ministry at the Fairview Church of God in Seattle in 1978. He served at Fairview Church until 1991, when he became senior pastor at North Anderson Church of God, now known as Madison Park. He also hosts the weekly international radio broadcast *ViewPoint* for Christians Broadcasting Hope of the Church of God. Jim, his wife Maureen, and their four sons now call Anderson home.

David Markle has been senior pastor of Park Place Church of God in Anderson, Indiana, since 2001. Prior to that time, he served as associate professor of religion and Christian ministries at Warner Pacific College in Portland, Oregon. For more than twenty years, he served in youth and pastoral ministries in Oregon, Indiana, Michigan, and North Carolina. He is a graduate of Asbury Theological Seminary (D. Min. in preaching), Anderson School of Theology (M. Div.), and Anderson University (BA). He and his wife, Peggy, are the parents of a daughter, Laura.

Lori Salierno is the founder and chief executive officer of Celebrate Life International, a non-profit organization dedicated to developing leaders of integrity. Lori travels extensively speaking to students, leaders, and women, equipping them to build lives of character; create positive relationships; stand strong in healthy habits; and multiply their influence among their peers. Through personal stories and the experiences of others, Lori brings biblical truths to life. Her fresh approach and creative ideas provide practical tools to live out Christianity in daily life. Lori received her doctorate in leadership development from Asbury

Theological Seminary. She and her husband, Kurt, live in the Atlanta areas, where Kurt pastors a ministry of Homeless, the Church in the Street.

David Sebastian has been the dean at the School of Theology, Anderson University, since July 1, 1995. He graduated from Warner Southern College, Anderson School of Theology, and Fuller Theological Seminary. He has been a senior pastor at North Hills Church of God in Phoenix, Arizona and Salem Church of God in Dayton, Ohio. He is married to the former Debbie Miller and they have two daughters—Julie, graduated from Anderson University, May 2001, and Amy who is a student at Anderson University.

Fredrick and Kay Shively live in Anderson, Indiana, where they attend Park Place Church of God. Fred is professor of Bible and religious studies at Anderson University and directs the ministry education program. They are both graduates of Anderson University (College). Fred holds M.Div. and Doctor of Ministry degrees from Fuller Seminary. He pastored churches in California and Oregon and has served as interim pastor in numerous congregations. He has written two books and several articles.

Kay has an MA in English from Ball State University. She taught high school and college English and served nineteen years on the national staff of Women of the Church of God. She has written curriculum for the Church of God and has published several articles. She is trained in conflict resolution and sexual and domestic violence prevention and serves as casework coordinator for clergy sexual misconduct for Indiana Ministries of the Church of God. She is self-employed as a writer, editor, and conference leader.

The Shivelys enjoy leading marriage enrichment retreats and international travel, having led many TRI-S (student travel) trips for Anderson University. They have two sons, a daughter-in-law, and one grandson.

Diana L. Swoope is the senior pastor of the Arlington Church of God in Akron, Ohio. Dr. Swoope is also the founder and principal of the Arlington Christian Academy which enrolls students from kindergarten through eighth grade. Pastor Swoope is a sought after speaker, traveling all across the United States and abroad, preaching and teaching the empowering message of the gospel of Jesus Christ. It is her strong desire to "united the hurting hearts of people, with the healing hands of God." She is the author of three books, *Shout, Jubilee!* (NIYC Publications, 1990), *Jesus Our Source,* (Warner Press, 1997) and her latest release, *Chosen and Highly Favored: A Woman's Sacred Call to Holiness* (Beacon Hill Press, 2001) Dr. Swoope, and her husband, Larry, reside in Copley, Ohio with their three children, Alecia, Allen, and Andreco.

Stan Toler is senior pastor of Trinity Church of the Nazarene in Oklahoma City, Oklahoma, and hosts the television program, "Leadership Today." He is model church instructor for INJOY Group—a leadership development institute for pastors where he conducts seminars throughout the U.S. He has written over 40 books. He graduated from Circleville Bible College, Th.B, in 1973; completed a Th.M. in 1975 at Florida Beacon Seminary; in 1988 earned a D. Min. from Maranatha Seminary; he also holds a B.A. from Southern Nazarene University (1988).